Original Tao

TRANSLATIONS FROM THE ASIAN CLASSICS

Original Tao

INWARD TRAINING

AND THE FOUNDATIONS OF TAOIST MYSTICISM

Harold D. Roth

Columbia University Press ~ New York

Chapter 2 contains a revised and expanded version of material published as chapter 8 in *The Religions of China in Practice*, edited by Donald Lopez, Jr. © 1995 by Princeton University Press.

Part of chapter 4 is based upon my article, "*Laozi* in the Context of Early Daoist Mystical Praxis," published as chapter 2 in the SUNY Press publication, *Religious and Philosophical Aspects of the Laozi*, edited by Mark Czikszentmihalyi and P. J. Ivanhoe, 1999. Used with the permission of the State University of New York Press, State University of New York. All rights reserved.

COLUMBIA UNIVERSITY PRESS
Publishers Since 1893

New York   Chichester, West Sussex

Library of Congress Cataloging-in-Publication Data

Roth, Harold David.
    Original Tao : inward training (nei-yeh) and the foundations of
Taoist mysticism / Harold D. Roth.
        p. cm. — (Translations from the Asian classics)
    Includes bibliographical references and index.
    ISBN 978–0–231–11564–3 (cloth: alk. paper) —978–0–231–11565–0
(pbk.: alk. paper)
    1. Nei yeh—Criticism, interpretation, etc. 2. Philosophy,
Taoist. 3. Meditation—Taoism. I. Nei yeh. II. Title.
III. Series.
BL1900.N45R67 1999
299'.51482—dc21   99–20737

FOR

ANGUS

AND

JÔSHU

Oh my teacher, my teacher!
You harmonize the myriad things but do not strive to be just.
You extend kindness to the myriad ages but do not strive to be humane.
You are elder than highest antiquity but do not strive to be venerable.
You shelter the heavens and sustain the earth.
You carve and shape the multitude of forms but do not strive to be skillful.

—*Chuang Tzu*, chapter 6: "Ta tsung shih" (The Great Ancestral Teacher)

Contents

Acknowledgments

This book represents the culmination of fifteen years of reflection on the origins and nature of early Taoist thought and ten years of writing articles on various aspects of it and how it could be systematically and critically studied. While working on this subject over the course of these years, I only gradually developed a sense of where it was leading me, and the result is but an imperfect reflection of the insights I gleaned and the advice of friends and colleagues that sustained me.

A paper written by Whalen Lai and read at the Second Meeting of the Society for Asian and Comparative Philosophy in Toronto in August 1983 first called my attention to *Inward Training* and its companion "Techniques of the Mind" texts. Subsequently, supported by a grant from the Social Sciences and Humanities Research Council of Canada, I had the wonderful opportunity to read through these works with Angus Graham at the School of Oriental and African Studies during his last year on the faculty there. This opportunity extended to developing a friendship with this remarkable man and to many evenings in discussions that ranged over a wide variety of topics, from the intricacies of the thought of the *Chuang Tzu* to conspiracy theories and spontaneous human combustion. There was a rare coterie of like-minded scholars at SOAS in those days that included my friends Paul Thompson and Sarah Allan, and I cannot begin to express my gratitude for all that these three friends taught me about classical Chinese thought and supportive, collegial scholarship.

After becoming established at Brown I was able to continue working with Angus Graham while he was a visiting professor here in 1988. I also began to renew two old interests of mine initially fostered during my undergraduate days at Princeton. To Tu Weiming and Fritz Mote I owe my initial tutelage in the problem of self-cultivation in early Chinese thought. And to Jock Reeder I owe my initial tutelage in the methods of critically examining the nature of mystical experience. At Brown I continued work on these subjects and was aided in the second of them by my work with Barney Twiss. Together we taught a number of courses over the years on various aspects of comparative mysticism and in the process had many engaging and beneficial discussions over a glass or two of single malt, a pleasure to which my British friends had introduced me during my years at SOAS.

As my ideas started to emerge on these topics, I was given a number of key opportunities to present them and receive feedback on them in public forums. Robert Buswell gave me my first invitation to speak about these ideas at the Southern California China Colloquium in February 1988 at USC, where I was particularly encouraged by Michel Strickmann's support. Robin Yates and Peter Bol invited me to the Pre-Modern China Seminar at Harvard a month later where I received further encouragement from several scholars, including Ben Schwartz. Later that year at the American Academy of Religion Annual Meeting Russell Kirkland invited me to talk on a panel on early Chinese religion, and Robert Henricks gave me an invaluable response to my ideas. Subsequent important papers were written at the invitation of Kidder Smith and our New England Symposium on Chinese Thought in 1989; Susan Cherniak at the 1994 Meeting of the Association for Asian Studies; Toshiaki Yamada and Livia Kohn at the First American-Japanese Conference on Taoist Studies in Tokyo in 1995; Victor Hori at McGill and Ch'en Ku-ying at the International Taoist Studies Research Conference in Peking, both in 1996; Scott Cook at the 1997 Meeting of the Association for Asian Studies; Paul Goldin at the Conference on Intellectual Lineages in Early China at the University of Pennsylvania in 1997; and Carl Bielefeldt at Stanford last year. All these invitations provided me with the opportunity to think and write about various aspects of early Taoism and to receive responses and challenges to my ideas that would spur me on.

During these years I found particular support for my work among a small group of close colleagues who read and critiqued most of the things I wrote and to whom I owe profound gratitude for all they did to help me clarify my always imperfect attempts to communicate my ideas: Sarah Queen, John Major, and Andy Meyer. Their support and encouragement gave me the strength to carry on in the direction in which I was heading even when I most doubted myself. I would also like to thank a number of other colleagues who provided stimulating criticism of various related research projects that eventually impacted on the final form of the work you are now reading: Roger Ames, Irene Bloom, Bill Boltz, Henry Rosemont, Jr., and Robin Yates.

It is often the case that the environment in which one teaches comes to have a profound effect on one's scholarship. This has certainly been true with my own work. Not only have my colleagues in the Department of Religious Studies aided and abetted my comparative analysis of mysticism, but they have been extremely helpful as well in introducing me to the methods of form, redaction, composition, and narrative criticism. Foremost among these is Stan Stowers, whom I can thank for stimulating discussions and influential references, and Anne Heyrman Hart, a former graduate student in the department with whom I spent many hours talking about these issues as they pertain to New Testament Studies. As it happened, just as I was beginning to study these important critical methodologies, several other scholars also began applying them to early Chinese thought. The researches of Michael LaFargue and Bruce and Taeko Brooks have been important intellectual influences on my own attempts to apply these Western critical methods to early Taoism.

As I began to envision writing a book about my emerging ideas on early Taoism and the significance of this long-overlooked work, *Inward Training*, I received important support of another kind from several sources. I spent a year's leave working under the aegis of a Fellowship for University Teachers from the National Endowment for the Humanities. In addition, over a period of five years I was constantly supported in my research and conference travel by an exceptional university administrator here at Brown, former Dean of the Faculty Bryan Shepp. His encouragement of my career meant a great deal to me: it made me feel part of a larger intellectual community. In this and in many other areas he was a model of a sensitive and thoughtful university administrator that I will always admire. I also wish to thank his successor, Kathryn Spoehr, who provided an invaluable subvention for the creation of the index to this book.

There are a number of other colleagues here at Brown who have given me intellectual and spiritual sustenance during the long gestation of this project. Principal among these are Dore Levy, who has helped me with just about everything imaginable during my years at Brown; Giles Milhaven, who always read my articles and expressed his admiration for them, all the while feigning ignorance of the subject; Wendell Dietrich, who secretly gave me the support I needed at critical times during my career; Jerry Grieder and Jimmy Wrenn, who rode to the rescue just in the nick of time; and, for a brief time, Mark Unno, who has a wisdom about the academy far beyond his years and whom I might have finally convinced about the central philosophy of Chuang Tzu. And I would certainly be remiss in ignoring the invaluable criticism and feedback I received from several generations of students at Brown during the many years I incorporated my evolving ideas on early Taoism into a whole range of courses in the undergraduate and graduate curriculums.

While I was actually writing this book in the spring of 1997, I spoke to no one outside my family, and to them only rarely. Nonetheless, during this time several scholars went out of their way to provide me with completed but unpublished manuscripts that I could not have done without. Chief among these is Don Harper, who kindly sent me copies of several major sections of his monumental work, *Early Chinese Medical Literature*, and Allyn Rickett, who did the same with relevant sections of the equally monumental second volume of his *Kuan Tzu* translation. I also benefited considerably from reading the manuscript of William Baxter's important study of the language of the *Lao Tzu* later published in the Kohn and LaFargue anthology, and I wish to thank these editors for providing it.

Once the first draft of this book was completed, several scholars thoroughly read and critiqued it and gave me invaluable criticisms on thought, grammar, organization, and argument, which have all found their way into the final version. For taking the time out of their always too busy schedules to do this I am deeply indebted to Bob Henricks and Sarah Queen, and to the two anonymous readers for Columbia University Press. I would also like to take this opportunity to thank a number of other friends and colleagues who read various portions of the book and gave me invaluable suggestions on how to improve it: Bill Boltz, Andy Meyer, Michelle Martin, Anne Hart, Aaron Stalnaker, and Jung Lee. My two brothers in arms, Greg Schopen, the Elder (by a lot) and Charles Lachman, the Younger (by a little), were also always there to hear some wild idea or other of mine at the strangest hours of the day and night. While I am sorely tempted to blame these people for all the inadequacies of the book and take credit for all its strengths, it would be neither fair nor intellectually honest to do so; nor would it set a scholarly precedent I would wish anyone to emulate, especially anyone whose own publications I might have aided over the years!

The publication team at Columbia University Press has been absolutely first rate. Jennifer Crewe, Publisher for the Humanities, initially encouraged and accepted the book and provided me with a contract I could readily embrace. Her complete trustworthiness at every step of the process restored my faith in the publishing business. Debra Soled edited the book with care and sensitivity. Leslie Kriesel fielded all aspects of the production with skill and flexibility. Freelancer Anne Holmes brought her considerable experience and erudition to the production of an extremely helpful index.

Finally, this book would not have been possible without the steadfast companionship of my wife, Lis, and the challenging devotion of our two sons, Zach and Gus. Lis was always there for me when I wasn't there for her because I was working on this book or some other project related to it. Zach gave me respite from my intense writing schedule through all the movies he took me to see and by challenging me to come up with presidential and sports trivia questions he could not answer. Gus provided a constant example of the kind of unself-conscious spontaneity that the early Taoists admired in the "childlike mind" and with many opportunities to exercise my "adultlike body." Also, my baby brother, Mitch, relieved me of the legal burdens of our late mother's estate so I could devote more attention to my work on this book. My gratitude to—and for—this extraordinary family knows no bounds.

Original Tao

Introduction

A Textual Revolution

During the past quarter century, a procession of long-lost texts has emerged from more than two millennia beneath the soils of China. Written on bamboo and silk and entombed at the burials of the local elite in North and South-Central China, these texts comprise three general types: (1) distinct (and very early) versions of works that have survived in the received tradition, such as the Ma-wang-tui (馬王堆) manuscripts of the *Lao Tzu* (老子);[1] (2) manuscripts of works known only from historical or literary sources that have not survived in the received tradition, such as the four texts attached to one of these *Lao Tzu* manuscripts at Ma-wang-tui and tentatively identified as the *Huang-ti ssu-ching* (The Four Classics of the Yellow Emperor, 黃帝四經);[2] and (3) texts previously unknown, such as the considerable corpus of medical texts unearthed at Ma-wang-tui.[3] Other texts whose significance is almost equal to those discovered at Ma-wang-tui have been excavated at such sites as Ting-chou (定州) in Hopei province, Yin-ch'üeh shan (銀雀山) in Shantung, and Chang-chia shan (張家山) and, most recently, Kuo-tien (郭店) in Hupei. These discoveries and their subsequent analyses by East Asian and Western scholars revolutionized our understanding of the origins and early development of Chinese religion, philosophy, and science.

This revolution has come not just from analyzing these texts themselves but from finding that many of them bear distinct and significant relationships to works in the received tradition that have not received much scholarly attention because of unclear intellectual filiations or because they have been regarded as derivative or even spurious. Chief among these are the *Lü-shih ch'un-ch'iu* (The Spring and Autumn Annals of Mr. Lü, 呂氏春秋), the *Huai-nan Tzu* (淮南子), the *Ho-kuan Tzu* (鶡冠子), and the work from which the present study is drawn, the *Kuan Tzu* (管子).[4] New theories have emerged about the relationships among these works and, most significantly, the Ma-wang-tui *Huang-ti ssu-ching*, leading the way in our reassessment of the early history of the Taoist tradition.[5] This book examines these theories and how they relate to the work translated and analyzed here: the collection of philosophical verses entitled *Nei-yeh* (Inward Training, 內業), which A. C. Graham has called "possibly the oldest mystical text in China."[6] One of the distinctive contributions of *Inward Training* to this discussion of Taoist origins is that it represents the earliest extant presentation of a mystical practice that appears in all the early sources of Taoist thought, including the *Lao Tzu*, the *Chuang Tzu* (莊子), and *Huai-nan Tzu*. As such it can truly be called "the original Tao."

Another distinctive contribution of *Inward Training* is that its theoretical discussion of this mystical practice employs concepts that appear in the surviving medical literature on physical and macrobiotic hygiene, the ancient Chinese practices for maintaining health and prolonging life. As Donald Harper points out, these practices include dietetics (that is, what or what not to eat), breath cultivation, exercise, and sexual cultivation, and their goals range from maintaining health to prolonging life and even to attaining some form of spiritual transcendence of death.[7] The parallels in technical terminology between *Inward Training* and certain texts within this general tradition raise the very intriguing problem of the role that its practitioners played in the early development of Taoism.[8]

"Textual Archaeology"

Although these retrieved texts have prompted scholars to rethink the origins and early development of Taoism, this study focuses on works that have long been part of the received tradition but not sufficiently appreciated. *Inward Training* is certainly one such text. Although not buried physically, it has been buried intellectually as a mystical work subsumed as one text among seventy-six in the voluminous collection, the *Kuan Tzu*, almost the entirety of which is devoted to political and economic thought.[9] While it has caught the attention of a few Chinese and Japanese scholars during the twentieth century, it has, until recently, been largely overlooked as an important early source of Taoist mysticism. Also not appreciated is the fact that, among all the works in the spectrum of late Warring States and early Han thought, it is the one that most closely parallels the *Lao Tzu* in both literary form and philosophical content. Far from being accidental, this parallel is of the utmost significance for our understanding of the origins of distinctively Taoist methods of mystical self-cultivation that have, arguably, persisted throughout the long history of this religion.

This book represents a study in "textual archaeology," or the uncovering of long-lost or long-overlooked texts and the interpretation of their significance. It attempts to recover the original meaning of *Inward Training* and explain its significance for the origins and early development of Taoism. In addition, it discusses how *Inward Training* became "entombed" within the Kuan Tzu collection and why so few people after the early Han were aware of it.

In essence, this book chronicles an experiment in historical hermeneutics, an attempt to reconstruct what *Inward Training* meant to the people who wrote it.[10] This experiment assumes, of course, that such a meaning can be derived from the ideas in the text and how they are presented in it and from comparing these ideas to other, contemporaneous works of a similar genre and viewpoint. It also assumes that the text was produced within a distinct sociological context and that its ideas derive from the life experiences of the people who wrote it. The following methodological perspective is employed to facilitate this analysis.

A "Mystical Hermeneutic"

This study examines *Inward Training* from the standpoint of the modern comparative study of mystical experience. The analytical tools drawn from this Western academic methodology can provide important insights into the evidence that the text of *Inward Training* contains for the religious practices and experiences that led to its creation. A clear understanding of the nature of mysticism will help to interpret the ideas in the text, as well as to see them in the larger context of early Taoist mysticism, and will enable us to distinguish how the early Taoist forms of mystical practice can be differentiated from apparently similar practices within the Chinese macrobiotic hygiene tradition. Accordingly, the text is approached from a "mystical hermeneutic."

One result of this is that the translation endeavors to illuminate the mysticism of *Inward Training* by maintaining this consistent interpretive viewpoint. A good example of how this "mystical hermeneutic" influences the translation is the ideograph *cheng* (正). Although in nonmystical contexts it functions as an adjective meaning "correct, regular, square" or a verb meaning "to regulate, to rectify, to correct," in *Inward Training* it functions as a verb that means "to square up, or to align." Used with objects like the four limbs (*ssu t'i*, 四體), body (*hsing*, 形), vital energy (*ch'i*, 氣), mind (*hsin*, 心), it refers to positioning the body in the squared posture of sitting meditation (with the knees touching the ground and forming a square pattern with the shoulders) and aligning one's breathing by allowing it to fall into a constant and regular pattern that the *Inward Training* authors believed was inherent and natural.

The Significance of *Inward Training*

Inward Training is a series of poetic verses devoted to the practice of guided breathing meditation and to the ideas about the nature of human beings and the cosmos that are directly derived from this practice. It is a mystical text because its authors followed this practice to depths not normally attained by daily practitioners of breathing for health and longevity, with whom they shared aspects of technical terminology and world view. These practitioners followed the "guiding and pulling" exercises spoken of critically in the *Chuang Tzu* and *Huai-nan Tzu* (and now exemplified by textual finds at Ma-wang-tui and Chang-chia shan) and other physical or physiological practices that involve dietary and sexual regimens. Harper refers to them as the tradition of "macrobiotic hygiene." The early Taoist authors of the *Chuang Tzu* and the *Huai-nan Tzu* took care to distinguish themselves from these macrobiotic hygiene practitioners, whom they said cultivated the physical but not the numinous. The main aim of these hygiene practitioners—who regarded the Chinese Methusaleh P'eng-tsu as their symbolic founder—was health and longevity. This book explores why early

Taoists felt it necessary to distinguish themselves from these macrobiotic hygiene practitioners by analyzing what they had in common with them and how they differed. Simply put, while both groups practiced guided breathing meditation, the early Taoists applied this practice much more assiduously. In *Inward Training*, the noetic insights attained from this assiduous application of breathing meditation are the basis of the distinctive cosmology of the text, a cosmology similar to that found in its more renowned companion, the *Lao Tzu*.

Beyond "Lao-Chuang"

Until recently, the traditional belief about the origins of Taoism has rarely been challenged. This tradition maintains that Taoism was founded by a shadowy sixth-century B.C. royal Chou archivist named Lao Tan (老 聃) or Lao Tzu ("Old Master," 老 子), who taught the Confucian rites and later wrote the famous text named for him. Lao Tzu was followed by Chuang Chou (莊 周), author of the *Chuang Tzu* and by other disciples to whom books are attributed, such as Lieh Tzu (列 子)and Wen Tzu (文 子). Together they formed a Taoist school of philosophy devoted to cosmology and mysticism that advocated, among other things, the acceptance of death as just one more change in the eternal cosmic process. During the Han dynasty (206 B.C.–A.D. 220), there was a gap of about three centuries when these ideas were co-opted by charlatan magicians who shared the commoners' superstititions about ghosts and spirits and who were concerned with such vulgar concepts as longevity and immortality. Afterward, Taoism re-emerged as the guiding philosophy of two millenarian rebellions, those of the Yellow Turbans and of the Celestial Masters. After these rebellions were quelled, the institutions they established formed the basis of the organized Taoist religion, which persists to this day. In this reading of history, the Taoist religion shares little but its name with the Taoist philosophy it has often claimed as its foundation and, indeed, if one follows this view of early Taoism, one has to agree. As A. C. Graham has so succinctly put it, "No doubt one may think of this church as debasing the pure doctrine of its founder, but the Christian churches never departed quite as far from the gospel as this."[11]

We now realize that such an understanding of the history of Taoism is grossly oversimplified and reflects largely the sensibilities of generations of Chinese literati and the Western scholars who studied under them.[12] Our understanding of the early history of Taoism is gradually being transformed so that this great gulf between "philosophical" and "religious" Taoism is coming to be seen as more apparent than real. We now know that Lao Tzu is a purely legendary figure with no solid historical basis. His text, *The Lao Tzu*, is truly apocryphal and, in its complete written form, dates from no earlier than the beginning of the third century B.C.; an incomplete version has recently been discovered at Kuo-tien in Hupei in a tomb dating back to approximately 300 B.C.[13] We know too that the texts attributed to his presumed disciples Lieh Tzu and Wen Tzu are likely fourth-century A.D. forgeries containing a bit of genuinely early material.[14] Finally, the *Chuang Tzu* is a highly stratified work containing at least four different philosophical voices, in addition to Chuang Chou's, that span the roughly two centuries preceding its final compilation circa 130 B.C.[15]

Furthermore, as mentioned above, the important archaeological discoveries of the past two and a half decades and the flurry of scholarly activity surrounding them are further transforming our understanding of early Taoism. In particular, the 1973 excavation of the tomb of a son of the Marklord of Tai at Ma-wang-tui in South-Central China has yielded an extraordinary cache of texts from around 200 B.C. It includes the two earliest manuscripts of the *Lao Tzu*, attached to one of which are four Taoistic essays on cosmology and politics featuring the legendary Yellow Emperor (Huang Ti) that many scholars think can be identified as predominantly products of the long-lost "Huang-Lao" (Yellow Emperor and Lao Tzu) lineage, an early Taoist philosophical lineage with Legalist tendencies that was previously known only through historical writings.[16] Textual parallels between these *Huang-ti ssu-ching* and other extant, but heretofore overlooked, works of early Taoism and the previous conclusions about Lao Tzu and his presumed disciples have led scholars to question the exclusivity—and even the very existence—of a "Lao-Chuang" school of Taoist philosophy in the late Warring States and early Han. Such questions indicate that, if we are to truly understand early Taoist thought and its relationship to the later Taoist religion, we must include a much wider range of early philosophical texts in our analysis.

After analyzing all the newly discovered texts and their connections to extant ones, some scholars still think in terms of a Lao-Chuang philosophical school that influenced a later Huang-Lao philosophical school.

But, in reality, all these discoveries lead us to question the very idea of a philosophical school at this point in time and, indeed, even the very idea of Taoism itself. The variety of theories that attempt to answer these fundamental questions is too great to detail here. Instead I would like to present how I have dealt with "Taoism" in the absence of "Lao-Chuang."

A survey of the full range of Warring States and early Han texts usually thought of as "Taoist," in both traditional bibliographies and recent scholarship, yields three general categories under which the distinctive ideas of these texts could be subsumed:[17]

1. *cosmology*: a cosmology based on the Tao as the predominant unifying power in the cosmos;

2. *inner cultivation*: the attainment of the Tao through a process of emptying out the usual contents of the conscious mind until a profound experience of tranquility is attained;

3. *political thought*: the application of this cosmology and this method of self-cultivation to the problems of rulership.

On the basis of these three categories, we can organize the textual sources of early Taoism into three general philosophical types or orientations: Individualist, Primitivist, and Syncretist.

The first type—represented textually by Chuang Chou's "inner chapters" of the *Chuang Tzu* and our text, *Inward Training*, and therefore datable to about the middle of the fourth century B.C.—is exclusively concerned with cosmology and the inner transformation of the individual leading to the mystical experience of attaining union with the Way that Benjamin Schwartz has called "mystical gnosis."[18] Here, this type is called "Individualist" because of its focus on self-cultivation and its virtual absence of social and political thought.

The second type includes the *Lao Tzu* and the "Primitivist" voice found in *Chuang Tzu* chapters 8–10 and the first part of 11. This type includes the cosmology and self-cultivation of the Individualist type, but adds a political and social philosophy that recommends the return to the simpler life-style associated with small agrarian communities. Following Schwartz and A. C. Graham, these early Taoist texts can be called "Primitivist" because of their advocacy of this vision of a simple society and politic.[19]

The third general philosophical orientation in the texts of early Taoism is here called the "Syncretist," after Graham's usage. It is richly represented by surviving texts such as the *Huang-ti ssu-ching* from Ma-wang-tui, several essays from the *Kuan Tzu*, the "Syncretist" voice in the *Chuang Tzu*, and the *Huai-nan Tzu*.[20] The hallmarks of this type are the presence of the same cosmology and philosophy of self-transformation as the former except that it is herein commended to the ruler as a technique of government, the emphasis on the precise coordination of the political and cosmic orders by the thus-enlightened ruler, and a syncretic social and political philosophy that borrows relevant ideas from the earlier Legalist and the Confucian schools while retaining the Taoist cosmological context. This last group of texts provided the basis for the influential definition of a "Taoist school" by the famous historian Ssu-ma T'an (司馬談, d. 110 B.C.), which some scholars prefer to label "Huang-Lao."[21]

The common thread that ties together these three philosophical orientations of early Taoism and that differentiates them from other early intellectual lineages is their shared vocabulary of cosmology and mystical self-transformation. This distinctive shared vocabulary helps distinguish the meaning of the category "Taoism" in this early period, a point made in greater detail throughout this book. Furthermore, this shared vocabulary, this common thread, derives from a common meditative practice first enunciated in *Inward Training*, which I call "inner cultivation." This inner cultivation practice and the cosmology that surrounds it seems to have been carried over into the mystical practices of the later Taoist religion, although the historical details by which this transmission occurred are so obscure that perhaps they will never be known for certain.

Moreover, chapter 5 shows that because they share evidence of this practice of inner cultivation, these three groupings of early Taoist texts were produced by actual historical groupings of individuals. These texts' commonalities are not the product of intellectual ferment in late Warring States China, but came about because they were part of a common tradition based on inner cultivation. That is not to say that there were any groups identifying themselves as "Individualist," and so on but, rather, that these texts were produced by master-disciple groups who all shared this practice. Thus these three groupings of texts reflect actual aspects or phases in the evolution of early Taoism.

Therefore *Inward Training* is best understood as the earliest extant statement of the one common mystical practice that ties together the three phases of early Taoism, including the texts heretofore regarded as the sole foundations of this tradition, the *Lao Tzu* and the *Chuang Tzu*. Furthermore, there is considerable reason to believe that it was actually written earlier than these two more famous works, as shown in chapter 5. As the oldest extant expression of this common mystical practice and as the first text of Taoism to be written down, *Inward Training* can truly be said to present "the original Tao."

CHAPTER ONE

The Text of
Inward Training

Nei-yeh (Inward Training, 內業) is a collection of poetic verses on the nature of the Way (Tao, 道) and of a method of self-discipline that I call "inner cultivation"—a mystical practice whose goal is a direct apprehension of this all-pervading cosmic force. It contains some of the most beautiful lyrical descriptions of this mysterious cosmic power in early Chinese literature and in both literary form and philosophical content is quite similar to the much more renowned *Lao Tzu* (also called the *Tao Te ching*). *Inward Training* contains a total of 1,622 characters and is thus about one-third as long as the *Lao Tzu*.

The title of this text well reflects its contents. The first character, *nei*, means simply "inner/inward." The second character, *yeh*, means "work, deed, achievement."[1] Hence the title has been translated as *The Workings of the Inner* by Jeffrey Riegel and *Inner Workings* by Allyn Rickett.[2] The notion of the inward is drawn from one of the central motifs of the text—the notion of an inner life of the mind and body, a life that, left to its own devices, will waste the great potential of human beings for physical, psychological, and spiritual fulfillment. However, if this inner life is led with self-discipline, it can lead to health, vitality, psychological clarity, a sense of well-being, a profound tranquility, and, ultimately, to a direct experience of the Way and an integration of this experience into one's daily life. To lead this disciplined life is the practice advocated by this text. It is for this reason that the modern commentator Chao Shou-cheng (趙守正), astutely observes:

> Inward Training means inner achievement. It refers to the practice [kung-fu, 工夫] by which one cultivates and nourishes the inner mind and preserves vital essence and vital energy. . . . While the author of this text points out the importance of proper drinking, eating, and physical movement, the most basic and emphatic point (of this practice) lies completely within the inner mind. Therefore he called it *Inward Training*.[3]

It is this discipline of the inner life of the mind that can genuinely be called the *Inward Training*.

The Literary Genre of *Inward Training*

The text of *Inward Training* consists of a series of verses, written almost exclusively in rhyme. These verses are devoted to expounding a practice of inner cultivation and the underlying cosmology of the Way on which it is based. Most of the lines of verse are tetrasyllabic, that is, they contain four syllables each of which is represented by one character, but other patterns of five or more syllables do sometimes occur. The rhymes occur most often at the end of every second line. For example:

I

1 凡物之精
The vital essence of all things:

2 此則為生。(sreng)
It is this that brings them to life.

3 下生五穀。
It generates the five grains below

4 上為列星。(seng)
And becomes the constellated stars above.

5 流<於>天地<之>間，
When flowing amid the heavens and the earth

6 謂之鬼神。(zdjien)
   We call it ghostly and numinous.

7 藏於胸中，
   When stored within the chests of human beings,

8 謂之聖人。(njien)
   We call them sages.

The rhymes occur here in the even lines. This is the most frequent, but by no means the sole, poetic pattern. For example:

II

1 是故 <民>「此」氣：
   Therefore this vital energy is:

2 杲乎如登於天。(ten)
   Bright!—as if ascending the heavens;

3 杳乎如入淵。(·wen)
   Dark!—as if entering an abyss;

4 <淖>「綽」乎如在於海。(xməɣ)
   Vast!—as if dwelling in an ocean;

5 <卒>「崒」乎如在於<己>「屺」。(kiəɣ)
   Lofty!—as if dwelling on a mountain peak.

6 是故此氣也
   Therefore this vital energy

7 不可止以力 (liak)
   Cannot be halted by force,

8 而可安以德；(tək)
   Yet can be secured by inner power.

9 不可呼以聲
   Cannot be summoned by speech,

10 而可迎以<音>「意」。(·iəɣ)
   Yet can be welcomed by the awareness.

11 敬守勿失：
   Reverently hold onto it and do not lose it:

12 是謂成德。(tək)
   This is called "developing inner power."

13 德成而智出，
   When inner power develops and wisdom emerges,

14 萬物 <果>「畢」得。(tək)
   The myriad things will, to the last one, be grasped.

Notice that this verse contains varying lengths of four, five, and six characters (and hence syllables). Notice too how the rhyme varies between the first and second parts (lines 1–5 and 6–14, respectively). In the former, the rhyme occurs at the end of each line, and in the latter the rhyme mostly occurs at the end of every other four- or five-character line. Notice as well the insertion of the conjunction "therefore" in lines 1 and 6. Such logical copulas are often seen as evidence of the work of the composer of an original text, in this case, the person who compiled it from a series of originally distinct verses.

Although extant editions have only two or three general divisions in the text, it is possible to identify distinct units based on semantic, syntactic, and phonological criteria. I have arranged the text into twenty-six separate verses, which makes my divisions closest to the eighteen verses (plus four subdivisions) of the Gustav Haloun/Jeffrey Riegel arrangement.[4] Other arrangements have been suggested, in particular, the arrangement of Ma Fei-pai (馬非白) into fifteen separate verses with some subdivisions that is also followed by Rickett.[5] Each of these units of rhymed verse can stand independently. Because of the variety in both the meter and the rhyme among them and the presence of a few interspersed prose comments, they appear to have been composed over a period of time and then brought together and written down by the compiler of the original written text. Riegel asserts that these poetic features of *Inward Training* would have facilitated memorization and recitation.[6] This suggests that they might have been transmitted orally for a period of time before they were assembled by this compiler.

This distinctive poetic form—Taoist philosophy presented within a series of verses that could have been independently and orally transmitted until they were assembled by a compiler of an initial written edition—is reminiscent of another work that has this same basic form, the *Lao Tzu*. Riegel is certainly struck by this parallel, as is Michael LaFargue, although the latter is much more interested in the philosophical parallels than the literary ones.[7] Given these parallels, the fact that in the received editions the text of *Inward Training* is not divided into distinct verses is not all that surprising. The oldest extant manuscripts of the complete *Lao Tzu*—those excavated at Ma-wang-tui—are not divided into the eighty-one *chang* (sections—often called chapters—章) found in all editions of the received tradition, but contain only a few section divisions.[8] This does not mean that there were no divisions into verses in the original written texts, but that the divisions were to be learned from the teacher with whom one studied the text. As Kao Yu (高誘, ?155–220) says about studying the *Huai-nan Tzu* with Lu Chih (盧植, d. 192) in about A.D. 175: "From him I received the proper punctuation of the text of the *Huai-nan Tzu*, and, as he recited it, he discussed the meaning in general terms."[9] Such a practice is very old.

In a recent article, William Baxter analyzes the structural and phonological characteristics of the *Lao Tzu* in an effort to provide a new approximate date for it.[10] In the process, he points out further similarities between the *Lao Tzu*, on the one hand, and *Inward Training* and two closely related texts, *Hsin-shu, shang* (Techniques of the Mind I, 心術上) and *Pai-hsin* (The Purified Mind, 白心), on the other. He has identified some basic rhetorical characteristics of the *Lao Tzu* that he also finds in these *Kuan Tzu* texts and maintains that, taken together, they constitute a distinct literary genre.[11] In addition, his analysis of the way in which the *Lao Tzu* preserves some of the traditional rhymes of the *Shih ching* (Book of Poetry, 詩經) that another early poetic collection, the *Ch'u tz'u* (Elegies of Ch'u, 楚辭) does not, leads him to the conclusion that the date of the *Lao Tzu* lies in between that of these two works, about 400 B.C.[12]

Baxter identifies the following rhetorical characteristics of the *Lao Tzu*:[13]

1. rhyme: frequent rhymes with no dominant pattern

2. rhythm: the rhymed parts of the *Lao Tzu* are often in four-character (tetrasyllabic) lines

3. semantic parallelism and antithesis: rhymed and unrhymed lines are often related through these two devices, with distinct subjects and predicates in line x having parallel meanings or antithetical meanings with those in line y, as in *Lao Tzu* 81.

4. Repetition of two types:

    a. chain repetition: "if x then y, if y then z"; this is the sorites structure discussed further in chapter 4 (*Lao Tzu* 59)

    b. repetition of the same word in several lines (*Lao Tzu* 19).

5. paradox (*Lao Tzu* 45)

6. absence of narration: in contrast to the *Analects*, the *Mencius*, and the *Chuang Tzu*

7. framing of a passage with introductory and concluding comments

8. the use of "transitional phrases" to mark boundaries between units of verse.

Baxter argues that unrhymed lines that demonstrate semantic patterning should also be considered verse.[14]

Baxter gives several examples of some of these rhetorical characteristics from *Inward Training*, *Techniques of the Mind* I, and *The Purified Mind*. They are sufficient to indicate that these texts, along with the *Lao Tzu*, are part of a distinct literary genre:

> For our purposes, the similarities in form among these texts are as important as the similarities in ideas, for they show that the *Lao Tzu* is not a text in a vacuum; rather, it represents a genre of which there are other examples. . . .[15]
>
> A reasonable conjecture would be that the *Lao Tzu* and similar texts emerged from a distinctive tradition of philosophical verse with strong oral elements and little concept of individual authorship.[16]

Although Baxter's observations are astute, his analysis has two minor problems that affect our understanding of the genre and dating of *Inward Training*. First, Baxter lumps all these *Kuan Tzu* texts together, thereby obscuring the distinctiveness of *Inward Training* as the only one of the group that is composed almost exclusively of rhymed verse. It is true that the list of rhetorical characteristics he finds in the *Lao Tzu* can also be found in all these *Kuan Tzu* texts together, but not all of them are in *Inward Training*.

Inward Training and the *Lao Tzu* both contain rhymed verse that is often tetrasyllabic. Although Allyn Rickett points out that both texts share the use of "irregular rhymes" in a general sense, the most common irregular rhymes of the former are not found in the latter.[17] Both texts show an absence of narration, but the framing of verses so common in the *Lao Tzu* is found only twice in the twenty-six verses of *Inward Training* (in verses V and VI). Moreover, *Inward Training* contains syntactic parallelism but not the semantic parallelism and antithesis that Baxter finds in the *Lao Tzu*. In addition, Baxter recognizes that "transitional phrases" such as the connective conjunction *shih ku* (therefore, 是故), which links verses or units of verse, are common in the *Lao Tzu*; yet there are only three instances of such connectives in *Inward Training* (verses II, V, and VII). Finally, the two types of repetition he sees in the *Lao Tzu* are virtually absent from *Inward Training*, with one exception (verse VIII, ll. 6–13 contains a sorites-style chain).

Second, while recognizing that the *Lao Tzu* is structured "to form a succession of short, paragraph-like units of verse sometimes loosely framed by elements which function as introductions, transitions, or summaries," Baxter underplays the significance and sophistication of these nonverse elements. This sophistication, however, has been well understood by LaFargue, who demonstrates how the philosophical verse in the *Lao Tzu* is often embedded within a literary matrix of introductory and concluding comments and linking lines that tie together what may have originally been distinct units of verse or individual aphoristic sayings.[18] LaFargue presents an extremely detailed analysis of the way in which each chapter of the *Lao Tzu* was "artfully composed" as a "sayings collage," and he includes in this a list of the distinctive rhetorical characteristics used by the "composers" of these chapters.[19] Many of these are found in Baxter's article, but LaFargue has been able to provide a more detailed and sustained analysis of these features that augments Baxter's list.

These differences are important for they indicate that, while the *Lao Tzu* and *Inward Training* are both examples, as Baxter says, of this "distinctive tradition of early philosophical verse," the *Lao Tzu* is a more sophisticated composition than *Inward Training*. As we shall see in chapter 5, this has definite implications for their relationship and their relative dating.

The Nature and Filiation of the *Kuan Tzu* Collection

While *Inward Training* has been almost completely ignored by scholars and Taoist adepts for almost two millennia, the recent archaeological discoveries of the past quarter century and the renewed interest in defining the origins of Taoism has led to a flurry of scholarly interest in this text and its three companions in the *Kuan Tzu* collection that had produced a wide variety of theories about its dating and authorship. The following surveys these theories before presenting my own ideas on this subject.

Inward Training is one of four related texts often considered together in the *Kuan Tzu*, a complicated collection that originated in the state of Ch'i c. 300 B.C. and to which material may have been added until as late as 26 B.C., when Liu Hsiang (劉 向) established the extant recension. It now contains seventy-six *p'ien* (chapters, 篇) arranged in 24 *chüan* (books, 卷), and its extant editions are subdivided into eight sections of varying length.²⁰ For the most part, each chapter contains one distinct text, as opposed to being a separate chapter in one large integral text.²¹ For this reason I consider the *Kuan Tzu* a collection of distinct texts and therefore treat each text as an independent work in a collection rather than as a chapter of a book. In addition to *Inward Training*, the other three texts are *Techniques of the Mind*, parts I and II, and *The Purified Mind*. They are all grouped together in one of the eight sections of the *Kuan Tzu* collection, the section entitled "Tuan-yü" (Short Discourses, 短 語) as chapters 36, 37, and 38, respectively. By contrast, *Inward Training* is found in another of the eight sections, "Ch'ü yen" (Minor Statements, 區 言), as chapter 49. Because of uncertainties over the dating of the individual texts in the *Kuan Tzu* collection and the nature of Liu Hsiang's editorial activity, the significance of these groupings is still unclear. While *Inward Training* focuses almost exclusively on the distinctively Taoist meditative practice I call "inner cultivation" and thus should be classified as an "Individualist" Taoist work, the three others focus on their application to the problems of government and can be classified as "Syncretist."

Since these four "Techniques of the Mind" texts are the only texts in the *Kuan Tzu* collection devoted to inner cultivation and its application, scholars tend to consider them together, without clearly differentiating the distinctive Individualist orientation of *Inward Training*. This, plus a lack of clarity about relative dating of the four and how they relate to one another, in addition to what I now think are misguided attempts to classify them in terms of philosophical "schools," has contributed significantly to a general failure to appreciate the uniqueness of *Inward Training*.

The *Kuan Tzu* collection itself has also passively contributed to this general failure because the remainder of its constituent texts is devoted largely to political and economic matters and because the entire work has been traditionally attributed to the famous minister whose name it bears, Kuan Chung (管 仲), who served the duke Huan (桓 公), the seventh-century B.C. ruler of the state of Ch'i (齊). Some of its texts advocate the implementation of a system of rewards and punishments to order the bureacracy and the human polity associated with the doctrines of "Legal-ism" (*fa-chia,* 法 家). Others deal with the specifics of economic policy and with various other aspects that fall under the general heading of "tech-niques of statecraft." The intellectual filiation of these texts and the collec-tion as a whole have been the subject of heated debate among modern scholars. Recently, some of them, working with the new information pro-vided by the Ma-wang-tui *Four Classics of the Yellow Emperor*, have discerned differences between the Legalist teachings in the *Kuan Tzu* and the classi-cal Legalism of Shang Yang (商 鞅, 385–338 B.C.) and now think that some of its texts—even the entire work—can more accurately be classified as "Huang-Lao." For example, Hu Chia-ts'ung (胡 家 聰) provides a chapter-by-chapter analysis in which he identifies which of the *Kuan Tzu*'s texts are Huang-Lao Taoist works and which are Legalist works.[22] Kanaya Osamu (金 谷 治) argues that, despite the diversity of topics, themes, and con-cepts in the collection, it has an overall systematizing philosophy that can be identified as Huang-Lao Taoist thought, which for him is a blend of Taoism and Legalism.[23]

In view of this diversity of opinion among modern scholars with ac-cess to the newly excavated texts of the past quarter century, it is no wonder that traditional Chinese bibliographers also had difficulty catego-rizing the book: During the Han dynasty it was placed in the section of Taoist works in the dynastic bibliography written in about 50 A.D., but from the Sui dynasty on, it was classified as "Legalist." This latter classifica-tion further buried the text of *Inward Training* because most people who consulted the *Kuan Tzu* were interested in it for its political and economic thought. Scholars and adepts looking for material on Taoist cosmology and self-cultivation would have—and generally did—turn to works like the *Lao Tzu* and the *Chuang Tzu* for their inspiration.

The Formation of the *Kuan Tzu* Collection

The question of how the text of *Inward Training* came to enter the *Kuan Tzu* collection is most intriguing and defies a definitive answer. We can begin to understand some of the issues surrounding the question by further understanding the circumstances of the creation of this collection.

During the fourth and third centuries B.C., rulers of the distinct kingdoms that constituted what is traditionally called the Warring States began to gather at their courts the representatives of a wide variety of intellectual lineages whom they thought might have teachings that might help them rule their domains more efficiently and successfully. With the exceptions of the Confucian and Mohist lineages, their origins are obscure, but in general they belonged to a class of *shih* (土), usually translated as "scholars," who filled the various bureaucratic positions within these states and whose numbers increased dramatically during these centuries. These scholars were the literate descendants of the class of knights of the many smaller states conquered by the larger ones and who were now unaffiliated. They thus sought positions in whichever state would employ them.[24]

Some of these scholars carried with them to the various local courts a text that was central to their intellectual lineage and that helped define them as members of it. What is not generally recognized by modern scholarship is that these scholars also often carried with them a distinctive collection of practices or "techniques" (*shu*, 術) that were also characteristic of their particular lineages and that they employed in whatever bureaucratic positions they were able to obtain.[25] At these local courts, they often competed with one another for official patronage and, in order to outdo their rivals, developed various techniques of rhetorical persuasion. They thus became, in the now-famous words of Angus Graham, the "disputers of the Tao."

The first formal assemblage of a group of these scholars at one of these local courts for which we now have a reasonable record occurred in the state of Ch'i in the capital city of Lin tzu. According to Ch'ien Mu (錢穆) this began during the reign of the king Wei (威王, r. 358–320 B.C.) or perhaps even during that of his predecessor, the duke Huan of the T'ien family (田桓公, r. 375–58 B.C.), which usurped the throne of Ch'i in 384 B.C.[26] However, most other scholars fix the beginning no later than the reign of the king's successor, the king Hsüan (宣王, r. 320–301 B.C.). This is probably because it was during his reign that specific buildings were constructed for these scholars. According to the *Shih chi* (Records of the Grand Historian, 史記), the king Hsüan gathered a group of scholars numbering seventy-six in all and gave them official positions without specific administrative responsibilities and comfortable living quarters in a district of the capital near the city's western gate, called the "Chi-men" (稷門). This district, called "Chi-hsia" (beneath the Chi gate, 稷下), was where these men lived and gathered to exchange ideas and debate about the merits of their respective positions.[27] This collection of scholars is known in Chinese history as the "Chi-hsia Academy," although whether it possessed the level of institutional organization that would merit such a term remains unknown. The academy was in eclipse for some years around 285 B.C., but revived for almost two decades under the king Hsiang (襄王, r. 284–64 B.C.).

We know the names of as many as seventeen scholars who participated in the intellectual exchanges at Chi-hsia, some of whom are significant for our study of *Inward Training*. According to the *Records of the Grand Historian*, these include the following who are said to have studied the "Huang-Lao techniques of the Way and its inner power": Shen Tao (慎到, 350–275 B.C.) from the state of Chao (趙); T'ien P'ien (田駢, 350–275 B.C.) and Chieh Tzu (接子, 350–275 B.C.) from Ch'i; and Huan Yüan (環淵, 360–280 B.C.) from Ch'u (楚).[28] In addition, others said to have stayed there during the more than six decades of its existence include the Huang-Lao thinkers P'eng Meng (彭蒙, 370–310 B.C.) from Ch'i; Sung Hsing (宋鈃, 360–290 B.C.) from Sung (宋); and Yin Wen (尹文, 350–285 B.C.) from Ch'i; the Confucians Mencius (孟子, 390–305 B.C.) and Hsün Tzu (荀子, 330–245 B.C.); Tsou Yen (鄒衍, 305–240 B.C.), the systematizer of "naturalist" (yin-yang and Five Phases) cosmology who was also from Ch'i; and perhaps even Chuang Tzu (莊子, 365–290 B.C.).

We should also not fail to mention the presence in the Ch'i court of another group of scholars who are not generally classified among the philosophers but who were nevertheless extremely influential here and throughout China during the fourth and third centuries B.C. They were the practitioners of the various technical and esoteric arts (literally, formulas and techniques: *fang shu,* 方術) that included medicine, macrobiotic hygiene (which comprises dietetics, breath cultivation, and physical exercises), divination, astrology and calendrics, and even demonology.[29] Their writings are often linked with Tsou Yen, who is credited with extracting elements of a coherent cosmology from them. By the second century B.C., this cosmology of yin and yang and the Five Phases of *ch'i* had entered the writings of the philosophers to such an extent that it continued to be the dominant cosmological scheme in China from that point on.

We have reliable evidence that a physician named Wen Chih (文摯) was in Ch'i during the reign of the kings Wei and Min (湣, r. 300–284 B.C.); the latter killed him for causing the king to "explode in anger" in order to cure him of an illness.[30] The *Records* also mention that the practitioners of these various arts, known as the *fang shih* (formula-scholars, 方士) from the states of Yen and Ch'i, were active during this time and that during the reigns of the kings Wei and Hsüan expeditions were sent to sea to look for the islands on which the immortals lived, presumably at their instigation.[31] While we have no way of ascertaining the degree of influence these *fang shih* had on the *Kuan Tzu* collection, their presence in Ch'i along with the philosophers mentioned above would have provided the opportunity for fertile contact between these two groups.

It is now generally accepted that the *Kuan Tzu* collection represents some of the concrete results of the work of the Chi-hsia Academy.[32] It certainly contains ideas that were later taken as representative elements of the teachings of the philosophers mentioned above, although it is now extremely difficult to delineate which—if any—of them wrote specific texts in the collection. What scholarship has attempted with some success is to date the texts included in this collection and to delineate those early ones that formed the core of the collection.

Given the earliest reference to the teachings of Kuan Chung is in the *Hsin shu* (New Writings, 新書) of Chia I (賈誼, 201–169 B.C.) and to the book of Kuan Chung is in the *Huai-nan Tzu* (淮南子, 139 B.C.), many scholars theorize that is was not until the middle of the third century B.C. that an early version of the *Kuan Tzu* collection began to circulate.[33] This corresponds roughly to the time of the decline of the Chi-hsia Academy. By the time Liu Hsiang edited it in about 26 B.C., there were already 564 chapters from at least four editions of the text that he reduced to 86 by removing all duplicates. Thus by about 250 B.C. an early core recension of the collection existed, to which material was added as it was transmitted into and through the Han dynasty, thus producing the partial and complete editions edited by Liu Hsiang.

Kanaya Osamu proposes a detailed theory of strata in the book that is, for the most part, independent of both the order and the sections in which the chapters occur in the extant recension. He maintains that the majority of the *Kuan Tzu* collection comes from the middle and late Warring States period, 361–221 B.C. Some texts were added in the brief interregnum between the Ch'in and Han, 206–202 B.C., and others were added until the period when the court of Huai-nan was flourishing in the early Han dynasty, 150–122 B.C.[34] Thus Kanaya details the four strata in Table 1.1, with chapters listed in a rough chronological order:

Table 1-1
The Strata of the *Kuan Tzu*

STRATUM	CHAPTERS
1. From the beginning and middle periods of the Chi-hsia Academy (c. 345–285 B.C.)	1, 20, 2, 3, 24, 59, 36, 5, 8, 55, 14–16
2. From the last period of the Chi-hsia Academy (c. 285–235 B.C.)	7, 4, 6, 18–20, 40, 37, 49, 38, 12–13, 42, 17, 45–46, 48, 30–31, 64, 66, 27–29, 44, 52–53, 11, and 35
3. From the Ch'in–Han interregnum (206–202 B.C.)	51, 67, 41, 85, 39
4. Early Han dynasty (202–122 B.C.)	68–79, 75–78, 80–84

Thus it appears that in Kanaya's scheme, about two-thirds of the *Kuan Tzu* collection was written before the fall of the state of Ch'i to the Ch'in in 221 B.C. that signaled the final unification of the empire under Ch'in Shih Huang-ti, the first emperor of the Ch'in dynasty.

The Dating and Authorship of *Inward Training*

The problem of the dating and authorship of *Inward Training* is intimately connected to that of two other texts from the *Kuan Tzu* collection, *Techniques of the Mind* I and II. All three works have close conceptual and textual parallels, which contain important information about the dating and authorship of *Inward Training*. Another text traditionally included in this group, *The Purified Mind,* is more distantly related to the others and contains no additional data relevant to these two questions.[35]

Techniques of the Mind I consists of two distinct parts: a series of discrete statements, many in rhymed verse, and a prose commentary on each statement. Both parts focus on the application of the inner cultivation program of *Inward Training* to the problems of government and share the intellectual concerns and technical vocabulary of late Warring States and early Han Syncretic Taoism.[36]

About two-thirds of *Techniques of the Mind* II is made up of passages that parallel the middle section of *Inward Training*, which deals primarily with inner cultivation practice. These parallel passages are presented in a different order and often contain variant readings. The remainder of the text is almost exclusively in prose, presents a philosophical position quite similar to that of *Techniques of the Mind* I, and frames and contextualizes the *Inward Training* parallels.

Considerable scholarly debate has arisen over the relationship between *Inward Training* and its two companion texts, centering on whether *Inward Training* is ancestral to the others or derived from them. The resolution of this question is of critical significance for the dating and authorship of *Inward Training*. The scholarly opinions on these questions can be summarized as follows:

1. All three texts were written by the Chi-hsia Huang-Lao thinkers Sung Hsing, Yin Wen, and their disciples (Kuo Mo-jo, 郭沫若).[37] This has been the most influential opinion in China throughout the twentieth century. Kuo thinks that that all three date to about 320 B.C. He argues that each of the two most closely related texts, *Inward Training* and *Techniques of the Mind* II, is a distinct version of Sung Hsing's lectures that were later recorded from memory by two different disciples. The differences in the order of their many parallel passages are caused by the scrambling of the text of *Techniques of the Mind* II during its transmission.[38]

2. They were not written by Sung and Yin but by other Huang-Lao Taoists (or "Taoist-Legalists") from Ch'i.[39] Scholars who hold this theory disagree widely on the dating varying from c. 320 to 200 B.C.

3. Because all three texts share irregular rhymes with other Taoist texts of Ch'u origin such as the *Lao Tzu*, the *Chuang Tzu*, and the *Four Classics*, they were written by authors from this state who either journeyed to Ch'i or whose writings were later incorporated into

the *Kuan Tzu* collection. *Inward Training* is the oldest of the group (fourth century B.C.). The verses in part A of *Techniques of the Mind* I are from the early third century B.C. and were compiled when the commentary in Part B was written at Huai-nan c. 150 B.C. At this time *Techniques of the Mind* II, derived from a damaged version of *Inward Training*, was also written (Allyn Rickett).[40]

4. All three were written by the Chi-hsia Taoists Shen Tao, T'ien P'ien, and their disciples (Ch'iu Hsi-kuei [裘 錫 圭]).[41] Kanaya Osamu rejects authorship by Shen and argues, instead, for T'ien.[42] In his opinion, *Inward Training* was derived from the other two texts in about 250 B.C.[43]

5. All three texts were written by disaffected followers of Chuang Tzu who went to Ch'i and studied at Chi-hsia (Li Ts'un-shan [李 存 山]).[44]

The above theories contain important insights as to the date and authorship of *Inward Training* and its companions. There is little doubt that these texts were written by Taoists at Chi-hsia, as most scholars concur, but if we rely on their theories, the dating of the texts and identity of the authors remain unresolved. In my opinion, the key to resolving these issues lies in determining the relative dating of the two texts that most closely parallel each other, *Inward Training* and *Techniques of the Mind* II. An analysis of the linguistic features of each text clearly indicates that *Inward Training* is a fourth-century B.C. text and that the others are derived from it.[45]

The antiquity of *Inward Training* is further supported by the evidence of its distinctive literary structure as a composition of originally independent, rhymed verse much like the majority of the material in the *Lao Tzu*.[46] This type of rhythmic and rhymed verse is a sign of oral transmission and harkens back to a time before literacy moved beyond government bureaucracies in the latter half of the fourth century B.C.[47] Further, *Inward Training* does not contain the kind of sustained argumentation found in third-century B.C. philosophical essays, and it shows only a loose principle of organization between its verses rather than a connection through a sustained argument. The absence of the correlative cosmology of yin and yang and the five phases, characteristic of third-century B.C. texts, further underscores its antiquity.

In addition to determining that *Inward Training* was the oldest of the three texts, I was also able to explain the reason for the intriguing parallels between it and *Techniques of the Mind* II. I discovered that *Techniques of the Mind* II is an original prose essay in which the author *deliberately* extracted and rearranged the verses from *Inward Training* for the purpose of advocating the techniques and philosophy of inner cultivation as part of the arcana of rulership. It thus complements *Techniques of the Mind* I, and it is no accident that the two are placed together in the *Kuan Tzu* and labeled as parts of one essay.

This theory that the *Techniques of the Mind* II compiler deliberately abridged, edited, and rearranged the material he used from *Inward Training* has the advantage of explaining the features of both texts without resorting to the explanation that one of the texts was damaged, as Kuo and Rickett have contended. It also fits well with what we know of the relative dating of the two works based on their linguistic features.

Moreover, the newly discovered *Lao Tzu* parallels, found in 1993 at Kuo-tien in Hupei province, contain evidence that is quite valuable for the dating of these texts.[48] They consist of thirty-three distinct passages that have parallels in thirty-one of the chapters of the *Lao Tzu*. These passages are found in three bundles of bamboo strips; the first contains twenty passages, the second eight, and the third five. After these five is another text heretofore unknown in China that the scholars who first studied this material entitled "T'ai-i sheng shui" (Grand Unity Generates Water, 太一生水). These parallel passages to the *Lao Tzu* occur in a completely different order from the one in the received *Lao Tzu*. The tomb has been given the approximate date of 300 B.C.[49]

The *Lao Tzu* parallel passages from Kuo-tien include both material on self-cultivation and an advocacy of this practice as part of the arts of rulership. Some of the more overtly political passages from *Lao Tzu* are not found in this material, and neither are most of the military passages.[50] In my opinion, their discovery does not indicate the existence of an already complete *Lao Tzu* at this time but, rather, testifies to one or more distinct attempts to compose verses based on those from an oral tradition we can call Taoist.[51] *Inward Training* is another such attempt, albeit a less sophisticated one. Because of the stylistic and philosophical similarities between these two works, the dating of the Kuo-tien tomb can serve as a *terminus ante quem* for dating *Inward Training* and rounds out our picture of the relative dating of it and companion texts from the *Kuan Tzu*.

This picture is that *Inward Training* is the oldest of the group and is a genuine fourth-century B.C. work. While it is difficult to say with certainty, its exclusively verse format and absence of political thought would support an early date—say mid-fourth century at the latest. The first part of *Techniques of the Mind* I contains verses that are almost as old, but since they begin to advocate the application of the inner cultivation program of *Inward Training* to the task of governing and show evidence of interaction with rival intellectual positions, I would date them to about 300 B.C. The commentary contained in the second part of *Techniques of the Mind* I shows the influence of the *Lao Tzu* and so must be dated to a later time after this work began to be influential in intellectual circles in about 250 B.C. It was probably completed at the same time *Techniques of the Mind* II was compiled from *Inward Training* after a Syncretic Taoist intellectual position had been established. Note that these approximate dates almost completely cover the span of time that the Chi-hsia Academy was in existence in Ch'i.[52]

How do these conclusions about the relative dating of these three texts influence our understanding of their authorship? To begin with, nothing discovered about their relative dates prevents them from being considered Taoist texts that are part of the same intellectual tradition. Since they are included in the *Kuan Tzu* collection that originated in Ch'i, their relative dates and close relationship do not contradict a Ch'i origin.

As for Rickett's interesting observation about their common use of irregular rhymes, a general use that they share with other Taoist texts presumed to come from Ch'u and to be indicative of a Ch'u dialect, while this evidence is compelling, there are questions about whether it is possible to identify such a dialect because of scholarly disagreement over what constitutes an irregular rhyme.[53] Moreover, if all these texts are products of the same intellectual tradition, perhaps the common distinctive rhymes are *not* the result of their being produced in the same geographic region but, rather, of certain literary standards accepted within this tradition. These distinctive rhymes would have been established by the oldest rhymed texts within this tradition, in my analysis, *Inward Training* and the *Lao Tzu*. Later authors would have used rhymes drawn from these two works. Indeed, the research of William Baxter that indicates these works constitute a distinct literary genre supports this theory. The implication of these doubts is that Rickett's theory of Ch'u authorship needs to be considered further.[54]

There seems little reason to adhere any longer to Kuo Mo-jo's theory that *Inward Training* and its companions were produced by the school of

Sung Hsing and Yin Wen. The most telling criticism of this theory is that while these texts are filled with mystical teachings, there is nothing whatsoever of this nature attributed to Sung and Yin in existing sources.[55] Furthermore, Kuo's arguments for his position rely heavily on the attribution to Sung and Yin of a doctrine of "purifying the mind" (pai-hsin, 白 心) in Chuang Tzu 33.[56] However, as Graham has shown, the use of this term in the Chuang Tzu is part of an introductory formula in which the author summarizes their teachings in his own words and is not to be attributed to them as a specific doctrine.[57]

As for Li Ts'un-shan's theory that all three texts were written by disaffected disciples of Chuang Tzu, all this theory is based on is certain common themes and technical terms they share with the Chuang Tzu. The case would be much more compelling if these points were in common *only* with the Chuang Tzu. However, many scholars have shown these texts share common themes and technical terms with other early Taoist works. These commonalities indicate membership within one general Taoist tradition, but they do not support a link with the Chuang Tzu alone.

Finally, the theories of Ch'iu Hsi-kuei and Kanaya Osamu linking the texts with Shen Tao and T'ien P'ien, or with T'ien P'ien alone, deserve further examination. While the extant writings of Shen do not bear out his interest in mystical themes, that is not the case for T'ien's testimony.[58] If Kanaya is right in asserting that the Chuang Tzu 33 summary of the teachings of these two is based much more on T'ien's than on Shen's, then we do find mystical ideas such as occur in our three texts associated with T'ien.[59] Significantly, in Chuang Tzu 33, these include the psychological concepts of attaining equanimity and of attaining the Way, of being impartial, and of discarding knowledge and abandoning the self—all of which derive from mystical practice.[60] Only the first two of these are found in Inward Training (see, for example, verses III and XVII), but the others are important ideas in Techniques of the Mind I and constitute what Kanaya calls the Taoist teachings of the "techniques of adaptation" (yin chih shu, 因 之 術).[61] The dialogue between T'ien P'ien and the king of Ch'i in the Annals of Mr. Lü essay 17.8, "Chih-i" (Grasping the One, 執 一) throws an interesting light on these questions:

T'ien P'ien was expounding the Techniques of the Way [Tao-shu, 道 術] to the king of Ch'i. The king responded to him, saying, "What I

possess is the state of Ch'i. I wish to ask you about governing Ch'i."
T'ien P'ien answered him, saying: "There is nothing about governing
in my words, yet they can be used to attain [the ability to] govern.
This is like the trees in the forest. The forest has no lumber in it, but
it can be used to obtain lumber. I wish that the king would simply
take from within himself the means of governing the state of Ch'i."
P'ien's teachings here were still shallow; if he had given more extensive teachings how would it be that only the state of Ch'i could have
been governed?

> Alternations and transformations respond and come forth
> Yet all have [underlying] patterns.
> If by adapting to their innate natures you employ things
> Then none will not be suitable and appropriate.
> This is what Ancestor P'eng used to be long-lived,
> What the Three dynasties used to flourish,
> What the Five Emperors used to be brilliant,
> And what Shen Nung used to be vast.[62]

When he says that his teachings contain nothing about governing, T'ien
is likely referring to the techniques of inner cultivation with which he is
associated in *Chuang Tzu* 33. Here he seems to be urging the king to apply
these techniques to the political tasks he is facing. Through them he can
find the inner abilities he needs to govern.

This dialogue is framed by comments from the author of this essay,
who can be classified as a Syncretic Taoist and perhaps a member of T'ien's
own tradition.[63] According to him, while T'ien did expound the basic
"Techniques of the Way" to the king, he did not go far enough in explaining the political application of these techniques: By cultivating a sense of
inner equilibrium and impartiality, rulers can clearly see the underlying
patterns of things amid the profusion of their transformations and see as
well their underlying natures. By seeing these patterns and adapting to
their innate natures, they can govern effectively by assigning tasks and
responsibilities to people that are never unsuitable or inappropriate. These
teachings show precisely the kind of application of the methods of inner
cultivation outlined in *Inward Training* to the problems of rulership that I
believe is characteristic of Syncretist Taoism, including the importance of
adapting to the innate natures of things and assigning suitable tasks.[64] This

is an excellent example of what Kanaya calls "the techniques of adaptation" that he finds in *Techniques of the Mind* I and indicates a philosophical similarity between its author and the author of this *Annals of Mr. Lü* essay.

This passage suggests the possibility that T'ien and his lineage are responsible for initiating the application of the methods of inner cultivation techniques of *Inward Training* to the problems of government. Whether T'ien himself is their author is difficult to say since much of the technical terminology and metaphors of these texts are absent from what little has survived of his teachings. Nonetheless, it is quite plausible that T'ien's lineage is responsible for writing the two *Techniques of the Mind* texts that apply inner cultivation to governing and contain some of his identified interests because of the philosophical similarities between these two texts and *Annals of Mr. Lü* 17.8. Also, the dates of his life span (350–275 B.C.) make this plausible, given our previous dating of the texts.[65] Unfortunately this evidence is not sufficiently substantial to establish the authorship of *Inward Training*; it can only be suggestive.

A Confucian *Inward Training*?

The *Han shu i-wen chih* ("Bibliographical Monograph" in the History of the Former Han Dynasty) lists a work entitled *Inward Training* among its Confucian texts.[66] It had fifteen chapters, and the author was unknown. This has led to speculation about a Confucian version of *Inward Training* that circulated separately from the *Kuan Tzu* collection. While it is known that certain texts now included in this collection did circulate independently during the Han dynasty, we have no other references to such a work in extant sources.

What we do have, however, is a unique verse in our extant *Inward Training* that evinces an interest in applying the principles of Taoist inner cultivation to a Confucian context:

XXII

1 凡人之生也，(sreng)
   As for the vitality of all human beings:

2 必以平正。(tjieng)
   It inevitably occurs because of balanced and aligned [breathing].

3 所以失之
The reason for its loss

4 必以喜怒憂患.
Is inevitably pleasure and anger, worry and anxiety.

5 是故止怒莫若詩；
Therefore, to bring your anger to a halt, there is nothing better than poetry;

6 去憂莫若樂；
To cast off worry there is nothing better than music;

7 節樂莫若禮；
To limit music there is nothing better than the rites;

8 守禮莫若敬；(ki'eng)
To hold onto the rites there is nothing better than reverence;

9 守敬莫若靜。(dzjieng)
To hold onto reverence there is nothing better than tranquility.

10 內靜外敬，(ki'eng)
When you are inwardly tranquil and outwardly reverent

11 能反其性。(sjieng)
You are able to return to your innate nature

12 性將大定。(deng)
And this nature will become greatly stable.

While A. C. Graham took this verse as evidence that *Inward Training* pre-dated the antagonisms between Confucianism and Taoism, there are both structural and philosophical reasons to suspect that lines 5–12 of this verse represent a later Confucian or Confucian-inspired interpolation.

Structurally, they are introduced by the connective conjunction, *shih ku* (therefore) and appear to constitute a separate unit added to lines 1–4 as a rough commentary. Lines 5–12 comment on only two of the problematic emotions in line 4, anger and worry. Pleasure and anxiety are ignored. Instead of commenting on pleasure and anger, lines 6–9 contain a sorites chain argument linking poetry, music, the rites, and reverence. Lines 5–7 interrupt the rhyme. Lines 5–9 are linked together by a common syntactic structure that occurs nowhere else in the passage (x 莫若 y). Indeed, virtually the only occurrence in *Inward Training* of the character *jo* (若) in the sense of "like, as," one of Bernhard Karlgren's indicators of both the Lu dialect and of a third-century B.C. text, occurs in these lines.[67] This is further suggestive of a later date for these lines or perhaps of a Confucian origin for them. It thus appears that lines 5–12 constitute an independent unit that had only a cursory resemblance to lines 1–4.

In addition, there are philosophical reasons to doubt the originality of lines 5–12. First, their discussion of the Confucian concepts of poetry, music, and the rites, is unique in the text.[68] Throughout the remainder of the text the authors commend inner cultivation practice, not Confucian practices, as the way to overcome the deleterious effects of emotions. This kind of positive use of Confucian ethical practices is otherwise unheard of in Taoist sources of the fourth century B.C. Witness the satires of Confucius in the Inner Chapters of *Chuang Tzu* and the vitriolic criticism of his teachings in *Lao Tzu* 18–19. Moreover, lines 11–12 discuss the concept of *hsing* (innate nature), which is otherwise unknown in Taoist texts until the middle of the third century B.C.[69] These lines about returning to one's innate nature echo the Syncretic Taoist *Huai-nan Tzu*, but seem clearly out of place here.[70] Finally, the phrase "inwardly tranquil and outwardly reverent" (*nei-ching wai-ch'ing*) closely parallels the famous "inner sageliness, outer kingliness" (*nei-sheng wai-wang*, 內 聖 外 王) of *Chuang Tzu* (33/14) that also finds parallels in other sources of the mature Syncretic Taoism called "Huang-Lao" in the early Han.[71] It also seems out of place in a fourth-century B.C. text like *Inward Training*. So although it is remotely possible that lines 5–12 were part of the original *Inward Training*, on balance, it is highly unlikely.

However, this is not to say that there was no interest in Confucian circles in applying Taoist inner cultivation practices to Confucian self-cultivation. Indeed, Jeffrey Riegel argues that the extant *Chung-yung* (Doctrine of the Mean, 中 庸) is a record of an early Han dynasty discussion of the ideas and merits of an earlier, now lost work, that was part of the lineage of Tzu Ssu (子 思), the grandson of Confucius. This earlier lost work, which he thinks was similar in form to *Inward Training*, represented precisely such a Confucian application of Taoist methods.[72] Moreover, Confucian interest in psychological techniques is also found in several other sources. First, there is the "Wu-hsing p'ien" (Section on the Five Conducts, 五 行 篇) discovered at Ma-wang-tui on the same silk scroll as one of the two *Lao Tzu* manuscripts.[73] An earlier version of this text was also found at Kuo-tien.[74] It contains the entire "canon" section of this later work but none of the commentary. The text stresses the cultivation of the inner mind in order to discover the roots of the Confucian virtues of humaneness, rightness, rectitude, wisdom, and sagacity and is considered a document from the Tzu Ssu–Mencian line of Confucianism.[75] Indeed, both the Kuo-tien and Ma-wang-tui manuscripts contain the famous admonition to "be watchful in your aloneness" found in the *Doctrine of the Mean,* thus linking these works together in a Tzu Ssu–Mencius line. In addition, some passages in the *Hsün Tzu* show that he was aware of these inner cultivation methods and even advocated them:

凡治氣養心之術，莫徑由禮，莫要得師，莫神一好。
In summary, of all the methods of regulating the vital breath and nourishing the mind, none is more direct than proceeding according to ritual principles, none more essential than obtaining a good teacher, and none more intelligent than unifying one's likes.[76]

For Hsün Tzu, inner cultivation could be accomplished by practicing these "external" Confucian virtues. For the Tzu Ssu lineage, it seems that inner cultivation was directed toward discovering Confucian virtues within the mind and then developing them through practice. Although these Confucian texts and *Inward Training* may have shared a common interest in psychological functioning and perhaps even a similarity in methods of breath cultivation, their goals are distinctively different. The Taoist inner cultivation practice advocated in *Inward Training* and evidenced in many other sources of early Taoism was aimed at a complete emptying of the mind of its normal conscious contents so that one could become aware of the subtle and mysterious Way that lies within.

We must also recognize the possibility that these lines or perhaps the entire verse was added by Liu Hsiang from the work called *Inward Training* in the *Han shu* (History of the Former Han Dynasty) when he compiled the eighty-six-chapter *Kuan Tzu* collection in about 26 B.C. Perhaps this verse was damaged in all his editions and he added it because he saw a parallel. It is, of course, also possible that the so-called Confucian *Inward Training* had absolutely nothing to do with our *Kuan Tzu* chapter or that it represented a Confucian application of its principles and methods. This question may never be answered, but, in view of all the archaeological discoveries in recent decades, one never knows.

CHAPTER TWO

A Critical Edition and Translation of
Inward Training

The Critical Edition of *Inward Training*

As I have previously written, establishing a critical edition of a text must be based on a solid foundation in textual history.[1] In the case of the *Kuan Tzu,* the beginnings of such a foundation are present in the writings of two Western sinologists, Gustav Haloun and Piet van der Loon.[2] Both deal capably with issues involving the origins and textual transmission of the *Kuan Tzu* collection and with the establishment of the recension from which all extant editions have descended. However, neither scholar provides the filiation analysis of all the extant editions of the text that would enable us to find the minimum number of extant editions with the widest range of possibly authentic textual variations.

Fortunately, we do have the brilliant work of Kuo Mo-jo, Hsü Wei-yü (許維遹), and Wen I-to (聞一多), which was improved upon by Kanaya Osamu.[3] Although they have not been able to make a complete search for all extant editions of the *Kuan Tzu*, they have made great strides toward identifying the major editions and clarifying their filiation. Work remains to be done in the identification of other editions and sorting of all editions into lineages to determine which are ancestral and which are derivative, yet their studies provide an excellent basis for establishing a critical edition.

All this research on the textual history of the *Kuan Tzu* has been admirably summarized by Allyn Rickett in two works.[4]

The process of establishing a critical edition consists of two basic steps, *recensio* and *emendatio*.[5] The first comprises gathering and sifting through the extant witnesses to a text, principally its extant editions, to determine which will be consulted. Often scholars simply take the oldest editions for their critical text. This is fine as far as it goes, but without a complete filiation analysis one can never be certain that a later edition has not preserved important variants from an earlier—and now lost—edition.[6]

In their work Kuo, Hsü, and Wen identified twenty-two extant editions of the Kuan Tzu, of which they used the five they considered the most important probably because they were the oldest, although they do not say for sure. Seventeen extant editions are descended from these five editions, twelve of them from the Chao edition. Using the first edition below as their base-text or "lemma," they then listed all textual variants in these five editions.

1. YANG CHEN (楊枕) REDACTION OF CIRCA 1284 (YC)

There is some uncertainty about the date of printing because the Yang preface provides only a Sung dynasty cyclical date: Ta Sung *chia-shen* (大宋甲申). Because this edition also includes another preface by Chang Nieh (張嵲) dated 1139, this cyclical date must be after 1139. The *chia-shen* year occurred twice during the Sung after 1139: in 1164 and 1224. Kuo thinks Yang was a Sung sympathizer who printed this edition in the last years of the Southern Sung but added the preface during the early Yüan dynasty, in 1281 (the *chia-shen* year during the reign of Kublai Khan, founder of the Yüan dynasty). If Kuo is right about Yang's sympathies, would he not have meant the *chia-shen* year of what was formerly the Sung dynasty? This would then give a date of 1284. We shall use this for our tentative date.[7]

This is acknowledged by Kuo and Kanaya as the best of the extant editions. It has many important descendants, including the Chao Yung-hsien edition (see below). A traced facsimile was made by Chang Ying (張瑛) in 1879, and a photolithographic reproduction was published in the *Ssu-pu ts'ung-k'an* in 1923. Although Kuo thinks it was based on an exemplar of the original redaction, judging from the case of the *Huai-nan Tzu* edition in the *Ssu-pu ts'ung-k'an* it is more likely to have been made from the Chang Ying facsimile.[8]

2. Liu Chi (劉績) Redaction of c. 1500 (LC)

Kuo's opinions about this redaction are clouded by his inability to date its editor, Liu Chi, whom he thinks is likely to have been a Liao scholar.[9] However, Kanaya and I both concur in dating him to the early Ming.[10] His *Huai-nan Tzu* edition is dated 1501.

3. Chu Tung-kuang's (朱東光) *Chung-li ssu tzu chi* (中立四子集) edition of 1579 (CLST)

This is based directly on a reprint of the Liu Chi redaction.[11] Without personally examining it I cannot say if another edition was consulted, as it was in the case of Chu's edition of the *Huai-nan Tzu*, also included in the same series.[12]

4. The Old Edition Without Commentary of c. 1530 (Old)

The information provided by Kuo makes it clear that this edition was based on a yellow-paper reprint of the Liu Chi edition that deleted the commentary. It contains a tell-tale textual variant also found in that edition, the omission of one character from *Techniques of the Mind* II that had erroneously entered the commentary in the yellow-paper reprint. Since the commentary was deleted in this edition, so was this character.[13] It contains no dates but because it is a direct ancestor of the An-cheng T'ang (安正堂) edition with the same publishing date as their *Huai-nan Tzu* edition of 1533, I estimate its date as 1530.[14] Kuo includes it because he thinks it is pre-Ming because of his confusion about the dates of Liu Chi.

5. Chao Yung-hsien (趙用賢) Edition of 1582 (CYH)

This has been the most prolific edition of the *Kuan Tzu*, as the ultimate ancestor of twelve of the twenty-two editions examined. An 1875 reprint of it by the Chekiang Publishing Company in its *Erh-shih erh tzu* (Twenty-Two Philosophers, 二十二子) collection was included in the *Ssu-pu pei-*

yao. However, Kuo thinks that it is ultimately based on the Yang Chen redaction.[15]

Based on these five editions, Kuo, Hsü, and Wen identified eleven textual variations in *Inward Training*, almost all of which involve obvious errors that can be determined from context and help us establish directionality of variation. These variations are summarized in Table 2.1. The location of each variation is given for the critical texts included below in this chapter.[16]

Table 2.1

Textual Variations in the Five Principal Editions of *Inward Training*

NUMBER	LOCATION	YANG CHEN	LIU CHI	OLD	CLST	CHAO
1.	V.11	被	彼	= LC	= LC	= LC
2.	VI.8	omission	故	= LC	= LC	= YC
3.	VII.1	正	政	= LC	= LC	= YC
4.	XI.3	靜	盡	= LC	= LC	= YC
5.	XII.2	照	昭	= LC	= LC	= YC
6.	XIV.15	心之中	心心之中	= LC	= LC	= YC
7.	XVIII.6	弟兄	兄弟	= LC	= LC	= YC
8.	XIX.6	能止乎能已乎	omission	= LC	= LC	= YC
9.	XIX.8	而之己乎	而得之己乎	= LC	= LC	= LC
10.	XXVI.5	臧	藏	= LC	= LC	= YC
11.	XXVI.10	匈中	中匈	= LC	= LC	= YC

The Yang and Chao editions agree on nine of these variations, and the other three editions agree on all eleven. The two variations on which the Chao edition agrees with the others, but not the Yang edition, are obvious errors in the latter.

Based upon this admittedly incomplete data and analysis, it appears that there are only three distinct lines of descent of the *Kuan Tzu* from the Sung dynasty or earlier recension that must have been ancestral to all extant editions. The ancestral redactions in these three lines of descent are the Yang Chen, Liu Chi, and the Chao Yung-hsien editions. This data allows the development of the following *stemma codicum*:

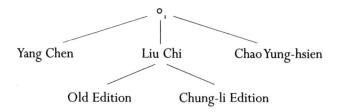

| Yang Chen | Liu Chi | Chao Yung-hsien |

| Old Edition | Chung-li Edition |

Thus the rule for determining the readings in o$_1$, the hypothetical ancestor of the twenty-two extant editions examined by Kuo, Hsü, and Wen is that when two of the three ancestral redactions agree on a reading, that is the reading in o$_1$. This enables us to decide all the above textual variations.[17]

With these variant readings decided, we can now proceed to the second stage in establishing a critical text, *emendatio*. This stage consists of emending the remaining readings to determine which are correct. The splendid collection of the emendations of forty-two Chinese and Japanese scholars included in the Kuan Tzu chi-chiao of Kuo Mo-jo, Hsü Wei-yü, and Wen I-to is an invaluable resource for this stage of the text-critical process. However, the commentary included in most extant editions—commonly attributed to Fang Hsüan-ling (房玄齡, 578–648), but probably written by Yin Chih-chang (尹知章, d. 718)—is of little value. It is best consulted for emending variant readings in the text that are sometimes not repeated in the commentary. Even for that, however, it must be used with caution.

The base-text for this translation is the *Ssu-pu ts'ung-k'an* edition of the *Kuan Tzu,* which is a photolithographic reproduction of a Ch'ing facsimile of the Yang Chen edition. Emendations are indicated according to the following notations: <A>: delete character A; 「B」: insert character B; A (B): character A is to be read as B: this is used most often for phonetic loan characters, characters that were traditionally substituted for other homophonous ones but do not have the same meaning. Explanations of the emendations are made in the notes to the Chinese text. In establishing this critical text I have consulted five important sources for emendations to the readings in this edition, listed chronologically as follows.

1. Kuo Mo-jo, Hsü Wei-yü, and Wen I-to, *Kuan Tzu chi-chiao* (官子集校).

2. Jeffrey Riegel, "The Four 'Tzu Ssu' Chapters of the *Li Chi*," which contains the text-critical notes of Gustav Haloun from a manuscript given the author by Dennis Twitchett.

3. Chao Shou-cheng, *Kuan Tzu t'ung-chieh* (管子通解).

4. Ma Fei-pai (馬非白, also known as Ma Yüan-tsai [馬元材]), "*Kuan Tzu* Nei-yeh p'ien chi-chu" (管子內業篇集注).

5. Endō Tetsuō (遠藤哲夫), *Kanshi* (管子), Shinshaku kambun taikei edition.

The *Inward Training* section of the book by Kuo, Hsü, and Wen contains comments by seventeen of the most important Chinese and Japanese text-critical scholars primarily from the eighteenth, nineteenth, and twentieth centuries, in addition to those of the authors. These scholars are: Liu Chi (劉績, fl. c. 1500), Wang Nien-sun (王念孫, 1744–1832), Igai Hikohiro (豬飼文博, 1761–1845), Wang Yin-chih (王引之, 1766–1834), Sung Hsiang-feng (宋翔鳳, 1776–1860), Ch'en Huan (陳奐, 1786–1863), Yasui Mamoru (安井衡, 1799–1876), Yü Yüeh (俞樾, 1821–1907), Ting Shih-han (丁士涵, fl. c. 1860), Tai Wang (戴望, 1837–73), Ho Ju-chang (何如璋, 1838–91), Chang P'ei-lun (張佩綸, 1848–1903), T'ao Hung-ch'ing (陶鴻慶, 1859–1918), Yao Yung-kai (姚永概, 1866–1923), Chang Ping-lin (章炳麟, 1868–1936), Liu Shih-p'ei (劉師培, 1884–1919), and Li Che-ming (李哲明, *chin-shih*, 1892). My critical edition lists only the emendations from these scholars that I accept and does not present those with which I do not agree. However, I have carefully considered every variant reading and emendation, following a principle of parsimony in accepting the fewest possible in order to make sense of the text.

Inward Training is found in chapter 49 of the *Kuan Tzu*, which in the *Ssu-pu ts'ung-k'an* edition is in book 16. All page and line numbers are to this chapter.

Inward Training is written almost exclusively in rhymed verse, as is the *Lao Tzu*. However, even the relatively few unrhymed lines often contain the four-syllable meter characteristic of the rhymed lines. Given the uncertain state of our knowledge of pronunication during the fourth century B.C. and of the possible existence of regional dialectical variations, it seemed pointless not to treat the few unrhymed lines in the text as verse. Indeed, as seen in chapter 1, William Baxter would categorize rhythmic parallel prose within this genre of philosophical literature as verse anyway. Instead, I provide pronunciations for the rhyming characters after each line of the Chinese text so that readers can see exactly which lines rhyme and which probably do not. Pronunciations follow rhyming characters and are taken from the ancient Chinese reconstructions of Chou Fa-kao (周

法高). [18] I have divided the text into distinct verses whenever a particular line of thought seemed to come to an end and when the rhyme or metrical pattern was completed. The original text was likely continuous, as are the two Ma-wang-tui manuscript editions of the *Lao Tzu*. Nonetheless, just as the *Lao Tzu* has been divided into chapters consisting of distinct verses, so too can *Inward Training*. Such divisions were undoubtedly part of the original text but were indicated, not in the text itself, but by how it was recited by masters to their students.

Technical Terminology

My translation and interpretation of the text of *Inward Training* is based on my understandings, sometimes unique, of the meaning of some key technical terms, as follows.

The translations of some of these key technical terms takes us into two very vexing areas in the history of Western philosophy: those involving the tenuous distinctions between energy and matter and between mind and body. Without engaging these problems in detail, suffice it to say that, in the early Chinese world view reflected in these early Taoist writings, such distinctions were not made with the same degree of concreteness and inflexibility that we are accustomed to.

Our conceptually distinct line between energy and matter is blurred in the traditional Chinese notion of *ch'i*, translated here as "vital energy" or as "vital breath" in contexts in which the breathing meditation is being discussed. In the very earliest texts, *ch'i* refers to the vapors or steam arising from the heating of water and watery substances and not much later appear as the actual air that we breathe. Hence many scholars have translated *ch'i* as "vapor." But to do this underplays its association with biological life and vitality. By the time of the *Huai-nan Tzu*, in 139 B.C., *ch'i* is the universal energy/matter/fluid out of which all phenomena in the universe are constructed, both the physical and the psychological. One can see here a cosmic continuum in which the heaviest and most turbid *ch'i* is found in the most solid and dense matter such as mountains and rock and in which the most ethereal *ch'i* is found in what we would call psychological and spiritual phenomena such as the most profound inner experiences of tranquility and in the ghostly entities that survive physical death. However, this notion of a continuum fails to capture the association of *ch'i* with life and vitality, for in these early Chinese contexts the more ethereal *ch'i* is found in the vitalizing fluids associated with all living things. Human beings are made up of systems containing varying densities of *ch'i*, such as the skeletal structure, the skin, flesh and musculature, the breath, the "Five Orbs" (*wu-tsang*, 五 臟) of *ch'i* that form our inner physiology and include the physical organs of the lungs, kidneys, liver, gallbladder, and spleen and the various psychological states comprising our constantly changing continuum of experience from rage and lust to complete tranquility. This last group demonstrates the remarkably modern notion that psychological states have physiological substrates. Although our modern understanding of physiology is markedly different from this and the early Chinese believed in a full integration between the physical and the psychological, the basic principle remains. This principle—which is central to Chinese medical theory—leads to various practices associated with later institutionalized Taoism, in which the physiological substrates are manipulated or influenced to achieve desired psychological or psychospiritual ends.

The most concentrated and yet refined and ethereal *ch'i* in our sources is called *ching*, translated here as "vital essence." It is, without a doubt, one of the central concepts of *Inward Training* and therein appears as both the life-giving essence contained in the seeds of all living things and as the physiological substrate associated with profound tranquility in sages leading directly to their sagacity. It is spoken of with awe and can truly be understood as the concrete manifestation of the Way's power to generate the living. As the source of the vital energy in human beings, it is the basis of our health, vitality, and psychological well-being. In some passages, it is given a cosmological dimension and is spoken of in language similar to that used for the Way. This is true to such an extent that commentators such as Ma Fei-pai and Chang Shou-cheng assert that the two terms are synonymous.[19] That is, the Way is actually a vital essence itself, thus giving it a very physiological, very "materialistic" character.

The term *hsin* (literally, "heart") is, for the early Chinese, the locus of the entire range of conscious experience, including perception, thought, emotion, desire, and intuition. It is another of those key philosophical terms that spans our definitive split between mind and body and so is commonly translated as either "heart" or "mind" or some combination thereof. Just as the *wu-tsang* include more than just physical organs, *hsin* means not just the physical heart but the entire sphere of vital energy that flows through and includes it. For this reason and because the *hsin* is not solely associated with emotion as it is for us, here the term is translated as "mind" and carries a concrete physiological connotation.

The *shen*, often translated as "spirit/spiritual" (noun/stative verb) and, following Willard Peterson, previously translated as "numen/numinous" (meaning a divinity or spirit), is, for the *Inward Training* authors, used to identify a foundational layer of mystical awareness that lies within human beings.[20] It is another concept that bridges our accustomed notions of mind and body in a way analogous to that in which the term *ch'i* bridges our ideas of energy and matter. The Chinese concept includes parts of the ranges of meanings of the English terms commonly used to translate it— spirit, soul, psyche, daemon—but none of these fully captures its range of meanings in Chinese. For the ancient Chinese, it is ultimately unfathomable, as is clearly stated in the "Hsi-tz'u" (Appended Statements, 繫辭) commentary of the *I ching* (Book of Change, 易經): "Where yin and yang do not penetrate, we call it the numinous" (陰陽不測謂之神).[21] Yet it provides humans with metaphysical knowledge such as precognition and is the locus of the mystical intuition called *shen ming*, translated here as "numinous clarity." As a most profound level of consciousness, it is experienced only fleetingly, and, according to *Inward Training*, one must take determined steps to to bring stillness and tranquility to our normal consciousness in order to retain it within our experience. In *Inward Training* and in associated works like chapter 7 of *Huai-nan Tzu*, it is said to have a "physiological substrate" of vital essence (*ching*). In the *Huai-nan Tzu*, this substrate is further identified as the *ching-shen* (numinous essence), the closest modern approximation being "psychic energy," an unusually apt translation adopted almost sixty years ago by W. K. Liao in his translation of the *Han-fei Tzu*.[22] An important development of the *Huai-nan Tzu* is that the *shen* is not only the locus and source of all higher and "mystical" forms of consciousness but also the ultimate organizing force behind the more mundane everyday perception and knowledge of the external world and is also called the "fount of knowledge." The *Huai-nan Tzu*'s ideas on self-cultivation are examined in chapter 5.

The translation as "numen/numinous" (noun/adjective) instead of "spirit/spiritual" has several advantages: 1. it retains the sense of an other power superceding the individual will that Graham's "daemonic" has, but none of the former term's malign connotation in common English usage;[23] 2. it retains the aura of something mystical or holy that is implied by *shen*.

The term "spiritual" has a broader range of meanings in English, and its nominal form "spirit" has many connotations for us (e.g., Holy Spirit, spirit-matter dichotomy) that are foreign to the Chinese concept of *shen*. Using "numen/numinous," which are closely related to "spirit/spiritual" but lack their inappropriate connotations, should enable the English reader to grasp more clearly the range of meanings of *shen*. The evolution of the understanding of this term in Taoist sources deserves a fuller study than can be undertaken here.

I have consistently translated *t'ien* (天) as "the heavens" rather than the standard "heaven." This translation more accurately reflects the naturalistic connotations of this term in this and many other early Taoist texts. The vault of the heavens was a numinous place wherein the detailed movements of the various celestial deities played out their nightly dramas. The kind of detailed astronomical observations in early works like the "T'ien-wen" (Heavenly Patterns, 天文) essay in the *Huai-nan Tzu* indicated a deep involvement and fascination with the activities of the heavens and a tremendous sense of awe and repect for its powers. Because these powers and activities were utterly spontaneous and natural, they became models for other sorts of natural impulses and abilities. Thus we find that adjectival uses of this term carry such connotations, e.g., "heavenly (or heavenlike) nature" (*t'ien-hsing*).[24]

Finally, a word on the concept of Tao, the "Way" things are in all early Chinese schools of thought. For Taoists, this Way is the ultimate power in the cosmos, paradoxically transcendent yet immanent. As a unitive principle beyond the grasp of any specific thing in the cosmos (and sometimes referred to simply as "the One" or by such metaphors as the "unhewn" [*p'u*, 樸] and the "simple" [*su*, 素]), it mysteriously operates within it to facilitate the generation of all phenomena and to serve as the inner guiding force throughout every moment of their lives. Although it is ineffable and so cannot be known as an object, the early Taoist sources maintain that it can be merged with, accorded with, or, in other words, directly experienced. Such an experience occurs only after the arduous practices referred to, sometimes metaphorically, in the selections below, and sometimes involves total self-transcendance.

Translation of *Inward Training*

I

1 The vital essence of all things:
2 It is this that brings them to life.
3 It generates the five grains below
4 And becomes the constellated stars above.
5 When flowing amid the heavens and the earth
6 We call it ghostly and numinous.
7 When stored within the chests of human beings,
8 We call them sages.

1 凡物之精
2 此則為生。(sreng)[25]
3 下生五穀
4 上為列星。(seng)
5 流 <於> 天地 <之> 間，[26]
6 謂之鬼神 (zdjien)
7 藏於胸中，
8 謂之聖人。(njien)

1 Therefore this vital energy is:[27]
2 Bright!—as if ascending the heavens;
3 Dark!—as if entering an abyss;
4 Vast!—as if dwelling in an ocean;
5 Lofty!—as if dwelling on a mountain peak.

6 Therefore this vital energy
7 Cannot be halted by force,
8 Yet can be secured by inner power [Te].
9 Cannot be summoned by speech,
10 Yet can be welcomed by the awareness.
11 Reverently hold onto it and do not lose it:
12 This is called "developing inner power."
13 When inner power develops and wisdom emerges,
14 The myriad things will, to the last one, be grasped.[28] ·

1 是故 <民>「此」氣：[29]

2 杲乎如登於天。(ten)

3 杳乎如入淵。(·wen)

4 <淖>「綽」乎如在於海。(xməɣ)[30]

5 <卒>「崒」乎如在於 <己>「屺」。(kiəɣ)[31]

6 是故此氣也

7 不可止以力 (liək)

8 而可安以德；(tək)

9 不可呼以聲

10 而可迎以 <音>「意」。(·iəɣ)[32]

11 敬守勿失：

12 是謂成德。(tək)

13 德成而智出，

14 萬物<果>「畢」得。(tək)[33]

III

1 All the forms of the mind[34]

2 Are naturally infused and filled with it [the vital essence],

3 Are naturally generated and developed [because of] it.

4 It is lost

5 Inevitably because of sorrow, happiness, joy, anger, desire, and profit-seeking.

6 If you are able to cast off sorrow, happiness, joy, anger, desire, and profit-seeking.[35]

7 Your mind will just revert to equanimity.

8 The true condition of the mind

9 Is that it finds calmness beneficial and, by it, attains repose.

10 Do not disturb it, do not disrupt it

11 And harmony will naturally develop.

1 凡心之形 (geng)

2 自充自盈。(ɣieng)

3 自生自成。(djieng)

4 其所以失之 (失 st'jiet)

5 必以憂樂喜怒欲利。(lier)

6 能去憂樂喜怒欲利，(lier)

7 心乃反 <濟>「齊」。(tser)[36]

8 彼心之情 (dzjieng)

9 利安以寧。(neng)

10 勿煩勿亂

11 和乃自成。(djieng)

IV

1 Clear! as though right by your side.

2 Vague! as though it will not be attained.

3 Indiscernable! as though beyond the limitless.

4 The test of this is not far off:

5 Daily we make use of its inner power.

6 The Way is what infuses the body,

7 Yet people are unable to fix it in place.

8 It goes forth but does not return,

9 It comes back but does not stay.

10 Silent! none can hear its sound.

11 Suddenly stopping! it abides within the mind.

12 Obscure! we do not see its form.

13 Surging forth! it arises with us.

14 We do not see its form,

15 We do not hear its sound,

16 Yet we can perceive an order to its accomplishments.

17 We call it "the Way."

1 ＜折折＞(暫暫) 乎如在於側。(tsiək)[37]

2 忽忽乎如將不得。(tək)

3 渺渺乎如窮無極。(giək)

4 此稽不遠。

5 日用其德。(tək)

6 夫道 ＜者＞ 所以充形 ＜也＞。[38]

7 而人不能固。(kaɣ)

8 其往不復。

9 其來不舍。(stiaɣ)

10 ＜謀＞「寂」乎莫聞其音。(·iəm)[39]

11 卒乎乃在於心。(sjiəm)

12 冥冥乎不見其形。(geng)

13 淫淫乎與我俱生。(sreng)

14 不見其形，(geng)

15 不聞其聲，(st'jieng)

16 而序其成：(djieng)

17 謂之道。

1 The Way has no fixed position;

2 It abides within the excellent mind.

3 When the mind is tranquil and the vital breath is regular,

4 The Way can thereby be halted.

5 That Way is not distant from us;

6 When people attain it they are sustained

7 That Way is not separated from us;

8 When people accord with it they are harmonious.

9 Therefore: Concentrated! as though you could be roped together
   with it.

10 Indiscernible! as though beyond all locations.

11 The true state of that Way:

12 How could it be conceived of and pronounced upon?

13 Cultivate your mind, make your thoughts tranquil,

14 And the Way can thereby be attained.

1 夫道無所：(iaɣ)

2 善心安 (焉) <愛>「處」。(t'jaɣ)⁴⁰

3 心靜氣理，(liəɣ)

4 道乃可止。(tiəɣ)

5 彼道不遠；(ɣɣwan)

6 <民>「人」得以產。(srian)⁴¹

7 彼道不離；(lia)

8 <民>「人」因以 <知>「和」。(gwa)⁴²

9 是故 <卒「卒」>「萃萃」乎其如可與索。(sak)⁴³

10 <眇眇>「渺渺」乎其如窮無所。(·siaɣ)⁴⁴

11 <被>「彼」道之情：(dzjieng)⁴⁵

12 惡 <音>「意」與聲。(·stjieng)⁴⁶

13 修心靜 <音>「意」；(·iəɣ)⁴⁷

14 道乃可得。(tək)

1 As for the Way:

2 It is what the mouth cannot speak of,

3 The eyes cannot see,

4 And the ears cannot hear.

5 It is that with which we cultivate the mind and align the body.[48]

6 When people lose it they die;

7 When people gain it they flourish.

8 When endeavors lose it they fail;

9 When they gain it they succeed.

10 The Way never has a root or trunk,

11 It never has leaves or flowers.

12 The myriad things are generated by it;

13 The myriad things are completed by it.

14 We designate it "the Way."

1 道也者：

2 口之所不能言也，

3 目之所不能視也，

4 耳之所不能聽也。(t'eng)

5 所以修心而正形也。(geng)

6 人之所失以死，

7 所得以生也。(sreng)

8 事之所失以敗，

9 所得以成也。(djieng)

10 凡道：無根無莖，(greng)

11 無葉無榮。(·iweng)

12 萬物以生，(sreng)

13 萬物以成。(djieng)

14 命之曰道。

VII

1 For the heavens, the ruling principle is to be aligned.

2 For the earth, the ruling principle is to be level.

3 For human beings the ruling principle is to be tranquil.

4 Spring, autumn, winter, and summer are the seasons of the heavens.

5 Mountains, hills, rivers, and valleys are the resources of the earth.

6 Pleasure and anger, accepting and rejecting are the devices of human beings.[49]

7 Therefore, the Sage:

8 Alters with the seasons but doesn't transform,

9 Shifts with things but doesn't change places with them.

1　天主正；(tjieng)
2　地主平；(bieng)
3　人主 <安> 靜。(dzjieng)⁵⁰
4　春秋冬夏，天之時也。(diəɣ)
5　山陵川谷，地之 <枝>「材」。(dzeɣ)⁵¹
6　喜怒取予，人之謀也。(mjwəɣ)
7　是故，聖人
8　與時變而不化，(xrwa)
9　從物「遷」而不移。(ria)⁵²

VIII

1 If you can be aligned and be tranquil,

2 Only then can you be stable.

3 With a stable mind at your core,

4 With the eyes and ears acute and clear,

5 And with the four limbs firm and fixed,

6 You can thereby make a lodging place for the vital essence.

7 The vital essence: it is the essence of the vital energy.

8 When the vital energy is guided, it [the vital essence] is generated,

9 But when it is generated, there is thought,

10 When there is thought, there is knowledge,

11 But when there is knowledge, then you must stop.

12 Whenever the forms of the mind have excessive knowledge,

13 You lose your vitality.

1 能正能靜 (dzjieng)
2 然后能定。 (deng)
3 定心在中，
4 耳目聰明，
5 四肢堅固： (kaɣ)
6 可以為精舍。 (st'jiaɣ)
7 精也者，氣之精也。 (tsjieng)
8 氣 <道>「導」乃生 (sreng)，[53]
9 生乃思，
10 思乃知，
11 知乃止矣。
12 凡心之形： (geng)
13 過知失生。 (sreng)

1 Those who can transform even a single thing, call them "numinous";

2 Those who can alter even a single situation, call them "wise."

3 But to transform without expending vital energy; to alter without expending wisdom:

4 Only exemplary persons who hold fast to the One are able to do this.[54]

5 Hold fast to the One; do not lose it,

6 And you will be able to master the myriad things.

7 Exemplary persons act upon things,

8 And are not acted upon by them,

9 Because they grasp the guiding principle of the One.

1 一物能化，謂之神。

2 一事能變，謂之智。

3 化不易氣，變不易智；

4 唯執一之君子能為此乎。

5 執一不失，(st'jiet)

6 能君萬物。(mjwət)

7 君子使物，(mjwət)

8 不為物使。(sliəɣ)

9 得一之理。(liəɣ)

X

1 With a well-ordered mind within you,

2 Well-ordered words issue forth from your mouth,

3 And well-ordered tasks are imposed upon others.

4 Then all under the heavens will be well ordered.

5 "When one word is grasped,

6 All under the heavens will submit.

7 When one word is fixed,

8 All under the heavens will listen."

9 It is this [word "Way"] to which the saying refers.[55]

1 治心在中：
2 治言出於口，
3 治事加於人。
4 然則天下治矣。

5 一言得 (tək)
6 而天下服： (bjwək)
7 一言定 (deng)
8 而天下聽。(t'eng)

9 <公>「此」之謂也。 [56]

1 When your body is not aligned,

2 The inner power will not come.

3 When you are not tranquil within,

4 Your mind will not be well ordered.

5 Align your body, assist the inner power,

6 Then it will gradually come on its own.[58]

1 形不正， (tjieng)

2 德不來。(ləɣ)

3 中不靜 (dzjieng)

4 心不治。(dəɣ)

5 正形攝德 (tək)

　＜天仁地義則＞[59]

6 淫然而自＜至＞「來」。(ləɣ)[60]

XII

1 The numinous [mind]: no one knows its limit;
2 It intuitively knows the myriad things.[61]
3 Hold it within you, do not let it waver.
4 To not disrupt your senses with external things,
5 To not disrupt your mind with your senses:
6 This is called "grasping it within you."

1 神 ＜明之＞「莫知」極 (gʼiək)⁶²
2 照乎知萬物。
3 中 ＜義＞守不忒。 (tʼək)⁶³
4 不以物亂官，
5 不以官亂心。
6 是謂中得。(tək)

1 There is a numinous [mind] naturally residing within;

2 One moment it goes, the next it comes,

3 And no one is able to conceive of it.

4 If you lose it you are inevitably disordered;

5 If you attain it you are inevitably well ordered.

6 Diligently clean out its lodging place[64]

7 And its vital essence will naturally arrive.

8 Still your attempts to imagine and conceive of it.

9 Relax your efforts to reflect on and control it.

10 Be reverent and diligent

11 And its vital essence will naturally stabilize.

12 Grasp it and don't let go

13 Then the eyes and ears won't overflow

14 And the mind will have nothing else to seek.[65]

15 When a properly aligned mind resides within you,

16 The myriad things will be seen in their proper perspective.[66]

1 有神自在＜身＞。(dzəɣ)[67]

2 一往一來：(ləɣ)

3 莫之能思。(sjiəɣ)

4 失之必亂；

5 得之必治。(diəɣ)

6 敬除其舍：

7 精將自來。(ləɣ)

8 ＜精＞「靜」想思之；(思 sjiəɣ)[68]

9 寧念治之。(治 diəɣ)

10 嚴容畏敬：(k'ieng)

11 精將＜至＞「自」定。(deng)[69]

12 得之而勿捨：(st'jiaɣ)

13 耳目不淫，

14 心無他圖。(daɣ)

15 正心在中，

16 萬物得度。(daɣ)

1   The Way fills the entire world.

2   It is everywhere that people are,

3   But people are unable to understand this.

4   When you are released by this one word:[70]

5   You reach up to the heavens above;

6   You stretch down to the earth below;

7   You pervade the nine inhabited regions.

8   What does it mean to be released by it?

9   The answer resides in the calmness of the mind.[71]

10 When your mind is well ordered, your senses are well ordered.

11 When your mind is calm, your senses are calmed.

12 What makes them well ordered is the mind;

13 What makes them calm is the mind.

14 By means of the mind you store the mind:

15 Within the mind there is yet another mind.

16 That mind within the mind: it is an awareness that precedes words.

17 Only after there is awareness does it take shape;

18 Only after it takes shape is there a word.

19 Only after there is a word is it implemented;

20 Only after it is implemented is there order.

21 Without order, you will always be chaotic.

22 If chaotic, you die.

1 道滿天下。(graɣ)
2 普在民所，(·siaɣ)
3 民不能知。(tieɣ)
4 一言之解；
5 上察於天，
6 下極於地。
7 蟠滿九州。
8 何為解之？
9 在於心安。
10 我心治，官乃治。(diəɣ)
11 我心安，官乃安。(·an)
12 治之者心也。
13 安之者心也。
14 心以藏心：
15 心之中又有心 <馬>「焉」。(·ian)[72]
16 彼心之心 <音>「意」以先言。(ngjan)[73]
17 <音>「意」然后形；(geng)
18 形然后言；(ngjan)
19 言然后使 (sli)。
20 使然后治。(djəɣ)
21 不治必亂；
22 亂乃死。

1 For those who preserve and naturally generate vital essence

2 On the outside a calmness will flourish.

3 Stored inside, we take it to be the well spring.

4 Floodlike, it harmonizes and equalizes[74]

5 And we take it to be the fount of the vital energy.

6 When the fount is not dried up,

7 The four limbs are firm.

8 When the well spring is not drained,

9 Vital energy freely circulates through the nine apertures.[75]

10 You can then exhaust the heavens and the earth

11 And spread over the four seas.

12 When you have no delusions within you,

13 Externally there will be no disasters.

14 Those who keep their minds unimpaired within,

15 Externally keep their bodies unimpaired,

16 Who do not encounter heavenly disasters

17 Or meet with harm at the hands of others,

18 Call them Sages.

1 精存自生，(sreng)

2 其外安榮。(·iweng)

3 內藏以為泉原。(ngjwan)

4 浩然和平，(bieng)

5 以為氣淵。(·wen)

6 淵之不涸，(gak)

7 四體乃固。(kaɣ)

8 泉之不竭，(giat)

9 九竅遂 <通> 「達」。(dat)[76]

10 乃能窮天地，(dia)

11 被四海。(xməɣ)

12 中無惑意，

13 外無邪菑。(tsiəɣ)

14 心全於中，

15 形全於外，(ngwar)

16 不逢天菑，

17 不遇人害：(gar)

18 謂之聖人。

1 If people can be aligned and tranquil,

2 Their skin will be ample and smooth,

3 Their ears and eyes will be acute and clear,

4 Their muscles will be supple and their bones will be strong.

5 They will then be able to hold up the Great Circle [of the heavens][77]

6 And tread firmly over the Great Square [of the earth].

7 They will mirror things with great purity.

8 And will perceive things with great clarity.[78]

9 Reverently be aware [of the Way] and do not waver,

10 And you will daily renew your inner power,

11 Thoroughly understand all under the heavens,

12 And exhaust everything within the Four Directions.

13 To reverently bring forth the effulgence [of the Way]:

14 This is called "inward attainment."

15 If you do this but fail to return to it,

16 This will cause a wavering in your vitality.

1 人能正靜:

2 皮膚裕寬,

3 耳目聰明, (miwang)

4 筋信 (伸) 而骨強。 (gjang)[79]

5 乃能戴大圜

6 而履大方, (pjwang)

7 鑒於大清,

8 視於大明。 (miwang)

9 敬慎無忒:

10 日新其德。 (tǝk)

11 遍知天下,

12 窮於四極。 (giǝk)

13 敬發其充,

14 是謂內得。 (tǝk)

15 然而不反;

16 此生之忒。 (tǝk)

XVII

1 For all [to practice] this Way:

2 You must coil, you must contract,

3 You must uncoil, you must expand,

4 You must be firm, you must be regular [in this practice].[80]

5 Hold fast to this excellent [practice]; do not let go of it.

5 Chase away the excessive; abandon the trivial.[81]

6 And when you reach its ultimate limit

7 You will return to the Way and its inner power.

1 凡道：

2 必周必密，

3 必寬必舒， (st'jaɣ)

4 必堅必固。 (kaɣ)

5 守善勿舍， (st'iaɣ)

6 逐淫＜澤＞「釋」薄。 (bwak)[82]

7 既＜知＞「致」其極， (giək)[83]

8 反於道德。 (tək)

XVIII

1 When there is a mind that is unimpaired within you,

2 It cannot be hidden.

3 It will be known in your countenance,

4 And seen in your skin color.

5 If with this good flow of vital energy you encounter others,

6 They will be kinder to you than your own brethren.

7 But if with a bad flow of vital energy you encounter others,

8 They will harm you with their weapons.

9 [This is because] the wordless pronouncement

10 Is more rapid than the drumming of thunder.

11 The perceptible form of the mind's vital energy

12 Is brighter than the sun and moon,

13 And more apparent than the concern of parents.

14 Rewards are not sufficient to encourage the good;

15 Punishments are not sufficient to discourage the bad.

16 Yet once this flow of vital energy is achieved,

17 All under the heavens will submit.

18 And once the mind is made stable,

19 All under the heavens will listen.

1 全心在中，

2 不可蔽匿。 (niək)

3 ＜和＞「知」於形容，[84]

4 見於膚色。 (siək)

5 善氣迎人，

6 親於弟兄。 (xiwang)

7 惡氣迎人，

8 害於戎兵。 (piwang)

9 不言之聲， (·stjieng)

10 疾於雷鼓。 (kwaɣ)

11 心氣之形: (geng)

12 明於日月，

13 察於父母。 (maɣ)

14 賞不足勸善。

15 刑不足懲＜過＞「惡」。 (·ak)[85]

16 氣＜意＞「壹」得 (·ək)[86]

17 而天下服。 (bjwək)

18 心＜意＞「壹」定 (deng)

19 而天下聽。 (t'eng)

XIX

1 By concentrating your vital breath as if numinous,
2 The myriad things will all be contained within you.
3 Can you concentrate? Can you unite with them?
4 Can you not resort to divining by tortoise or milfoil
5 Yet know bad and good fortune?
6 Can you stop? Can you cease?
7 Can you not seek it in others,
8 Yet attain it within yourself?[87]
9 You think and think about it
10 And think still further about it.
11 You think, yet still cannot penetrate it.
12 While the ghostly and numinous will penetrate it,
13 It is not due to the power of the ghostly and numinous,
14 But to the utmost refinement of your essential vital breath.
15 When the four limbs are aligned
16 And the blood and vital breath are tranquil,
17 Unify your awareness, concentrate your mind,
18 Then your eyes and ears will not be overstimulated.
19 And even the far-off will seem close at hand.

₁ ＜搏＞「搏」氣如神，[88]

₂ 萬物備存。

₃ 能專，能一乎。 (·jiet)

₄ 能無卜筮

₅ 而知＜吉凶＞「凶吉」乎。 (kjiet)[89]

₆ 能止乎，能已乎。 (riəy)[90]

₇ 能勿求諸人

₈ 而「得」之己乎。 (kiəy)[91]

₉ 思之思之

₁₀ 又重思之。

₁₁ 思之而不通，

₁₂ 鬼神將通之。

₁₃ 非鬼神之力也。 (liək)

₁₄ 精氣之極也。 (giək)

₁₅ 四體既正， (tjieng)

₁₆ 血氣既靜， (dzieng)

₁₇ 一意＜搏＞「搏」心。 (sjiəm)

₁₈ 耳目不淫。 (riəm)

₁₉ 雖遠若近。

XX

1 Deep thinking generates knowledge.

2 Idleness and carelessness generate worry.

3 Cruelty and arrogance generate resentment.

4 Worry and grief generate illness.

5 When illness reaches a distressing degree, you die.

6 When you think about something and don't let go of it,

7 Internally you will be distressed, externally you will be weak.

8 Do not plan things out in advance

9 Or else your vitality will cede its dwelling.

10 In eating, it is best not to fill up;

11 In thinking, it is best not to overdo.

12 Limit these to the appropriate degree

13 And you will naturally reach it [vitality].

1 思索生知。

2 慢易生憂。

3 暴傲生怨。

4 憂鬱生疾。

5 疾困乃死。

6 思之而不捨 (st'iaɣ)

7 内困外薄, (bwak)

8 不蚤（早）為圖。 (daɣ)

9 生將巽舍。 (st'aɣ)

10 食莫若無飽,

11 思莫若勿致。 (tjier)[92]

12 節適之齊,

13 彼將自至。 (tjier)

XXI

1 As for the life of all human beings:

2 The heavens bring forth their vital essence,

3 The earth brings forth their bodies.

4 These two combine to make a person.

5 When they are in harmony there is vitality;

6 When they are not in harmony there is no vitality.

7 If we examine the Way of harmonizing them,

8 Its essentials are not visible,

9 Its signs are not numerous.

10 Just let a balanced and aligned [breathing] fill your chest

11 And it will swirl and blend within your mind,

12 This confers longevity.

13 When joy and anger are not limited,

14 You should make a plan [to limit them].

15 Restrict the five sense-desires;

16 Cast away these dual misfortunes.

17 Be not joyous, be not angry,

18 Just let a balanced and aligned [breathing] fill your chest.

1 凡人之生也：(sreng)

2 天出其精，(tsjieng)

3 地出其形。(geng)

4 合此 <以> 為人。[93]

5 和乃生：(sreng)

6 不和不生。(sreng)

7 察和之道：(dəw)

8 其 <精>「情」不見，[94]

9 其徵不醜。(t'jəw)

10 平正擅匈 (胸)。(xjewng)

11 <論治>「淪洽」在心。[95]

12 此以長壽。(djəw)

13 <怨>「喜」怒「之」失度，[96]

14 乃為之圖。

15 節其五欲，

16 去其二凶。(xjewng)

17 不喜不怒，

18 平正擅匈（胸）。(xjewng)

XXII

1 As for the vitality of all human beings:
2 It inevitably occurs because of balanced and aligned [breathing].
3 The reason for its loss
4 Is inevitably pleasure and anger, worry and anxiety.
5 Therefore, to bring your anger to a halt, there is nothing better than poetry;
6 To cast off worry there is nothing better than music;
7 To limit music there is nothing better than the rites;
8 To hold onto the rites there is nothing better than reverence;
9 To hold onto reverence there is nothing better than tranquility.
10 When you are inwardly tranquil and outwardly reverent
11 You are able to return to your innate nature
12 And this nature will become greatly stable.[98]

1 凡人之生也， (sreng)
2 必以平正。 (tjieng)
3 所以失之
4 必以喜怒憂患。[97]
5 是故止怒莫若詩；
6 去憂莫若樂；
7 節樂莫若禮；
8 守禮莫若敬； (ki'eng)
9 守敬莫若靜。 (dzjieng)
10 内靜外敬， (ki'eng)
11 能反其性。 (sjieng)
12 性將大定。 (deng)

1 For all the Way of eating is that:

2 Overfilling yourself with food will impair your vital energy

3 And cause your body to deteriorate.

4 Overrestricting your consumption causes the bones to wither

5 And the blood to congeal.

6 The mean between overfilling and overrestricting:

7 This is called "harmonious completion."

8 It is where the vital essence lodges

9 And knowledge is generated.

10 When hunger and fullness lose their proper balance,

11 You make a plan to correct this.

12 When full, move quickly;

13 When hungry, neglect your thoughts;

14 When old, forget worry.

15 If when full you don't move quickly,

16 Vital energy will not circulate to your limbs.

17 If when hungry you don't neglect thoughts of food,

18 When you finally eat you will not stop.

19 If when old you don't forget your worries,

20 The fount of your vital energy will rapidly drain out.[99]

1 凡食之道：

2 大充「氣」傷， (st'jang)¹⁰⁰

3 而形 <不> <臧> 「戕」。 (dziang)¹⁰¹

4 大攝骨枯 (kaɣ)

5 而血洰。 (gaɣ)

6 充攝之間：

7 此謂和成。 (djieng)

8 精之所舍

9 <而> 知之所生。 (sreng)¹⁰²

10 飢飽 <之> 失度¹⁰³

11 乃為之圖。

12 飽則疾動；

13 飢則 <廣> 「曠」思； (sjiəɣ)¹⁰⁴

14 老則 <長> 「忘」慮。 (liaɣ)¹⁰⁵

15 飽不疾動，

16 氣不通 <於四> 末。 (mwat)¹⁰⁶

17 飢不 <廣> 「曠」思， (sjiəɣ)

18 <飽> 「食」而不 <廢> 「止」。 (tjiəɣ)¹⁰⁷

19 老不 <長> 「忘」慮。 (liaɣ)

20 <困> 「淵」乃速竭。 (giat)¹⁰⁸

XXIV

1 When you enlarge your mind and let go of it,
2 When you relax your vital breath and expand it,
3 When your body is calm and unmoving:
4 And you can maintain the One and discard the myriad disturbances.[109]
5 You will see profit and not be enticed by it,
6 You will see harm and not be frightened by it.
7 Relaxed and unwound, yet acutely sensitive,
8 In solitude you delight in your own person.
9 This is called "revolving the vital breath":
10 Your thoughts and deeds seem heavenly.[110]

1 大心而 <敢>「放」。 (t'jang)[111]

2 寬氣而廣。 (kwang)

3 其形安而不移: (ria)

4 能守一而棄萬苛: (ga)

5 見利不誘;

6 見害不懼。

7 寬舒而仁, (njien)[112]

8 獨樂其身。 (st'jien)

9 是謂 <雲>「運」氣。[113]

10 意行似天。 (t'en)

XXV

1 The vitality of all people
2 Inevitably comes from their peace of mind.
3 When anxious, you lose this guiding thread;
4 When angry, you lose this basic point.
5 When you are anxious or sad, pleased or angry,
6 The Way has no place within you to settle.
7 Love and desire: still them!
8 Folly and disturbance: correct them!
9 Do not push it! do not pull it!
10 Good fortune will naturally return to you,
11 And that Way will naturally come to you
12 So you can rely on and take counsel from it.
13 If you are tranquil then you will attain it;
14 If you are agitated then you will lose it.

1 凡人之生：

2 必以其歡。 (xwan)

3 憂則失紀；

4 怒則失端。 (twan)

5 憂悲喜怒： (naɣ)

6 道乃無處。 (t'jaɣ)

7 愛慾靜之。 (dzieng)

8 遇 (愚) 亂正之。 (tjieng)[114]

9 勿引勿推。 (twər)

10 福將自歸。 (kjwər)

11 彼道自來。 (ləɣ)

12 可籍與謀。 (mjwəɣ)

13 靜則得之， (tjiəɣ)

14 躁則失之。 (tjiəɣ)

1 That mysterious vital energy within the mind:

2 One moment it arrives, the next it departs.

3 So fine, there is nothing within it;

4 So vast, there is nothing outside it.

5 We lose it

6 Because of the harm caused by mental agitation.

7 When the mind can hold on to tranquility,

8 The Way will become naturally stabilized.

9 For people who have attained the Way

10 It permeates their pores and saturates their hair.[15]

11 Within their chest, they remain unvanquished.

12 [Follow] this Way of restricting sense-desires

13 And the myriad things will not cause you harm.

1 靈氣在心，

2 一來一逝。(djiar)

3 其細無內；

4 其大無外。(ngwar)

5 所以失之：

6 以躁為害。(gar)

7 心能執靜，(dzjieng)

8 道將自定。(deng)

9 得道之人：

10 理丞 (烝)「而」<屯>「毛」泄。(riar)[116]

11 匈 (胸) 中無敗。(brwar)

12 節欲之道，

13 萬物不害。(gar)

CHAPTER THREE

The Teachings of
Inward Training

A Thematic Overview of *Inward Training*

Before presenting a detailed study of the central ideas in *Inward Training*, this chapter offers a general overview of the main topics of its twenty-six verses.

Structure and Topics of *Inward Training*

Based on this analysis, *Inward Training* appears to have a deliberate—if somewhat loose—organizational structure. The first seven verses consider what might be called the philosophical foundations of inner cultivation practice. The next seven present the details of this practice. After this, four of the next five verses discuss the benefits of inner cultivation, the only exception being verse XVII, which gives further details of breathing practice. However, as will be seen, this verse *does* end with a most significant final benefit of breathing practice, the return to the Way and its inner power. The next four verses, XX–XXIII provide further refinements of inner cultivation practice, including a philosophy of eating. The final three verses appear to be summaries of inner cultivation and its benefits presented in a more general fashion than the instructions in verses VIII–XIV. This textual organization is followed below.

The Philosophical Foundations of *Inward Training*

COSMOLOGY: VITAL ESSENCE AND THE WAY

The two most important philosophical concepts in *Inward Training* are the closely related concepts of the vital essence (*ching*, 精) and the Way. The vital essence is that which brings life to all living things. Verse I reads:

1 The vital essence of all things:
2 It is this that brings them to life.
3 It generates the five grains below
4 And becomes the constellated stars above.
5 When flowing amid the heavens and the earth
6 We call it ghostly and numinous.
7 When stored within the chests of human beings,
8 We call them sages.

This verse establishes certain basic characteristics of the vital essence within a triune framework of the heavens, the earth, and human beings that is an important motif throughout the text. Here, *ching* is a generative substance of cosmic proportions that manifests itself in these three interrelated areas of the universe. Most important for *Inward Training*, when we can store it within our hearts/minds, we become sages. Verse VIII provides the following clear definition: "The vital essence: it is the essence of the vital energy." Thus it is a highly refined, concentrated, and subtle form of vital energy. Yet while it has these concrete properties, something about it defies intellectual understanding and categorization:

II

1 Therefore this [form of] vital energy [that is, the vital essence] is:[1]
2 Bright!—as if ascending the heavens;
3 Dark!—as if entering an abyss;
4 Vast!—as if dwelling in an ocean;
5 Lofty!—as if dwelling on a mountain peak.

As a cosmic power or force, the vital essence resembles the very Way itself:

IV

1 Clear! as though right by your side.
2 Vague! as though it will not be attained.
3 Indiscernable! as though beyond the limitless.
4 The test of this is not far off:
5 Daily we make use of its inner power.
6 That Way is what infuses the body,
7 Yet people are unable to fix it in place.
8 It goes forth but does not return,
9 It comes back but does not stay.
10 Silent! none can hear its sound.
11 Suddenly stopping! it abides within the mind.
12 Obscure! we do not see its form.
13 Surging forth! it arises with us.
14 We do not see its form,
15 We do not hear its sound,
16 Yet we can perceive an order to its accomplishments.
17 We call it "the Way."

Verse IV depicts the Way as the ineffable cosmic power familiar from other early sources of Taoism, the most important of which is the *Lao Tzu*. However, it has a more tangible presence in *Inward Training* than in the *Lao Tzu*. Although this vital essence cannot be perceived as an object, we not only see what it accomplishes; it is also a constantly moving power that seems to come and go within the human mind. Verse V details further how the Way resides within people:

1 The Way has no fixed position;
2 It abides within the excellent mind.

3 When the mind is tranquil and the vital breath is regular,
4 The Way can thereby be halted.
5 That Way is not distant from us;
6 When people attain it they are sustained
7 That Way is not separated from us;
8 When people accord with it they are harmonious.

9 Therefore: Concentrated! as though you could be roped together with it.
10 Indiscernable! as though beyond all locations.
11 The true state of that Way:
12 How could it be conceived of and pronounced upon?
13 Cultivate your mind, make your thoughts tranquil,
14 And the Way can thereby be attained.

Although constantly moving in and out of the mind, the Way can come to abide within it when one cultivates tranquility through the regular and systematic practice of breathing meditation. Though beyond dualistic concepts and pronouncements, it can be apprehended directly within this cultivated or "excellent" mind. These passages do not suggest that the Way is sometimes present within human beings and at other times absent. Rather, the Way is always present. However, the awareness of this presence enters the human mind only when it is properly cultivated. This emphasis on the potential of people to experience the Way is also paralleled in how *Inward Training* discusses the vital essence:

II

6 Therefore this vital energy [that is the vital essence]
7 Cannot be halted by force,
8 Yet can be secured by inner power [*Te*].
9 Cannot be summoned by speech,
10 Yet can be welcomed by the awareness.
11 Reverently hold onto it and do not lose it:
12 This is called "developing inner power."
13 When inner power develops and wisdom emerges,
14 The myriad things will, to the last one, be grasped.

Psychological Dimensions:
Tranquility, Inner Power, and the Numinous Mind

As the previous passages suggest, *Inward Training* defines inner power (*Te,*
德) in a very concrete psychological sense. It is linked to both the vital
essence and the Way. It is what enables the sage to secure vital essence,
and it is the perceptible manifestation of the Way within human experience. It cannot be controlled by force of will or use of language, thus
implying that it arises within awareness devoid of individual will and dualistic thought. In verse XI it is one definite result of the distinctive method
of inner cultivation advocated in *Inward Training*:

1 When your body is not aligned,
2 The inner power will not come.
3 When you are not tranquil within,
4 Your mind will not be well ordered.
5 Align your body, assist the inner power,
6 Then it will gradually come on its own.

Thus inner power gradually and naturally develops within you if you
place your body in the proper posture and thereby become tranquil. This
proper posture refers to the position for breathing meditation, a link repeated
in verse XVI. It therefore seems that, to the authors of *Inward Training*,
inner power was a quality of mental concentration that arose naturally,
along with tranquility, through the practice of breathing meditation. It is
also closely connected to the vital essence and the Way. One way to conceive
of the relationship between inner power and the vital essence is that the
latter appears to be the physiological substrate associated with the former;
one way to conceive of the relationship between the Way and inner power
is that inner power represents a quality of mind, discovered through the
tranquility attained through breathing practice, through which the presence of the Way that dwells within human beings is revealed to them.

Thus if inner power is a highly concentrated and tranquil state of mind
with an associated physiological substrate, the vital essence, and if the
Way is revealed within the mind through this inner power, then there is
also an extremely close relationship between the Way and the vital essence.
As cosmic powers, both are spoken of in similar terms. Verse XXVI pre-

sents a summation of the basic teachings of *Inward Training* in which the closeness of these two concepts is demonstrated further:

 1 That mysterious vital energy within the mind:
 2 One moment it arrives, the next it departs.
 3 So fine, there is nothing within it;
 4 So vast, there is nothing outside it.
 5 We lose it
 6 Because of the harm caused by mental agitation.
 7 When the mind can hold on to tranquility,
 8 The Way will become naturally stabilized.
 9 For people who have attained the Way
 10 It permeates their pores and saturates their hair.
 11 Within their chest, they remain unvanquished.
 12 [Follow] this Way of restricting sense-desires
 13 And the myriad things will not cause you harm.

This passage describes the Way as a kind of mysterious vital energy, or vital essence, that comes to actually permeate your entire being, to penetrate the very pores of your skin, when you attain tranquility. This does not mean, however, that the text supports a materialistic conceptualization of the Way. Rather, the vital essence appears to be the crystallization of the more abstract power or force that is the Way within the energetic systems constituting the human being and the entire cosmos. This is borne out by the opening verse of *Inward Training*, which explains the vital essence as the generative principle within all phenomena. In this text the power of the Way to generate all things is thus manifested as the vital essence.

Related to securing vital essence through the development of tranquility and inner power is the understanding of how the vital essence is actually generated within people. Verse VIII states that human beings generate it through the guiding of the vital energy. This guiding and circulating refines vital energy into vital essence, yet a recursive relationship exists between the two:

XV

 1 For those who preserve and naturally generate vital essence
 2 On the outside a calmness will flourish.
 3 Stored inside, we take it to be the well spring.

4 Floodlike, it harmonizes and equalizes
5 And we take it to be the fount of the vital energy.
6 When the fount is not dried up,
7 The four limbs are firm.
8 When the well spring is not drained,
9 Vital energy freely circulates through the nine apertures.

Here the vital essence, which in verse VIII is generated by the guiding and circulating of the vital energy, is itself the source of the vital energy, its very "well spring." Those who practice inner cultivation are able to generate vital essence and store it in the heart/mind "within their chests." Associated with this is a psychological calmness and a physical vitality that is created by the harmonizing and equalizing effect of this pooling of vital essence. This then generates vital energy and assures that it is properly circulated throughout the various physiological pathways envisioned in the early Chinese medical systems.² It is thus not surprising to find a seamless web in *Inward Training* connecting the psychological, physiological, and spiritual aspects of the human being. These spiritual aspects are often discussed in *Inward Training* in concepts and phrases closely related to the vital essence, the Way, and the inner power:

XIII

1 There is a numinous [mind] naturally residing within;
2 One moment it goes, the next it comes,
3 And no one is able to conceive of it.
4 If you lose it you are inevitably disordered;
5 If you attain it you are inevitably well ordered.
6 Diligently clean out its lodging place
7 And its vital essence will naturally arrive.
8 Still your attempts to imagine and conceive of it.
9 Relax your efforts to reflect on and control it.
10 Be reverent and diligent
11 And its vital essence will naturally stabilize.
12 Grasp it and don't let go
13 Then the eyes and ears won't overflow
14 And the mind will have nothing else to seek.
15 When a properly aligned mind resides within you,
16 The myriad things will be seen in their proper perspective.

This important passage is from one of five verses in *Inward Training* in which the term *shen*, here translated as "numinous mind," appears. In verses I and XIX it appears together with the term *kuei* (ghost, 鬼) and therein refers to the external spirits or numina of various things like mountains, rivers, and the ancestors. These spirits are the powers that descended into early Chinese shamans and shamanesses during their ritualized trances. Angus Graham argues that, by the time *Inward Training* was written in the fourth century B.C., these external powers, like the concept of the heavens, were becoming depersonalized. In the philosophical literature from this time on, the term *shen* "tends to be used as a stative verb rather than noun, of mysterious power and intelligence radiating from a person or thing."[3] The authors of *Inward Training* seem to make a distinction like Graham's when, in verse XIX, they say:

1 By concentrating your vital breath as if numinous,
2 The myriad things will all be contained within you.

Here the phrase "as if numinous" is particularly noteworthy. The text speaks not of some internal numen or spirit but, rather, of a spiritlike or numinous power that can foreknow. It details how the practice of concentrating and refining vital energy into vital essence leads to the ability to divine the future without tortoise shells or milfoil stalks. This foreknowledge also occurs without relying on ghostly or numinous powers either outside or within oneself but, rather, because of "the utmost refinement of your essential vital energy." So sages who have achieved this utmost refinement are numinous in that they, like the external spiritual powers, are filled with this vital essence.

That the term *shen* is used to describe a quality of mind or a special type of awareness in verse XIX is indicated not only by this passage but by a critical discussion of how to experience the Way "that fills all under the heavens" in verse XIV. In talking about how one becomes released from the fixed perspective of an individual human being by using the word "Way," the *Inward Training* authors state that there is a "mind within the mind" that is experienced when the mind is calm and well ordered:

15 Within the mind there is yet another mind.
16 That mind within the mind: it is an awareness that precedes words.
17 Only after there is awareness does it take shape;

18 Only after it takes shape is there a word.
19 Only after there is a word is it implemented;
20 Only after it is implemented is there order.

This verse suggests that the "mind within the mind" is a direct, nondual, awareness of the Way that resides within all human beings (it is "everywhere that people are, but people are unable to understand this"). This nondual awareness of the Way that constitutes the "mind within the mind" is also referred to in verse XIII as numinous. Hence I translate it as "numinous mind." Just as the arrival of the numinous mind at its lodging place in the tranquil and purified mind in verse XIII establishes a condition of psychological order, attaining the "mind within the mind" in verse XIV also establishes such order.

That this special mind is described as "spiritlike" or "numinous" is perfectly logical: As a nondual awareness of the Way, it cannot be fathomed by the dualistic intellect and as such fits the famous quotation from the "Hsi-tz'u" commentary of the *Book of Change:* "Where yin and yang do not penetrate, we call it the numinous."[4] It is further described as coming into and departing from consciousness, just as external spirits come into and depart from the mind of the shaman or from the ancestral temple. In terms of the various physiological forces that make up the human being and everything else within the cosmos, this nondual awareness is manifested as vital essence—the essential component of ghosts and spirits that dwell outside humans. Although in later texts like the *Huai-nan Tzu* the *shen* seems to be the locus of more prosaic aspects of awareness such as everyday perception,[5] in *Inward Training*, only this more rarefied, mystical awareness is indicated by this term.

One final characteristic associated with this numinous mind in verse XII is its "illumined knowing" (*chao chih,* 照知). This term refers to the ability immediately and intuitively to know all the myriad things. This ability derives from the fact that the numinous mind is the nondual awareness of the Way. Because this Way is inherent in all things, being aware of the Way imparts an immediate knowledge of the most foundational layer of every phenomenon perceived. This relates to the lines that begin verse XIX:

1 By concentrating your vital breath as if numinous,
2 The myriad things will all be contained within you.

All things are contained within those who realize the numinous mind because it is a nondual awareness of the Way. The Way not only is within all things, as the mysterious unifying foundation of the cosmos, but also contains all things.

The Practice of Inner Cultivation in *Inward Training*

The practices outlined in *Inward Training* aim to generate and retain vital essence through developing an inner tranquility and an inner power associated with attaining the numinous "mind within the mind," the nondual awareness of the Way. The text discusses in some detail how this is to be undertaken, but uses a specialized, "mystical language" to do so that must be carefully interpreted. It must be understood within the context of mystical practice (see chapter 4).

THE FOURFOLD ALIGNING

The attainment of tranquility (*ching*) is one of the central concepts and goals of *Inward Training*. Indeed, the term appears in eleven of the twenty-six verses. For the *Inward Training* authors, the attainment of tranquility is always preceded by the practice of *cheng* (正), which literally means "to square up" or "to center" something, but is translated here as "to align." The term implies adjusting or lining up something with an existing pattern or form. This is appropriate to the contexts in which this term is used in *Inward Training*. In fact, as their basic method of practice the authors of *Inward Training* advocate a "Fourfold Aligning": (1) aligning the body (*cheng-hsing*, 正 形); (2) aligning the four limbs (*cheng ssu t'i* [or *chih*], 正 四 體 ，肢); (3) aligning the vital energy (*cheng-ch'i,* 正 氣); and (4) aligning the mind (*cheng-hsin,* 正 心). The first two methods are addressed in the following passages.

VIII
1 If you can be aligned and be tranquil,
2 Only then can you be stable.
3 With a stable mind at your core,
4 With the ears and eyes acute and clear,

5 And with the four limbs firm and fixed,
6 You can thereby make a lodging place for the vital essence.

XI

1 When your body is not aligned,
2 The inner power will not come.
3 When you are not tranquil within,
4 Your mind will not be well ordered.
5 Align your body, assist the inner power,
6 Then it will gradually come on its own.

In these two passages, being aligned precedes being tranquil, and both are the basis for developing a stable or concentrated mind and inner power and, ultimately, for lodging the vital essence. The aligning spoken of here is a physical one, in which one sits with the limbs fixed in a stable posture.

"Aligning the body" and "aligning the four limbs" are closely related. From their basic meaning, they seem to refer to sitting in a stable posture in which the limbs are aligned or squared up with one another. Sitting in a stable position with the spine erect is a posture described in the macrobiotic hygiene texts of Ma-wang-tui and Chang-chia shan.[6] Therein, in such a posture, one practices a form of circulation of the vital energy. This is also the basic posture in which Buddhist meditation was practiced in India and China. Chuang Tzu also makes reference to such a posture in his famous passage on "sitting and forgetting." For these reasons and those provided by the larger context of *Inward Training*, "aligning the body" and "aligning the four limbs" appear to refer to a specific posture within which breath meditation was practiced. The meaning of the two phrases seems to suggest a posture in which the knees are touching the floor and perhaps the buttocks are seated on a thick cushion and the arms and shoulders are fixed in a position in which they line up to form a square pattern with the knees. While we cannot be certain of such details, passages like those in verses VIII and XI make it clear that the position was designed to keep the body stable while breathing practice was pursued. The summary of inner cultivation practice found in verse XXIV provides further evidence for this:

1 When you enlarge your mind and let go of it,
2 When you relax your vital breath and expand it,
3 When your body is calm and unmoving:

4 And you can maintain the One and discard the myriad disturbances.
5 You will see profit and not be enticed by it,
6 You will you see harm and not be frightened by it.
7 Relaxed and unwound, yet acutely sensitive,
8 In solitude you delight in your own person.
9 This is called "revolving the vital breath":
10 Your thoughts and deeds seem heavenly.

Here it is from the stability of the body's sitting in a calm and unmoving position that one practices the "revolving" or regular circulation of the vital breath. The *Inward Training* authors call this breathing practice "aligning the vital breath," the third of the "Fourfold Aligning." With your breathing relaxed and expanded by this practice, you let go of the various contents of your mind and become acutely sensitive. Verse XIX includes a related passage:

15 When the four limbs are aligned
16 And the blood and vital breath are tranquil,
17 Unify your awareness, concentrate your mind,
18 Then your eyes and ears will not be overstimulated.
19 And even the far-off will seem close at hand.

From this stable sitting posture, with the breathing tranquil, you can become concentrated on one thing, perhaps the One of verse XXIV. The "far-off that will seem close at hand" in the last line of XIX actually refers to the Way that this practice enables you to attain. Further support for this is found in verse V:

1 The Way has no fixed position;
2 It abides within the excellent mind.
3 When the mind is tranquil and the vital breath is regular,
4 The Way can thereby be halted.

When the mind is tranquil and the breathing is aligned with its inherent and regular natural guidelines (*li*, 理), the very Way itself can be experienced. Further advice on how to pursue this breathing practice and to attain its ultimate results is in verse XVII:

1 For all [to practice] this Way:
2 You must coil, you must contract,
3 You must uncoil, you must expand,
4 You must be firm, you must be regular [in this practice].
5 Hold fast to this excellent [practice]; do not let go of it.
5 Chase away the excessive; abandon the trivial.
6 And when you reach its ultimate limit
7 You will return to the Way and its inner power.

THE CULTIVATED MIND

The passages on inner cultivation practice discussed above all touch upon the establishment of a certain quality of mind that is the basis for experiencing the Way. It is called the "cultivated mind" (hsiu-hsin, 修心) in verse V, the "stable mind" (ting-hsin, 定心) in verse VIII, the "excellent mind" (shan-hsin, 善心) in verse V, the "concentrated mind" (chuan-hsin, 專心) in verse XIX, and the "well-ordered mind" (chih-hsin, 治心) in verses X, XI, XIII, and XIV. It is also referred to as the "aligned mind" (cheng-hsin, 正心), the fourth of our "Fourfold Aligning," in verse XIII. In this verse it is the mind into which the numinous mind comes:

1 There is a numinous [mind] naturally residing within;
2 One moment it goes, the next it comes,
3 And no one is able to conceive of it.
4 If you lose it you are inevitably disordered;
5 If you attain it you are inevitably well ordered.
6 Diligently clean out its lodging place
7 And its vital essence will naturally arrive.
8 Still your attempts to imagine and conceive of it.
9 Relax your efforts to reflect on and control it.
10 Be reverent and diligent
11 And its vital essence will naturally stabilize.
12 Grasp it and don't let go
13 Then the eyes and ears won't overflow
14 And the mind will have nothing else to seek.
15 When an aligned mind resides within you,
16 The myriad things will be seen in their proper perspective.

Thus the inconceivable numinous mind will come into the cultivated, the stable, the excellent, the concentrated, the aligned mind, the abode that has been "diligently cleaned out" through the aligning of the body and breathing. This cleaning out also entails emptying out the various normal contents of conscious experience, the emotions, the desires, the thoughts, and the perceptions. In many passages, *Inward Training* refers to the restriction or removal of each of these types of mental contents. Verse III speaks of the emotions and the desires:

1   All the forms of the mind
2   Are naturally infused and filled with it [the vital essence],
3   Are naturally generated and developed [because of] it.
4   It is lost
5   Inevitably because of sorrow, happiness, joy, anger, desire, and profit-seeking.
6   If you are able to cast off sorrow, happiness, joy, anger, desire, and profit-seeking,
7   Your mind will revert to equanimity.
8   The true condition of the mind
9   Is that it finds calmness beneficial and, by it, attains repose.
10   Do not disturb it, do not disrupt it
11   And harmony will naturally develop.

Indeed, this verse implies that the mind has a natural tendency to revert to equanimity (*ch'i*, 齊) or tranquility. Verse VII reiterates that this is so:

1   For the heavens, the ruling principle is to be aligned.
2   For the earth, the ruling principle is to be level.
3   For human beings, the ruling principle is to be tranquil.
4   Spring, autumn, winter, and summer are the seasons of the heavens.
5   Mountains, hills, rivers, and valleys are the resources of the earth.
6   Pleasure and anger, accepting and rejecting are the devices of human beings.

Temporally, the four seasons follow one another in sequence; although there is meteorological variation in any given year, this order remains.

Spatially, although there are topographical variations throughout the earth, the levelness of the ground is the mean or standard to which these features return. Human beings too have emotions and desires, but people always return to their inherent tranquility. Sages are those rare human beings who are able to accord with this inherent tendency. These two passages suggest that inner cultivation practice enables people to revert to something that is basic to them. It is a process of aligning with tendencies that are already present in their body, mind, and spirit. Other references to restricting or removing emotions and desires are found in verses VII, XX, XXI, XXIV, and XXVI.

There are fewer references to limiting perception and thought but they are, nonetheless, present. For example, the former is encountered in verses XIII ("the eyes and ears won't overflow") and XIX ("Unify your awareness, concentrate your mind; then your eyes and ears will not be overstimulated"), and a more veiled reference is in verse XVII ("Chase away the excessive"), which I take to refer to excessive sense perception. These lines imply that perception is not to be completely cast away, but to be limited and refined. This is supported by two references, in verses VIII and XVI, where being aligned and tranquil produces acute hearing and clear vision.

Thinking is also an impediment to attaining the well-ordered mind, particularly when it becomes excessive.

VIII
8 When the vital energy is guided, it [the vital essence] is generated,
9 But when it is generated, there is thought,
10 When there is thought, there is knowledge,
11 But when there is knowledge, then you must stop.
12 Whenever the forms of the mind have excessive knowledge,
13 You lose your vitality.

The forms of the mind here are the succession of mental states humans continually experience. Just as, in this passage, thinking is a problem when it becomes excessive, in verse XX it is a problem when it becomes obsessive.

6 When you think about something and don't let go of it,
7 Internally you will be distressed, externally you will be weak.

Like perceptions, thinking is not to be removed but merely to be restricted. The only exception to this is in the attempt to attain the numinous mind within, where, for the "cleaning out of the lodging place" in verse XIII, we are told to:

8 Still your attempts to imagine and conceive of it.
9 Relax your efforts to reflect on and control it.
10 Be reverent and diligent
11 And its vital essence will naturally stabilize.

So in the quest to realize the Way within that is the numinous "mind within the mind," thinking is to be abandoned because dualistic thought is somehow inimical to the Way.

V

11 The true state of that Way:
12 How could it be conceived of and pronounced upon?
13 Cultivate your mind, make your thoughts tranquil,
14 And the Way can thereby be attained.

THE ONE

Two verses in *Inward Training* deal with the One, which, as in the *Lao Tzu*, seems to be a metaphor for the Way. Verse XXIV discusses the One as follows:

XXIV

1 When you enlarge your mind and let go of it,
2 When you relax your vital breath and expand it,
3 When your body is calm and unmoving,
4 And you can maintain the One and discard the myriad disturbances.
5 You will see profit and not be enticed by it,
6 You will you see harm and not be frightened by it.
7 Relaxed and unwound, yet acutely sensitive,
8 In solitude you delight in your own person.
9 This is called "revolving the vital breath":
10 Your thoughts and deeds seem heavenly.

Here, maintaining the One (*shou-i,* 守 一) appears to be a meditative technique in which the adept concentrates on nothing but the Way, or some representation of it. It is to be undertaken when you are sitting in a calm and unmoving position, and it enables you to set aside the disturbances of perceptions, thoughts, emotions, and desires that normally fill your conscious mind. This passage is the earliest extant mention of this meditative technique that was to become a central practice in the later institutionalized Taoist religion. (Its significance is discussed in chapter 4.)

The One appears in a slightly different context in verse IX:

1 Those who can transform even a single thing, call them "numinous";
2 Those can alter even a single situation, call them "wise."
3 But to transform without changing your vital energy, to alter without expending wisdom:
4 Only exemplary persons who hold fast to the One are able to do this.
5 Hold fast to the One; do not lose it,
6 And you will be able to master the myriad things.

Verse IX looks more at the results of inner cultivation practice than at the details of practice described in the previous verse. Here only exemplary persons who "hold fast to the One" (*chih-i,* 執 一) can transform in response to other things or to the situation in which they find themselves because they see them from an underlying unity, that is, from the standpoint of the Way. The idea here seems similar to that of "pervading and unifying things" (*t'ung wei i*) in the famous chapter 2 of the *Chuang Tzu,* "Ch'i-wu lun" (Essay on Seeing Things as Equal, 齊 物 論).[7] Therein, sages, in embodying the Way, are able—like the Way—to see things as equal because they see the Way within them. So holding fast to the One entails retaining a sense or a vision of the Way as the one unifying force within phenomenal reality while seeing this reality in all its complexity.

Both verses are related to another that contains an epistemology of the Way and also relates to the earlier discussion of the numinous mind:

XIV

1 The Way fills the entire world.
2 It is everywhere that people are,
3 But people are unable to understand this.

4 When you are released by this one word:
5 You reach up to the heavens above;
6 You stretch down to the earth below;
7 You pervade the nine inhabited regions.
8 What does it mean to be released by it?
9 The answer resides in the calmness of the mind.
10 When your mind is well ordered, your senses are well ordered.
11 When your mind is calm, your senses are calmed.
12 What makes them well ordered is the mind;
13 What makes them calm is the mind.
14 By means of the mind you store the mind:
15 Within the mind there is yet another mind.
16 That mind within the mind: it is an awareness that precedes words.
17 Only after there is awareness does it take shape;
18 Only after it takes shape is there a word.
19 Only after there is a word is it implemented;
20 Only after it is implemented is there order.
21 Without order, you will always be chaotic.
22 If chaotic, you die.

This verse discusses the direct experience of the Way that pervades the entire cosmos but that most people do not realize. It is experienced as a nondual, numinous awareness "that precedes words" and lies deep within the "mind within the mind." To be released by the experience of the Way entails being freed from the temporal, spatial, and individual human confines symbolized in lines 5–7 by the heavens-earth-humans imagery.[8] This certainly appears to be a kind of unitive mystical experience (see chapter 4). This passage relates to the verses on the One in its discussion of the "one word."

Being released by the one word seems to involve the two related aspects of the One in verses XXIV and IX. The one word "Way" represents the One that exemplary persons "hold fast to" that enables them to "transform things" in the latter verse. The one word "Way" is also a verbal symbol or image of the Way retained by the mind after it is realized by experiencing the "mind within the mind" in verse XIV. As such a symbol, it could certainly serve as the object of the mental concentration entailed in the phrase "to maintain the One" (shou-i) in verse XXIV. This focus on the one word

"Way" could actually refer to a specific technique of concentration similar to the practice of repeating a mantra in Buddhist and Hindu forms of yogic meditation. While it is difficult to be certain of this interpretation, it makes sense in the context of mystical practice examined here in chapter 4.

Thus there is a recursive relationship here. By focusing on the one word "Way" while "revolving the vital breath" in the practice of inner cultivation you gradually calm the mind (verse XXIV). Through calming the mind and emptying it of its normal conscious contents, you "clean out the lodging place of the numinous mind" (verse XIII). This cleaning out enables you to realize the nondual awareness of the Way that is the "mind within the mind" and that releases you from the human perspective in verse XIV. After being released from this perspective, you inevitably return to the dualistic world, but retain a sense of your union with the Way by the "holding fast to the One" of verse IX. These are the several closely related aspects of the One discussed in the verses of *Inward Training*.

THE HOLISTIC BENEFITS OF INNER CULTIVATION

In addition to the spiritual and psychological benefits of the practice of inner cultivation presented in our analysis of *Inward Training*, this practice also has what might be deemed "physical" benefits, described in the second half of the text, primarily in verses XV–XXVI. Verse XV states that those who "preserve and naturally generate vital essence" will have an excellent circulation of vital energy. Verse XVIII shows how this circulation can influence other people.

XVIII
1 When there is a mind that is unimpaired within you,
2 It cannot be hidden.
3 It will be known in your countenance,
4 And seen in your skin color.
5 If with this good flow of vital energy you encounter others,
6 They will be kinder to you than your own brethren.
7 But if with a bad flow of vital energy you encounter others,
8 They will harm you with their weapons.
9 [This is because] the wordless pronouncement

10 Is more rapid than the drumming of thunder.
11 The perceptible form of the mind's vital energy
12 Is brighter than the sun and moon,
13 And more apparent than the concern of parents.
14 Rewards are not sufficient to encourage the good;
15 Punishments are not sufficient to discourage the bad.
16 Yet once this flow of vital energy is achieved,
17 All under the heavens will submit,
18 And once the mind is made stable,
19 All under the heavens will listen.

Thus the flow of vital energy within you is instantaneously apparent to all those with whom you interact. If you are in a bad mood, people will react to you with hostility. But if you have a good flow of vital energy, people will react with warmth and friendliness. Moreover, the sage who has mastered the practice of inner cultivation possesses a charisma that will influence others in a way that rewards and punishments cannot. This idea seems to inform the verses discussing how inner cultivation practice prevents you from being harmed by others, such as verse XXVI and the following passage from verse XV.

8 When the well spring [of vital essence] is not drained,
9 Vital energy freely circulates through the nine apertures.
10 You can then exhaust the heavens and the earth
11 And spread over the four seas.
12 When you have no delusions within you,
13 Externally there will be no disasters.
14 Those who keeps their minds unimpaired within,
15 Externally keep their bodies unimpaired,
16 Who do not encounter heavenly disasters
17 Or meet with harm at the hands of others,
18 Call them sages.

In this passage, the good flow of vital energy not only prevents others from harming you but also puts you in harmony with the greater patterns of the circulation of vital energy found in the heavens and the earth. This coordination of the heavens, the earth, and human beings is one of the dominant motifs in *Inward Training*. It is found in another passage that depicts further benefits of inner cultivation practice:

XVI

1 If people can be aligned and tranquil,
2 Their skin will be ample and smooth,
3 Their ears and eyes will be acute and clear,
4 Their muscles will be supple and their bones will be strong.
5 They will then be able to hold up the Great Circle [of the heavens]
6 And tread firmly over the [Great Square of the earth].
7 They will mirror things with great purity.
8 And will perceive things with great clarity.
9 Reverently be aware [of the Way] and do not waver,
10 And you will daily renew your inner power,
11 Thoroughly understand all under the heavens,
12 And exhaust everything within the Four Directions.
13 To reverently bring forth the effulgence [of the Way]:
14 This is called "inward attainment."
15 If you do this but fail to return to it,
16 This will cause a wavering in your vitality.

This passage approaches the benefits of inner cultivation holistically. There are the physical benefits in lines 2 and 4, the perceptual benefits in lines 3 and 8, psychological benefits in line 7, and the spiritual or mystical benefits in lines 10–12. It contains one of the dominant metaphors of *Inward Training*: interiority. The practice of inner cultivation is conceived of as taking place in the interior dimensions of the human person, but its benefits extend throughout all aspects of one's being.

All these aspects are embraced under the general term of vitality (*sheng*, 生). Through inner cultivation practice, one attains a vitality that puts one in accord with the harmonies of the cosmos. It is a vitality established by being grounded in the vital essence of the Way and the circulation of vital energy that it engenders. But here the *Inward Training* authors warn that it is possible to waste this excellent circulation of vital energy on things here unspecified but that other passages indicate consist of emotions, desires, and excessive perception and thought. If you do this but fail to return to reestablish your circulation of vital energy in the vital essence developed by tranquility, your vitality will waver and decline. The essentials of this position are summarized in verse XXV:

1 The vitality of all people
2 Inevitably comes from their peace of mind.
3 When anxious, you lose this guiding thread;
4 When angry, you lose this basic point.
5 When you are anxious or sad, pleased or angry,
6 The Way has no place within you to settle.
7 Love and desire: still them!
8 Folly and disturbance: correct them!
9 Do not push it! do not pull it!
10 Good fortune will naturally return to you,
11 And that Way will naturally come to you
12 So you can rely on and take counsel from it.
13 If you are tranquil then you will attain it;
14 If you are agitated you will lose it.

Verse XXI indicates that another important result of achieving a holistic vitality through inner cultivation practice is the attainment of longevity:

1 As for the life of all human beings:
2 The heavens bring forth their vital essence,
3 The earth brings forth their bodies.
4 These two combine to make a person.
5 When they are in harmony there is vitality;
6 When they are not in harmony there is no vitality.
7 If we examine the Way of harmonizing them,
8 Its essentials are not visible,
9 Its signs are not numerous.
10 Just let a balanced and aligned [breathing] fill your chest
11 And it will swirl and blend within your mind,
12 This confers longevity.
13 When joy and anger are not limited,
14 You should make a plan [to limit them].
15 Restrict the five sense-desires;

16 Cast away these dual misfortunes.
17 Be not joyous, be not angry,
18 Just let a balanced and aligned [breathing] fill your chest.

Given their commitment to a holistic vision of inner cultivation practice and its results, it is not surprising that the authors of *Inward Training* also put forth a philosophy of eating:

XXIII

1 For all the Way of eating is that:
2 Overfilling yourself with food will impair your vital energy
3 And cause your body to deteriorate.
4 Overrestricting your consumption causes the bones to wither
5 And the blood to congeal.
6 The mean between overfilling and overrestricting:
7 This is called "harmonious completion."
8 It is where the vital essence lodges
9 And knowledge is generated.
10 When hunger and fullness lose their proper balance,
11 You make a plan to correct this.
12 When full, move quickly;
13 When hungry, neglect your thoughts;
14 When old, forget worry.
15 If when full you don't move quickly,
16 Vital energy will not circulate to your limbs.
17 If when hungry you don't neglect thoughts of food,
18 When you finally eat you will not stop.
19 If when old you don't forget your worries,
20 The fount of your vital energy will rapidly drain out.

The holistic approach to attaining a harmony of physical, psychological, and spiritual dimensions in the process of self-cultivation in *Inward Training* provides early testimony to the practice later called "nourishing the vitality (or vital principle)" (*yang sheng*, 養生). In her seminal study of Taoism, Isabelle Robinet describes its importance:

Yangsheng . . . the art of "nourishing the vital principle" . . . consists of adopting a way of life ruled by physico-mental hygienic principles.

This is not specifically a Taoist art and derives from ancient Chinese practices; Taoists adopted, developed, and modified them. . . . Even when they seem to be eclipsed by new tendencies, the rules of this art remain a foundation of all Taoist practices in all eras.[9]

The very origins of the distinctively Taoist version of this central practice are in *Inward Training*.

CHAPTER FOUR

Inward Training

in the Context of Early Taoist Mysticism

The practices of self-discipline advocated in *Inward Training* and its companion texts parallel practices advocated in other textual sources of early Taoism. In fact, they are not altogether unlike those found in many other mystical traditions throughout the world. They are essentially apophatic—that is, they involve a systematic process of negating, forgetting, or emptying out the contents of consciousness (perceptions, emotions, desires, thoughts) found in ordinary experience based in the ego-self.¹ This systematic emptying leads to increasingly profound states of tranquility until one experiences a fully concentrated inner consciousness of unity, which is filled with light and clarity and is not tied to an individual self.

Some sources imply further that this condition of unitary consciousness is temporary and that upon returning to normal differentiating consciousness the concerns of the self that had previously characterized one's conscious experience are no longer present. Therefore the sage thus transformed becomes selfless, impartial, unmoved by common passions and prejudices, and singularly able to respond spontaneously and harmoniously to any situations that arise and to exert a numinous influence upon them. It is no wonder that the fruits of these practices became so desirable to those who governed. It promised a sagely, almost divine clarity and the attendant wisdom not only to govern efficaciously but to also achieve total personal fulfillment.

The culturally unique characteristics of this system of praxis involve the particular ways the early Taoists conceived of this process. Systematic breath-control practices, often while sitting in a stable position, as seen in *Inward Training*, involved for them the circulating and refining of the *ch'i*, the vital breath, producing an increasingly rarefied and concentrated form of it called the vital essence (*ching*), which seems to be thought of as the "material" counterpart of the psychological experience of tranquility, as well as the essential generative element in the material world. Since vital essence is expended in such daily activities as perception, thoughts, desires, and emotions, inner cultivation theory urges these activities to be kept to a minimum. By emptying the mind of these common experiences and cultivating tranquility, one will attain both the physical vitality and psychological well-being that come from having the entire human organism function spontaneously according to its inherent patterns or "natural guidelines" (*li*). At ultimate levels our sources speak of the rising of an intuitive awareness that is clairvoyant and noetic and is associated with the numen or numinous mind spoken of in *Inward Training*.

Inward Training, verse XIII, line 6, speaks metaphorically of this process as "diligently cleaning out the lodging place of the numinous" (敬除其舍)—the layer of the mind directly in touch with the Way—by thoroughly sweeping out its abode, the normal conscious mind. In other passages *Inward Training* refers to this as emptying the mind to make a lodging place for the Way and conceives of this apophatic process as developing "inner power." Uncovering the Way within is thus linked to developing increasing tranquility, which itself is the "inner power" that is the manifestation of the Way in human beings. This "inner power" can be thought of as a psychological condition of focused and balanced awareness from which the adept is able to respond spontaneously and harmoniously to whatever arises.

As the oldest surviving text of inner cultivation theory, *Inward Training* contains some of the earliest instances of important techniques of self-transformation, including passages on systematic breathing meditation and the proper posture for this meditation and on the meditative technique called "maintaining the One" (*shou-i*) that was so influential in later Taoist and Buddhist meditation.

This chapter analyzes the evidence for mysticism in *Inward Training* in light of the cross-cultural, comparative analysis of mystical experience, a scholarly discipline developed during the past century in the West. It examines how the mysticism of *Inward Training* relates to that in other sources of early Taoism, especially the *Lao Tzu* and the *Chuang Tzu,* long regarded as the foundations of the Taoist tradition. Finally, it contrasts the breathing meditation advocated in early Taoist sources with that found in the recently excavated texts of "macrobiotic hygiene" with which they share technical terminology and certain common assumptions.

What Is Mysticism?

Since the analysis of the mysticism found in *Inward Training* is the central focus of this chapter, it is critical to clarify this term and its varied aspects. Although the term "mysticism" has been uncritically used to refer to a wide variety of unusual human experiences from demonic visions to psychokinesis, and has been deplored as the antithesis of the rational, scholars of religion have developed a more focused definition.

The cross-cultural study of "mysticism" is a modern Western phenomenon that began with the publication of William James's *The Varieties of Religious Experience* in 1902.[2] This work argues that all religious systems in their many and varying complexities are founded on the collective religious experiences of individual practitioners.[3] Mystical experience, as a subset of religious experience, can be identified by the presence of several characteristics: (1) ineffability: they defy description; (2) noetic quality: they impart definitive knowledge about fundamental truths; (3) transiency: they pass quickly; and (4) passivity: despite taking steps to cultivate it, when one is actually having the mystical experience it is as if one's will is suspended and one feels "grasped and held by a superior power."[4] James distinguishes mystical experiences from other religious experiences that seem to share this last characteristic by emphasizing the transforming influence of the mystical experience: One is never again the same as before one had it. It is this transforming aspect that constitutes an unspoken fifth characteristic of mystical experience for James. Robert Gimello adds two important characteristics to this list: "a feeling of oneness or unity, variously defined" and a "cessation of *normal* intellectual operations or the substitution for them of some 'higher' or qualitatively different mode of intellect (e.g., intuition)."[5]

Following James's lead, scholars from Evelyn Underhill to Robert Forman have pursued the study of mysticism along the following two lines clearly adumbrated by Peter Moore:

The philosophical analysis of mysticism comprises two overlapping lines of inquiry: on the one hand the identification and classification of the phenomenological characteristics of mystical experience, and on the other the investigation of the epistemological and ontological status of this experience. The first line of inquiry is generally focused on the question whether the mystical experiences reported in different cultures and religious traditions are basically of the same type or whether there are significantly different types. The second line of inquiry centres on the question whether mystical experiences are purely subjective phenomena or whether they have the kind of objective validity and metaphysical significance that mystics and others claim for them.[6]

In other words, the former line deals with the nature and characteristics of mystical experience, and the latter deals with the various philosophical claims made on the basis of mystical experience. These overlapping lines of inquiry indicate that two fundamental aspects of mysticism are mystical experience and mystical philosophy.

Along the first line of inquiry, Walter Stace delineates two fundamental forms of mystical experience, "extrovertive" and "introvertive."[7] The extrovertive looks outward through the senses of the individual and sees a fundamental unity between this individual and the world, simultaneously perceiving the one and the many, unity and multiplicity. Stace and James give several examples of this form of mystical experience and discuss it as what one mystic called "cosmic consciousness."[8] Introvertive mystical experience looks inward and is exclusively an experience of unity, that is, an experience of the unitive or what some scholars (Forman and others) call "pure" or objectless consciousness.[9] For Stace this introvertive experience is the essence of mysticism, "the undifferentiated unity of pure ego that holds the manifold stream of consciousness together"; he sees it in Christian mystics such as John van Ruysbroeck and Meister Eckhart and in Hindu and Mahayana Buddhist mystics as well.[10] In his account, while mystical experiences have these two fundamental aspects, the many and varied conceptions that accompany them are the products of post-experiential cultural and religious categorization and are not inherent in the experiences themselves.

The work of James and Stace on the phenomenology of mystical experience has been strongly disputed by scholars such as Steven Katz.[11] Katz claims that the unique cultural characteristics that Stace sees as entering into the picture before and after the mystical experience but not *during* it are actually important determinants of the experience itself. Asserting that there are no such things as pure, unmediated, experiences, Katz argues that to delineate common phenomenological characteristics is fruitless because we have no way of ascertaining whether there are any. Yet Katz's position is, in turn, challenged by Robert Forman and Donald Rothberg, who contend that in many traditions it is precisely those cultural and religious categories that Katz believes constitute mystical experience that are stripped away during mystical practice.[12]

Along the second line of inquiry adumbrated by Moore, two basic forms or types of mysticism can be distinguished that take their distinctions from that which is unified within the mystical experience, Stace's "objective referant."[13] The first is "theistic," in which that with which one unifies is a single god or divine being, and the second is "monistic," in which that with which one unifies is a single abstract force or principle. In general (there are exceptions), theistic mysticism is found in Christianity, Judaism, Islam, and many schools of Hinduism, and monistic mysticism is found in Buddhism, some schools of Hinduism, and the early Taoism of *Inward Training,* the *Lao Tzu,* and other related texts. It is thus possible to have four different combinations of these phenomenological and ontological types: extrovertive and introvertive monistic mysticism, and extrovertive and introvertive theistic mysticism.

In addition to mystical experience and mystical philosophy, several other aspects of mysticism are relevant to our study of the *Inward Training.* Carl Keller provides a valuable definition of "mystical writings," which holds true for *Inward Training*:

> "Mystical writings" are texts which deal with ultimate knowledge: with its nature, its modalities, its conditions, its methods. . . . "Mystical writings" are thus texts which discuss the path towards realization of the ultimate knowledge which each particular religion has to offer, and which contain statements about the nature of such knowledge.[14]

Keller further distinguishes nine literary genres of mystical writings: aphorisms, biographies, reports on visions, commentaries, dialogues, instructions, prayers, religious poetry, and fiction.[15] Although Keller worked primarily from Western sources, some of these genres are represented in *Inward Training* and other early Taoist sources such as the *Lao Tzu*. Indeed, the verse sayings of these two texts can be classified as a form of religious poetry. *Inward Training* certainly contains "instructions" on inner cultivation practice. If we expand our sources to include the *Chuang Tzu*, we find aphorisms, commentaries, and dialogues present as well.[16]

Working from a broader range of textual sources than Keller that include works from the South Asian traditions of Hinduism and Buddhism, Peter Moore presents three categories of mystical writings: "first-order," autobiographical accounts of mystical experience; "second-order," impersonal accounts in which mystical experience is described in abstract terms; and "third-order," "accounts of a mainly theological or liturgical kind which although referring to some mystical object or reality do not refer, unless very obliquely, to mystical experience itself."[17] All three categories may be present in the same work.

Moore's categories are generally applicable to *Inward Training*, the *Lao Tzu,* and the other Taoist texts in the genre that William Baxter has identified. In these works, Moore's third category predominates, while there is less evidence for the second category and virtually none for the first. However, the fit is not perfect: Moore's third category suggests a more developed theological rhetoric than is found in these early Taoist sources. *Inward Training* primarily comprises philosophical verses about the nature of the world derived directly from the experiences of practitioners of the inner cultivation techniques that it also presents but do not contain direct reports of mystical experience. However, it has not yet become weighted down with the kinds of rigid rhetorical structures that Moore finds in this final category and that imply a much more advanced level of religious institutionalization than must have been present for the authors of *Inward Training* and the other early Taoist sources. For Moore, the kind of stereotypical rhetoric characteristic of this category makes it so far removed from actual mystical experience as to render it useless as a source for the philosophical analysis of mystical experience.[18] Yet he makes no provisions for the existence of a prestereotypical mystical philosophy directly derived from mystical experience that I think is well represented in *Inward Training* and the other early Taoist sources. Because of this failure to recognize nuances in this category of mystical writings, I cannot concur with his denigration of it as a source for the study of mystical experience.

Moore goes on to argue that a particularly crucial element of mysticism is the intimate connection between mystical experiences and what he calls "mystical techniques," the practices used to "induce" them.[19] He distinguishes between two primary techniques that represent the "immediate preconditions" for mystical experience, "meditation" and "contemplation." The former entails "the disciplined but creative application of the imagination and discursive thought to an often complex religious theme or subject-matter." The latter, a development of the former, entails the attempt "to transcend the activities of the imagination and intellect through an intuitive concentration on some simple object, image, or idea."[20] *Inward Training*'s method of "focusing on the One" while breathing in a systematic fashion seems to be an example of Moore's latter category of "contemplation." Moore's distinctions are instructive, particularly because the term "meditation" as used in Western religious contexts often implies a use of discursive thought focused on a problem that we do not see in South and East Asian sources. However, because the term "meditation" in common parlance as well as much of the scholarly literature is used for both activities that Moore distinguishes, I use "meditation" in this way to refer broadly to both general techniques, despite the astuteness of Moore's distinction.

Mystical techniques are further clarified in the writings of Forman and Rothberg. Forman, following the phenomenological tradition of James and Stace, argues that the "Pure Consciousness Event" (PCE—defined as a wakeful though contentless [nonintentional] consciousness)—his version of the latter's introvertive mystical experience—comes about through a systematic process of "forgetting."[21] This is elaborated upon by Rothberg:

> Robert Forman . . . has proposed a model of mystical development (in many traditions) as involving the "forgetting" (Meister Eckhardt's term) of the major cognitive and affective structures of experience. . . .
> In this process of "forgetting," there is an intentional dropping of desires, ideas, conceptual forms (including those of one's tradition), sensations, imagery, and so on. The end of this process is a contentless mystical experience in which the constructs of the tradition are transcended.[22]

Citing the twelve-year research project on meditative praxis in three Indo-Tibetan traditions by the psychologist Daniel Brown, Rothberg argues that in many traditions the spiritual path involves "a process of progressive deconstruction of the structures of experience."[23] Under this rubric Brown includes attitudes and behavioral schemes, thinking, gross perception, self-system, and "time-space matrix."[24] This is not to argue that the spiritual path is the same in every tradition. Indeed, as Rothberg contends, "each path of deconstruction or deconditioning is itself constructed or conditioned in a certain way."[25] Nor do he and Forman claim that pure consciousness is the only goal of all mystic paths. Indeed, the entire Forman collection intentionally passes over the important extrovertive aspect of mystical experience, unfairly denigrated by Stace and extremely important to the understanding of early Taoist mysticism.[26]

In a 1995 review essay, I argued for the presence of a "bimodal" mystical experience in early Taoism, particularly evident in the "inner chapters" of the *Chuang Tzu*.[27] The first mode is an introvertive unitive consciousness in which the adept is in complete union with the Way. This corresponds, in general, with Stace's "introvertive mystical experience" and with Forman's "Pure Consciousness Event." The second is an extrovertive transformed consciousness in which the adept returns to the world and retains, amid the flow of daily life, a profound sense of the unity previously experienced in the introvertive mode. This experience entails an ability to live in the world free from the limited and biased perspective of the individual ego. This second mode corresponds, in general, to Stace's "extrovertive mystical experience," although I regard it as a profound subcategory of it.[28] This bimodal character of mystical experience is, actually, quite prevalent in mystical experience across traditions, but it is often overlooked by scholars, who tend to focus on the introvertive mode exclusively. While evidence for its presence is not as strong in *Inward Training* as in the *Chuang Tzu*, it is most certainly there.

Finally, the philosophical analysis of mysticism there also pays a great deal of attention to mystical language, and the present discussion is concerned with one particular subset of it, the unique language that evolves within mystical practice. Brown witnessed this in his study of Tibetan monastic communities that held a body of teachings about the internal states attained through mystical practice to which an adept could compare his/her experience. He states:

In such traditions, where meditation practice is socially organized, a technical language for meditation experience evolved. This language was refined over generations. The technical terms do not have external referents, e.g., "house," but refer to replicable internal states which can be identified by anyone doing the same practice, e.g., "energy currents," or "seed meditations." Much like the specialized languages of math, chemistry, or physics, technical meditation language is usually intelligible only to those specialized audiences of yogis familiar with the experiences in question.[29]

Michael LaFargue sees this kind of language present in the *Lao Tzu*, and I concur.[30] I also see it in the other textual sources of early Taoism including, most important, *Inward Training*. The great challenge facing modern scholars who wish to study this specialized mystical language is to make sense of what it really meant to the people who used it. While this is not as much a problem when technical terms are primarily descriptive, as, for example, in Chuang Tzu's famous prescription for how to just "sit and forget," the more metaphorical the language becomes (for example, the idea of "cleaning out the lodging-place of the numinous" in verse XIII of *Inward Training* or in Chuang Tzu's phrase "merging with the Great Pervader"), the more challenging it is to interpret.[31]

Before applying these central elements of mysticism to *Inward Training*, it is necessary to clarify a particular terminological usage that could cause some confusion for specialist readers familiar with the scholarly literature on mysticism. As mentioned in chapter 2, the Chinese term *shen* is translated as "numen/numinous" instead of the more common "spirit/spiritual" to avoid confusion with Western meanings of these latter words. However, there is a technical usage of the word "numinous" among scholars of religion that began with Rudolph Otto, who used the term to describe the experience of the "wholly Other" in which an individual self is confronted with the supreme object of its religious devotion and trembles with awe and fascination.[32] This is the most basic *dualistic* religious experience, one in which a fundamental separation between human and divine is retained. Hence it does not qualify as a mystical experience in which such a fundamental separation does not occur or is overcome.

Here the translation "numen/numinous" is not being used in Otto's sense. Indeed, in *Inward Training* the numen or numinous mind is the locus of the nondual awareness of the Way, the monistic principle that pervades everything in the cosmos. As such a principle, it can never be "wholly Other" in Otto's definition because the Way is not transcendent in the same strong sense that God is in Christianity and Judaism. The Way is transcendent only in that it is present in all things and so is beyond any one of them. And it is transcendent in the sense that it is not normally perceived within the conscious mind, even though the authors of *Inward Training* believed that it resided at a deeper layer. In an analogous way, the numen or numinous "mind within the mind" as the locus of the Way in the deepest level of one's being, when it is finally perceived by the conscious self, is sensed as a power or force that is "other" in that it defies the attempt to control it by the will of the individual self. This is the sense of the meaning of *shen* that Graham hoped to capture with his translation of this term as "daemon/daemonic," which is unsuitable because of its malign connotations in common English. [33]

The Mysticism of *Inward Training*

We have seen that the central elements of mysticism are mystical practices or techniques, mystical experience, and mystical philosophy. Whether a given text is a "mystical writing" in which "mystical language" is found depends on our ability to identify these three elements within it. That *Inward Training* contains such elements is demonstrated in the following analysis.

MYSTICAL PRACTICE IN *Inward Training*

The primary mystical practice in *Inward Training* can be symbolically referred to by its distinctive phrase of "cleaning out the lodging-place of the numinous." This cleaning out is essentially an apophatic process in which one gradually and systematically removes the normal feelings, desires, thoughts, and perceptions that commonly occupy consciousness. In *Inward Training* the practice involves the attainment of tranquility through following the "Fourfold Aligning," namely, aligning the body, the four limbs, the breathing, and the mind (see chapter 3).

Indeed, the attainment of tranquility is one of the most important aims of inner cultivation practice in *Inward Training*. It is found in eleven of its twenty-six verses. The authors, however, made it very clear that this goal cannot be accomplished without first achieving the "Fourfold Aligning." Thus many passages insist that aligning (*cheng*) must precede tranquility (*ching*), as seen, for example, in verse XI:

1 When your body is not aligned,
2 The inner power will not come.
3 When you are not tranquil within,
4 Your mind will not be well ordered.
5 Align your body, assist the inner power,
6 Then it will gradually come on its own.

While stablizing body and mind through these alignings, the adept proceeds to "enlarge the mind and relax the vital breath" (verse XXIV) through a regular and systematic (verse V) breath-circulation (verse XXIV) that is also spoken of as a "coiling and uncoiling" (verse XVII). As part of this practice, one also "maintains [or focuses] on the One" through which one can "discard the myriads of disturbances" (verse XIX). In other passages these disturbances are enumerated as they are eliminated by inner cultivation: emotions and desires are removed (verses III, VII, XXI–XXIV, and XXVI), thinking is restricted (verse VIII) and or stopped (verse V), and perceptions are limited (verses XIII and XIX). The result of this is the development of equanimity (verse III), "inner power" (verses II, IV, XI, and XVI), and a profound tranquility (verses IV, V, VII, XI, XVI, XIX, XXII, and XXIV–XXVI) in which the mind is completely concentrated and the awareness is unified (verse XIX), and one becomes fully conscious of the constantly moving Way as an "awareness that precedes words" that emerges in the "mind within the mind" (verse XIV). This is also spoken of as "halting" or "grasping the Way" (verse V), "lodging the vital essence" (verses VIII and XIII), and "returning to the Way and its inner power" (verse XVII).

Because this inner cultivation practice gradually removes desires, emotions, and thoughts and restricts and attunes perception until one can directly perceive the Way, it exemplifies a "mystical technique" of "deconstruction" according to the definitions of Moore, Forman, and Rothberg. In addition, there are striking parallels between the general process and specific phases of inner cultivation and the stages of meditation found in traditional Hindu and Buddhist texts studied by Daniel Brown.[34] For example, sitting in a stable and erect position such as is advocated in *Inward Training* is one of the essentials of the preliminary stages of meditation in these texts. Further parallels between *Inward Training* and these South Asian religious sources can be found by examining Brown's typology of meditative stages outlined below.[35]

I. PRELIMINARY ETHICAL PRACTICES
This has no obvious parallels in *Inward Training*.

II. PRELIMINARY BODY/MIND TRAINING
This includes sitting in a stable posture, becoming aware of and later calming breathing and thinking.

III. CONCENTRATION WITH SUPPORT
This includes concentration on either an external or internal object leading to a reduction in mental contents of all kinds and the eventual resolving of mental activity into a simple, unified awareness often associated with light.

IV. CONCENTRATION WITHOUT SUPPORT
Continuing focus on a simple awareness of light leading to the collapse of the ordinary observer; sense of self-agency drops away; events simply occur by themselves; here is where the traditional Buddhist Eight Absorptions(*jhanas*) and the "psychic powers" (including foreknowledge) occur.

V. INSIGHT PRACTICE
Applying the inner concentration developed in the above stages to gaining insight into how the world of ordinary experience and the self are constructed; for Hindus and Tibetan Buddhists, an "experience of unity comes forth in which all the potential events of the universe come forth as a dimension of the same underlying substratum"(255).

VI. ADVANCED INSIGHT PRACTICE
A more profound level of Stage V that represents a profound shift in consciousness and an opening up of awareness to the level beyond the time/space matrix of awareness permanently freed from psychological structure.

The "Fourfold Aligning" of *Inward Training* parallels the entire second stage in Brown's summary. It is in this stage too that the concentration on breath-circulation from *Inward Training* could be classified. The meditative technique of "maintaining the One" from *Inward Training* and the general apophatic or deconstructive process that derives from its breathing meditation correspond to Brown's third stage. The tranquility thus engendered in *Inward Training* could be located in both his third and fourth stages along with the complete concentration of the mind and unification of the awareness found there as well. Finally, the direct apprehension of the Way as a liberating and nondual "awareness that precedes words" in *Inward Training* seems to parallel the experience of unity found in Brown's fifth stage in Hindu and Tibetan Buddhist writings. As might be expected given the diversity of cultural, religious, and historical circumstances, the fit between these South Asian sources and *Inward Training* is far from perfect. However, the fact that so many parallels appear in spite of these differences is striking.

Victor Mair has noted similar parallels between the evidence for breath meditation in the *Lao Tzu* and the systematic practice and surrounding philosophy of yoga that developed in India in the first millenium B.C.[36] Precise dates for this development are difficult to fix. However, evidence of breathing practices is found in some of the thirteen principal *Upanisads*, texts of metaphysical philosophy that are attached to the *Vedas* and thought to have been written between the eighth and fourth centuries B.C.[37] Mair also sees textual parallels between the *Lao Tzu* and the later Hindu epic narrative, the *Bhagavad-gita*, which dates from no earlier than the fourth century B.C. Because of these textual parallels and the gathering archaeological evidence for a much earlier date for commercial contact between the peoples of the Indian subcontinent and China than has previously been established (going back to early in the first millenium B.C. and perhaps even earlier), Mair asserts that Indian yoga is the principle formative influence on Chinese Taoism.

> Those who take the trouble to read attentively the early Indian texts just cited, particularly the classical *Upanisads*, will realize that they foreshadow the entire philosophical, religious, and physiological foundations of Taoism, but not its social and political components, which are distinctively Chinese.[38]

Mair's arguments from textual parallels and commercial contact are not persuasive evidence that the meditative practice of *Inward Training* and other early Taoist sources derived from Indian yoga. Rather, these arguments suggest parallel developments in different cultures at different times, which occurred because of the application of similar methods of psychophysical cultivation by human beings, who, despite their cultural differences were affected by these techniques in generally similar ways. Systematically deconstructing cognitive structures through sitting breath meditation seems to yield similar experiences of tranquility and of a unified awareness, despite distinct cultural differences. This should not be surprising since neurophysiologists who have studied meditation have found similar results.[39] It should also not be surprising that these results should be conceived of differently according to different cultural and religious conceptual categories. By examining the common practices in addition to the apparently similar mystical concepts that derive from them we can avoid the charges of ignoring cultural differences that scholars such as Katz level against those who examine these mystical philosophies alone. Certain human practices, such as sitting, breathing, focusing the awareness, and becoming tranquil, are found in people despite the cultural categories by which they understand these experiences. Studying these practices offers a better understanding of the experiences they yield than approaching them by ideas alone.

Moreover, despite providing evidence of early commercial contact between India and China, Mair has not been able to show any archaeological evidence that religious practices and ideas were transmitted along with trade. Perhaps they were, and perhaps some day we will find evidence of this. But until we do, Mair's evidence and arguments simply indicate the *possibility* of an Indian influence, not the *necessity* of it. Until such a time, it is prudent to refer to the early Taoist mystical practice as "inner cultivation," rather than "Taoist yoga," whose use implies the accuracy of the Mair hypothesis. Using this appellation further distinguishes this practice from the macrobiotic hygiene practices with which it shares some technical terminology.

MYSTICAL EXPERIENCE IN *Inward Training*

In this light it would be of further interest to examine the applicability of Stace's categories of mystical experience to *Inward Training*. If this text is categorized as what Moore calls a "third-order mystical writing," or one in which mystical experience is referred to only "very obliquely"—if at all—there is little direct evidence for Stace's introvertive mystical experience. While experiencing complete tranquility or a unified awareness might seem to qualify as introvertive mystical experiences on bare phenomenological grounds, phrases that speak of the ultimate result of inner cultivation practice as "halting or grasping the Way" or returning to the Way and its inner power," which also involve the "objective referent" mentioned by Stace, provide more solid evidence. However, one verse in *Inward Training* seems to be more of a "second-order" mystical writing according to Moore's definition and provides the most direct evidence of Stace's unitive mystical experience.

XIV

1 The Way fills the entire world.
2 It is everywhere that people are,
3 But people are unable to understand this.
4 When you are released by this one word:
5 You reach up to the heavens above;
6 You stretch down to the earth below;
7 You pervade the nine inhabited regions.
8 What does it mean to be released by it?
9 The answer resides in the calmness of the mind. . . .

14 By means of the mind you store the mind:
15 Within the mind there is yet another mind.
16 That mind within the mind: it is an awareness that
     precedes words.
17 Only after there is awareness does it take shape;
18 Only after it takes shape is there a word.
19 Only after there is a word is it implemented;
20 Only after it is implemented is there order.
21 Without order, you will always be chaotic.
22 If chaotic, you die.

This verse implies that, through the direct apprehension of the reality of this "one word," the Way, we are freed from the usual spatial and temporal restrictions and experience a union with the entire world. Although this looks like Stace's extrovertive mystical experience and certainly could entail that, the argument that being released by the Way derives from an experience deep within the mind seems to imply that this experience is actually an internal one of union with the Way.

   It is certainly an experience of an awareness that precedes words and hence language, the intellect, and the dualistic structures common to the psyche. As such it would fall into Forman's category of "Pure Consciousness Event." When considered along with the other statements in the text about attaining or returning to the Way through inner cultivation practice, this verse seems to provide the clearest testimony for Stace's category of introvertive mystical experience and for Forman's "Pure Consciousness Event." It is also linked conceptually with the testimony to extrovertive mystical experience in the text, both with its lines about being freed to merge with the cosmos (ll. 1–7) and in the epistemology of the One that is implied in others (ll. 15–20). If the Way is directly experienced as a nondual unitive awareness that results from apophatic inner cultivation practice, these lines indicate that some aspect or memory or vision of this Way with which one has united can be retained when one returns to normal dualistic consciousness. I see this at the basis of the central idea of "holding fast to the One" (*chih-i*) that is found in verse IX:

> 3 . . . to transform without expending vital energy; to alter without expending wisdom:
> 4 Only exemplary persons who hold fast to the One are able to do this.
> 5 Hold fast to the One; do not lose it,
> 6 And you will be able to master the myriad things.
> 7 Exemplary persons act upon things,
> 8 And are not acted upon by them,
> 9 Because they grasp the guiding principle of the One.

Here holding fast to the One without letting go of it gives a sage the ability to "master the myriad things" and influence them without exerting any effort at all. Since the One, or the Way, is present in all phenomena (verses IV–VI), if you can directly apprehend it within yourself and retain it throughout your interactions with things in the world, you can master them because you know their very foundation, their most essential element.

Indeed, in the later *Huai-nan Tzu* this ability to influence and even transform other things was conceived of as occurring through a mysterious resonance between the highly refined vital essence of a sage-ruler and the vital essences that occur in all things.[40] The basis for what the *Huai-nan Tzu* calls this "numinous transformation" is found in this passage from *Inward Training*. This transformation can occur without deliberate intentional activity by sages because they have directly experienced how the Way is the guiding principle of themselves and of all phenomena. The retention of this experience of the Way qualifies as an extrovertive mystical experience. Indeed, it could very well serve as the basis for the phrase made famous by the *Lao Tzu*: "[the sage] takes no action and yet nothing is left undone" (*wu-wei erh wu pu-wei,* 無為而無不為). While I have always understood this to refer to the lack of intentional and self-based activity, its meaning could also include this notion of the sages' ability to transform things numinously through this mysterious resonance.

Further benefits that accrue from inner cultivation practice are mentioned in *Inward Training;* and these benefits are evidence of the extrovertive mystical experience for several reasons. After experiencing the temporary loss of self in the introvertive mystical experience, when you return to viewing the world from within this self again you are no longer attached to its limited perspective. So, for example, verse XXIV says that "you will not be enticed by profit or be frightened by harm" because you are no longer attached to the perspective of the individual self that is normally so enticed and so frightened. The verse goes on to say that "your thoughts and deeds seem heavenly," which means that, like heaven, you will be spontaneously responsive because this natural inclination is not interfered with by the self-conscious deliberation that often accompanies the individual self. Verse XVI says that following inner cultivation will allow you eventually to "mirror things with great purity and perceive things with great clarity" for this same reason: the lack of self-conscious deliberation that derives from holding onto the sense of loss of self and union with the Way that follows from the introvertive mystical experience or the "Pure Consciousness Event."

Although such psychological qualities do not predominate in Stace's description of extrovertive mystical experience, they appear in the work of other scholars, such as Evelyn Underhill and Katsuki Sekida, who are much more attuned to the varieties of such an experience and how it affects daily life. Indeed, Underhill regards the development of these qualities of what she calls "the unitive life"—and not the experience of union with the divine—as the very pinnacle of mysticism.[41] Sekida presents a similar argument: "If we accept that there is an object in Zen practice," he writes, "then it is this freedom of mind in actual living."[42] These qualities of mind are the concrete results of gaining the broadened perspective on the individual self afforded by the introvertive mystical experience and its retention.

One final aspect of inner cultivation that is unique to *Inward Training* when examined from the cross-cultural perspective are the distinctive physical and physiological benefits that develop from this practice. Vitality, efficient circulation of vital energy, strong bones, supple muscles, and so on are part of the holistic benefits of inner cultivation conceived of by the *Inward Training* authors. They show their familiarity with the conceptual schema of the early techniques of physical and macrobiotic hygiene aimed at nourishing vitality and prolonging life, in which breath cultivation was also an important practice. That they took such cultivation to a deeper and more profound level should not obscure their debt to these techniques.

MYSTICAL PHILOSOPHY IN *Inward Training*

To the extent that they conceptualize the mystical practices and experiences of the authors of *Inward Training*, the ideas presented here can be classified as mystical philosophy. In addition to these, undoubtedly the most important mystical ideas in *Inward Training* are the Way that is unified within the "mind within the mind" and the vital essence, the concrete representation of the Way within the physiological systems that constitute the human being in all its levels—physical, psychological, and spiritual.

James, Stace, and others recognize that paradoxicality and ineffability are two primary characteristics of mystical experience and of the concepts derived from it. The three verses devoted to the Way in *Inward Training* are filled with such statements. Ineffability is first seen in verse VI.

1 As for the Way:
2 It is what the mouth cannot speak of,
3 The eyes cannot see,
4 And the ears cannot hear.

It is further called vague and indiscernable (verse IV, ll. 2–4), silent and obscure (verse IV, ll. 10 and 12), and indiscernable again (verse V, l. 10). It is also said to have neither root nor trunk, leaves nor flowers (verse VI, ll. 10–11), a sign that it cannot be analyzed—nor does it function—according to the normal laws of sequential causation in the plant life that flourishes in the natural world.

Yet despite this mysterious and indefinable quality, it is, paradoxically, seen as very concrete. For example, it is described as "Clear! as though right by your side" (verse IV, l. 1), not distant (verse V, l. 5), and something with which you could be roped together (verse V, l. 9). Indeed, it is further described as something that abides within the mind (verse IV, l. 11, and verse V, l. 2), something that arises with me (verse IV, l. 13), and something that infuses the body (verse IV, l. 6). And, of course, we "daily make use of its inner power" (verse IV, l. 5). Yet despite its concreteness it cannot be fixed in place because it constantly "goes forth but does not return, comes back but does not stay" (verse IV. ll. 7–9).

In addition to these paradoxical descriptions of its simultaneous ineffability and concreteness, it is also important on both the individual and cosmic levels. For example, people are sustained when they attain it (verse V, l. 6) and harmonious when they accord with it (verse V, l. 8). It is the basis for the entire practice of inner cultivation (verse VI, l. 5), and it is so important that verse VI states:

6 When people lose it they die;
7 When people gain it they flourish.
8 When endeavors lose it they fail;
9 When they gain it they succeed.

It is further described in the same verse as the power or force through which all things are generated and develop to completion.

The authors of *Inward Training* propose a program of self-discipline by which this ineffable Way can be grasped, halted, fixed, or directly experienced within the mind in a nondual "awareness that precedes words." This fact yields a clue to its paradoxical ineffability and concreteness. It is ineffable and generally imperceptible because it is a force—or perhaps, in modern terms, an energy—that simply cannot be known dualistically. As verse V puts it: "The true state of the Way, how could it be conceived of or pronounced upon?" Yet even though it cannot be known as an object, it can be both sensed through its accomplishments (verse IV, l. 16) and felt as a vital essence that pervades the body and mind while constantly moving through them. Indeed, this vital essence is described using similar locutions in verse II:

1 Therefore this vital energy is:
2 Bright!—as if ascending the heavens;
3 Dark!—as if entering an abyss;

4 Vast!—as if dwelling in an ocean;
5 Lofty!—as if dwelling on a mountain peak.

6 Therefore this vital energy
7 Cannot be halted by force,
8 Yet can be secured by inner power.
9 Cannot be summoned by speech,
10 Yet can be welcomed by the awareness.
11 Reverently hold onto it and do not lose it:
12 This is called "developing inner power."
13 When inner power develops and wisdom emerges,
14 The myriad things will, to the last one, be grasped.

Lines 1–5 employ the identical rhetorical structure of a vivid adjective followed by an "as if" clause used to describe the Way in verse IV, ll. 1–3 and ll. 10–13 and verse V, ll. 9–10. It is also linked with the inner power that is the manifestation of the Way and is something that cannot be controlled by an act of the will but can only be "welcomed by the awareness." The vital essence is thus a mystical idea very closely related to the Way that gives it a concrete representation or aspect within the natural world and helps explain its paradoxical characteristics. This concreteness, conceived in terms of the philosophy of ch'i, provides further evidence that the authors of *Inward Training* were aware of the conceptual world of the teachers of macrobiotic hygiene, who were also steeped in this philosophy.

Inward Training and the *Lao Tzu*

The parallels between *Inward Training* and the *Lao Tzu* are considerably more extensive than the shared literary genre that William Baxter has insightfully recognized. There are distinct parallels as well in mystical philosophy and mystical practice. Both texts share a conception of the Way as the ultimate power through which all the myriad things are generated and through which they complete their development. Thus the Way is repeatedly described in the *Lao Tzu* as the "beginning," the "mother" (verses 1 and 20)[43] or "ancestor" of the myriad things (verse 4), the "father of the multitude" (verse 21) and the "mother of heaven and earth" (verse 25). The myriad things "entrust their lives to it, and yet it does not act as their master" (verse 34). "The Way gives birth to them, nourishes them, matures them, completes them, rests them, rears them, supports them, and protects them" (verse 51). Likewise, *Inward Training*, verse VI, describes the Way as follows: "The myriad things are generated by it" and "The myriad things are completed by it." While the *Lao Tzu* has much more to say about the Way, the message is the same.

Both texts, likewise, handle the concept of *Te* (inner power) in similar fashions. In *Inward Training* it is that aspect of the Way that we "daily make use of" (verse IV) and it develops as we refine the vital breath into the vital essence through breath meditation (verse II). This link between inner power and the vital essence also occurs in verse 55 of the *Lao Tzu*, where one "who is filled with an abundance of inner power" is compared to the newborn babe in whom the vital essence is at its height. However, more often inner power in the *Lao Tzu* is a more abstract concept paired with the Way as its nurturing aspect (verse 51), as a quality that arises in those who have attained the Way (verse 28), and as the quality of the Way itself by which it generates and completes all things but does not try to dominate them (verses 10 and 51). As such it can be thought of as a more concrete aspect of the Way as it is manifested within the world, and the relationship between these two concepts in the *Lao Tzu* parallels that in *Inward Training*.

The abstract/concrete contrast between *Tao* and *Te* shows a paradoxical relationship noted here in detail in the mystical philosophy of *Inward Training*, where the Way is described as both ineffable yet concrete. These paradoxical qualities are much more fully elaborated on in the mystical thought of the *Lao Tzu*. The famous first two lines state: "The Way that can be spoken of is not the constant Way. The name that can be named is not the constant name." Additional locutions closely parallel *Inward Training*, for example, *Lao Tzu,* verse 14:[44]

1 We look at it but do not see it;
2 We name this "the minute."
3 We listen to it but do not hear it;
4 We name this "the rarefied."
5 We touch it but do not hold it;
6 We name this "the level and smooth."

Verse 21 reads:

2 As for the nature of the Way—it's shapeless and formless.
3 Formless! Shapeless! Inside there are images.
4 Shapeless! Formless! Inside there are things.
5 Hidden! Obscure! Inside there are essences [*ching*, 精].

Compare these descriptions with those in *Inward Training*, verse VI:

1 As for the Way:
2 It is what the mouth cannot speak of,
3 The eyes cannot look at,
4 And the ears cannot listen to.

And those in verse IV:

1 Clear! as though right by your side.
2 Vague! as though it will not be attained.
3 Indiscernable! as though beyond the limitless.
4 The test of this is not far off:
5 Daily we make use of its inner power . . .
10 Silent! none can hear its sound.
11 Suddenly stopping! it abides within the mind.
12 Obscure! you do not see its form.
13 Surging forth! it arises with me.

Although the descriptions of the Way in the two texts are similar, they
are never identical. One important contrast is in the way in which *Inward
Training* interweaves the paradoxical qualities of ineffability and concreteness, in every other line in verse IV, ll. 1–3 and ll. 10–13, and also in verse
V, ll. 9–10. The authors of the *Lao Tzu* seem to emphasize the ineffable
qualities of the Way much more than the concrete ones, although the
latter are not omitted. For example, in verses 34 and 51 concrete activities
of the Way are described, including the generation and completion of the
myriad things. But, in the *Lao Tzu*, even such concrete activities are often
given more mysterious descriptions, for example, in verse 4.

1 The Way is empty
2 When you use it, you never need fill it again
3 Like an abyss! It seems to be the ancestor of the myriad things.

and in verse 34:

1 The Way floats and drifts
2 It can go left or right
3 It accomplishes its tasks and completes its affairs, and yet
   for this it is not given a name.

Thus while the *Lao Tzu* has general descriptions of the Way's activities, there is virtually nothing in the *Lao Tzu* to parallel the concrete representation of the Way in terms of the early physiological concepts of vital energy and vital essence found in *Inward Training*. Perhaps also related to this is the strong emphasis on the mind and on the practice of inner cultivation in *Inward Training*, an emphasis with few parallels in the *Lao Tzu*. However, although there appear to be few parallels, they are not entirely absent. Indeed, the ones that are present give clear indication that the authors of the *Lao Tzu* followed mystical techniques similar to those advocated in *Inward Training*.

The emphasis on the importance of attaining tranquility that predominates in *Inward Training* is also found in the *Lao Tzu*. The term occurs in seven of its eighty-one verses, and its importance can be seen in verse 16, which states that to "maintain tranquility is the central (practice)" (*shou-ching tu yeh,* 守靜督也).

Just as tranquility is attained in *Inward Training* through the apophatic practices of inner cultivation, the *Lao Tzu* also contains references to such practices, although, for the most part, they occur rather unsystematically. These practices, as mentioned above, involve removing knowledge, desire, perception, and emotions; they find parallels in the *Lao Tzu* in the following passages.

1. *Knowledge*—verse 19: "eliminate sageliness, discard knowledge and eliminate learning"; verse 20: "eliminate learning [and] there will be no sorrow"; verse 48: the pursuit of learning is contrasted with the pursuit of the Way, and we are urged to do less and less of the former.

2. *Desires*—verse 1: we are told that if we are "constantly without desires" then we will see the subtlety of the Way; verse 19: we are urged to "manifest the Unadorned" (*hsien-su,* 見素) and "embrace

the Unhewn" (*pao-p'u*, 抱樸), which are further defined as being selfless and desireless, respectively; the latter link is reiterated in verse 37, which also speaks of the Unhewn as being "nameless," and in verse 57.

3. *Perception*—verse 12: "The Five Colors blind the eyes, the Five Tastes confuse the palate, the Five Tones deafen the ears. . . . Therefore in their self-control, sages focus on the belly [symbolizing breath meditation] and not the eye"; verse 52: one attains the mother by "blocking the openings and closing the doors." This advice is reiterated in verse 56, where the ultimate result of this elimination of sense-perception is called the "profound merging" (*hsüan-t'ung*, 玄同). I have elsewhere concluded that this is a metaphor for the introvertive mystical experience of union with the Way.[45]

4. The emotions are virtually ignored in the *Lao Tzu*. The few uses have nothing to do with apophatic practice.

The phrase "maintaining tranquility is the central (practice)" from the *Lao Tzu,* verse 16, is one example of an important locution related to inner cultivation practice that is shared by both *Inward Training* and the *Lao Tzu*:

VERB (maintain/hold fast to/embrace) OBJECT (tranquility/the One/the Way).

We find it in verses IX ("hold fast to the One": *chih-i,* 執一) and XXIV ("maintain the One": *shou-i,* 守一) of *Inward Training.* Recall that the former is an important exhortation involved in extrovertive mystical experience, and the latter is a meditative concentration undertaken when one is "revolving the vital breath." Both aspects are also seen in the *Lao Tzu*'s use of this distinct locution, for example, the following uses:

1. *Verse 5:* "maintain the central (practice)" (*shou yü chung,* 守於中) to counteract excessive learning, which seems to refer to the attainment of tranquility as the central practice in verse 16.

2. *Verse 10:* "embrace the One" (*pao-i,* 抱一), which seems to imply retaining a sense of the unity achieved in the introvertive mystical

experience of merging with the Way when one is immersed in daily living.

3. *Verse 14*: "hold fast to the Way of the present" (*chih chin chih Tao,* 執 今 之 道) to manage present things and know the ancient beginning: retain a sense of union with the Way when immersed in daily living.

4. *Verse 15*: "guard the Way" (*pao Tao,* 葆 道): in this context, which talks of stilling the muddy water (of consciousness) to make it clear, this looks like a form of meditative concentration.

5. *Verse 22*: "hold fast to the One" (*chih i,* 執 一): the sage who retains a sense of union with the Way can nurture all under the heavens because he is unattached to his individual self.

6. *Verse 32*: "maintain the nameless Way" (*shou [wu-ming chih] Tao,* 守 無 名 之 道): the myriad things will spontaneously submit to rulers who retains a sense of union with the Way.

7. *Verse 37*: "maintain the nameless Way": the myriad things will spontaneously transform for rulers who retain a sense of union with the Way. These two verses seem to be close in meaning to verse IX of *Inward Training,* in which those who hold fast to the One can transform things and influence events through a mysterious resonance engendered by their rarified vital essence. This could very well be related to *wu-wei.*

8. *Verse 52*: "maintain the mother" (*shou-mu,* 守 母): if you focus on the Way (the mother of all things) while you cut off perception, you will attain it, be able to know all things, and avoid harm and toil.

Thus both *Inward Training* and the *Lao Tzu* employ this distinctive locution for both a technique of meditative concentration and a symbol of retaining the sense of union with the Way in daily living, which appears to be a kind of extrovertive mystical experience. In her excellent study of the phrase *shou-i* in later Taoism, Livia Kohn shows that it entailed both these aspects and more.[46]

The most explicit reference to inner cultivation practice in the *Lao Tzu* is found in verse 10, in the critical section that discusses an example of this distinctive locution, "embracing the One":

1 Amid the daily activity of the psyche,[47] can you embrace the One and not depart from it?

2 When concentrating your vital breath until it is at its softest, can you be like a child?

3 Can you sweep clean your Profound Mirror so you are able to have no flaws in it?

4 In loving the people and governing the state, can you do it without using knowledge?

5 When the Gates of Heaven open and close, can you become feminine?

6 In clarifying all within the Four Directions, can you do it without using knowledge?

This passage is probably the most important evidence for breathing meditation in the *Lao Tzu* and it contains three close parallels to *Inward Training*.

First, the phrase "embracing the One," which can be interpreted to refer to retaining a sense of union with the Way amid the turmoil of daily life, parallels *Inward Training,* verse IX, in which the phrase "holding fast to the One" seems to imply the same thing.

Second, the phrase "concentrate the vital breath" (*chüan-ch'i,* 專氣) refers to the general practice of breath meditation in *Inward Training.* It is also found in verse XIX, which speaks of the results of such breath concentration as attaining the numinous mind, a unified awareness, and the ability to know the future. These results occur because concentrating the vital breath allows one to refine it until it becomes the rarefied vital essence. The *Lao Tzu* also speaks of making the vital breath soft—which is reminiscent of the advice to "relax and expand the vital breath" in verse XXIV of *Inward Training.* The specific wording in these parallel phrases is not as important as the general picture of meditation in this line, which attests to the likelihood that the authors of the *Lao Tzu* were advocating a practice of breathing meditation similar to that found in *Inward Training.*

The final parallel is contained in the phrase "sweep clean your Profound Mirror" (*ti ch'u hsüan chien,* 滌除玄鑒) in line 3. This phrase is extremely close in meaning to the important metaphor for apophatic practice in the inner cultivation tradition first seen in verse XIII of *Inward Training,* "to reverently clean out the lodging place [of the numinous]" (*ching-ch'u ch'i she,* 敬除其舍). This metaphor shares the syntax and key verb (*ch'u,* 除) with the *Lao Tzu,* verse 10. An almost identical metaphor is repeated in the related *Kuan Tzu* essay *Techniques of the Mind* I, where emptying the mind of desires is symbolized as "sweeping clean" (*sao-ch'u*, 掃除) the abode of the numinous.[48]

The meaning of the "Profound Mirror" is rather abstruse; it is a perfect example of the type of metaphorical mystical language that abounds in these texts and that Brown sees in his South Asian sources as referring to specific mental states known to the community of adepts who followed the practices through which they attained these states. D. C. Lau interprets the Profound Mirror as the mind, and this would fit well with the two parallel phrases in the *Kuan Tzu*.[49] However, more may be implied here than just the mind.

The mirror is one of the most important metaphors in Chinese religious thought. It is often seen as symbolizing the clarified mind of the sage, which reflects things exactly as they are without even an iota of personal bias.[50] This meaning is also found in verse XVI of *Inward Training*, which says that people who practice inner cultivation will be able to "hold up the Great Circle of the heavens, tread firmly over the Great Square of the earth, mirror things with great purity and perceive things with great clarity" (*chien yü ta-ch'ing, shih yü ta-ming:* 鑒於大清, 視於大明). This refers not just to the mind but to a numinous cognition that develops in those who follow inner cultivation techniques. The *Lao Tzu* metaphor of the Profound Mirror also seems to refer to such a numinous mind free from flaws. However, in the *Lao Tzu*, the implication is that this mirror is inherently profound and is simply covered over by dust.

The mirror covered by dust is a central metaphor for the "discovery model" of innate nature and is often found in Taoist and Buddhist sources. Perhaps its earliest occurrence is in chapter 5 of the *Chuang Tzu*, and it has become a central element in Ch'an (Zen) Buddhist lore with its story of the succession of the Sixth Patriarch.[51] Implicit in this metaphor is the idea that through apophatic practice one discovers an inherently pristine innate nature that has been covered over by the "dust" of passions and ideas. This contrasts with the "development model" in which one develops the as-yet unrealized tendencies for perfection inherent in innate nature as potentialities. Mencius's notion of the Four Sprouts of the Confucian virtues that are inherent in human nature is an excellent example of this model.[52] *Inward Training* does not explicitly address the question of whether the mirroring activity of numinous cognition is *developed* through inner cultivation practice or is inherently there and simply *discovered*. However, the idea that the numinous mind is an awareness of the Way that resides within in the "mind within the mind" contains a strong implication of an inherent clarity that is discovered. This constitutes a further conceptual parallel with the *Lao Tzu*.

Whatever the case, these parallel phrases and similar metaphors offer further evidence for a common practice of inner cultivation in both the *Lao Tzu* and *Inward Training*. There is one final parallel, between the *Lao Tzu*'s idea of governing the people and clarifying everything without using knowledge in verse 10, ll. 4 and 6, with the idea in verse IX of *Inward Training* that those who hold fast to the One can transform things without expending vital energy and alter situations without expending wisdom. These and other phrases throughout both texts point to the numinous cognition of those sages who can "contain the myriad things within them" (*Inward Training*, verse XIX) and can "know all under the heavens" without ever venturing out their doors (*Lao Tzu*, verse 47).

Taken together, these parallels demonstrate that the authors of both the *Lao Tzu* and *Inward Training* followed a common apophatic practice, a mystical technique through which they directly experienced the foundations of their distinctive mystical philosophy—the Way and its inner power. This is not to say that there are not differences between the two texts. In addition to those already detailed—including the more elaborate, metaphysical, and frequent descriptions of the Way and its inner power in the *Lao Tzu*—*Inward Training* does not explicitly employ the term "emptiness" (*hsü,* 虛), which is so central to the *Lao Tzu*. Of course, the apophatic practice of "cleaning out the lodging-place of the numinous" from *Inward Training* is one by which the mind is emptied, yet this term does not appear.

In addition, *Inward Training* does not contain the striking metaphors for the Way for which the *Lao Tzu* is famous: the valley spirit, the ravine, and the mysterious female. Nor does *Inward Training* utilize the *Lao Tzu*'s distinctive metaphors for sages and their psychospiritual cultivation, such as the empty vessel, the babe who has not yet smiled, the Unadorned, and the Unhewn. Indeed, the entire subject of sages, what they do, and how they appear to others is also completely absent from *Inward Training*. And, of course, *Inward Training* contains virtually no political philosophy, a major concern of the *Lao Tzu*. (The significance of all these omissions is analyzed in chapter 5.)

These differences, however, cannot obscure the fact that the authors of both texts shared a common practice of inner cultivation. Although this practice is the central focus of *Inward Training* and is mentioned infrequently and unsystematically in the *Lao Tzu*, the commonality of this practice can no longer be doubted. These two early Taoist works are not unique; all early Taoist works show evidence of such a practice.

Inward Training and the *Chuang Tzu*

The parallels between *Inward Training* and what has traditionally been regarded as the second foundational text of Taoism, the *Chuang Tzu,* are so extensive as to merit a separate study. This discussion focuses on passages that demonstrate that the authors of the *Chuang Tzu* and *Inward Training* shared a common practice of inner cultivation. Moreover, such common mystical techniques are easier to compare than the mystical experiences and the philosophies derived from them because they are discussed in more concrete language.

The *Chuang Tzu* contains three basic kinds of evidence for inner cultivation practice: (1) evidence of shared techniques and goals without identity in phrasing; (2) evidence of shared techniques and goals with identical or similar phrasing; (3) whole sentences or even passages that are identical or almost identical to those in *Inward Training*. This evidence occurs throughout the entire *Chuang Tzu* collection, but is particularly prevalent in chapters 2, 4, 6, 11, 15, and 19–23. These chapters span the three traditional divisions of the text, the "inner" (1–7), "outer" (8–22), and "miscellaneous" (23–33) chapters. The first kind of evidence predominates in the "inner chapters," while the latter two predominate in the remainder of the book. They also derive from four of the different authorial voices identified by Graham: Chuang Chou, the author of the "inner" chapters and the inspiration for the rest (chapters 2, 4, and 6), the "primitivist" whose ideology shares much with the *Lao Tzu* (chapter 11), the "school of Chuang Tzu"—the disciples of Chuang Chou (chapters 19–22), and the Syncretists, the final contributors to the book (chapter 15).[53] The significance of this is that inner cultivation is one of the most prevalent and significant influences in the *Chuang Tzu* collection.

In a recent essay I analyzed the considerable evidence for "bimodal" mystical experience in the *Chuang Tzu,* chapter 2, "Ch'i-wu lun" (Essay on Seeing Things as Equal).[54] In this chapter, extrovertive mystical experience occurs in an enlightened mode of consciousness referred to by the unique phrase "the 'That's it' which goes by circumstance" (yin-shih, 因是)—the author's distinctive label for the free and selfless cognition of perfected human beings who "pervade and unify" (t'ung wei-i, 通為一) everything in their world. This kind of cognition is one of the qualities of the numinous mind in *Inward Training* and other early sources of inner cultivation practice. In this essay, as in these other sources, it derives directly from the introvertive mystical experience that in the "inner chapters" is called "merging with the Great Pervader" (t'ung yü ta-t'ung, 同於大通). This cognition is the culmination of an apophatic practice like that in *Inward Training*, detailed in chapter 6 of the *Chuang Tzu*. In this famous passage, Confucius's favorite disciple, Yen Hui, ironically teaches his master how to "sit and forget" (tso-wang, 坐忘):

> (Confucius:) "What do you mean, just sit and forget?"
> (Yen Hui:) "I drop away organs and members, dismiss eyesight and hearing, part from the body and expel knowledge, and merge with the Great Pervader. This is what I mean by 'just sit and forget.'"[55]

To "drop away organs and members" (tuo chih t'i, 墮肢體) means to lose visceral awareness of the emotions and desires, which, for the early Taoists, have "physiological" bases in the various organs.[56] To "dismiss eyesight and hearing" (ch'u ts'ung ming, 黜聰明) means deliberately to cut off one's awareness of sense perceptions. To "part from the body and expel knowledge" (li-hsing ch'ü-chih, 離形去知) means to lose bodily awareness and remove all thoughts from consciousness. To "merge with the Great Pervader" means that, as a result of these practices, Yen Hui has become united with the Way.

This, the first of the two classical descriptions of mystical practice in the *Chuang Tzu*, speaks of a general technique of emptying the mind of its normal conscious contents that is shared with the apophatic practice of *Inward Training* but lacks any common phrases describing this technique. The second more closely resembles *Inward Training*. In it, Confucius instructs Yen Hui about how to attain the mental equanimity to teach the Way to a tyrant. Here Confucius advises Yen in how to practice the "fasting of the mind" (hsin-chai, 心齋):

> Unify your attention [i-chih, 一志]. Do not listen with the ears, listen with the mind. Do not listen with the mind, listen with the vital breath. The ears only listen to sounds.[57] The mind is only aware of its

objects.[58] But to focus on the vital breath is to be empty and await the arising of objects. It is only the Way that settles in emptiness. Emptiness is the fasting of the mind.[59]

The fasting of the mind is an apt metaphor for the apophatic practice of systematically removing the normal contents of consciousness. This passage provides a relatively concrete reference to a meditation practice in which one focuses on the breathing, rather than perceptions and thoughts. Here, to "unify your attention" seems to mean focusing on one thing. Instead of "listening" or paying attention to the various objects of perception, including sounds and the various other mental objects found in the mind, Confucius urges Yen to focus on his breathing. By paying attention to breathing, one no longer focuses on any mental object, these objects gradually disappear from consciousness, and the mind becomes empty. When the mind is empty, the Way settles within it (chi, 集).[60] In other words, one becomes aware of the Way, but not as an object. This is the "merging with the Great Pervader" spoken of in the previous passage.

Confucius's advice to Yen Hui here is similar to the general apophatic breath cultivation practice in *Inward Training*. One passage in verse XIX includes wording that is even closer.

15 When the four limbs are aligned
16 And the blood and vital breath are tranquil,
17 Unify your awareness, concentrate your mind,
18 Then your eyes and ears will not be overstimulated.
19 And even the far-off will seem close at hand.

Here too, by focusing on one thing ("unify your awareness": i-i, 一意), probably the breathing, when sitting in a stable posture, perceptions will be reduced and the "far-off" will seem close at hand, which refers to drawing one's mind ever closer to the Way. In addition, the *Chuang Tzu's* idea that the Way settles in emptiness resembles the oft-repeated idea in *Inward Training* that the constantly moving Way (and its vital essence) can be halted, stopped, or fixed, within the cultivated mind, that is, the mind made empty during breath meditation (see, for example, verses II and V).

The mostly primitivist chapter 11 of the *Chuang Tzu,* "Tsai yu" (To Preserve and Circumscribe, 在宥), contains two narratives that have embedded instructions on inner cultivation that are strikingly similar to the general practices and some of the specific phrases of *Inward Training*.[61] Although these two narratives are not generally regarded as Primitivist writings and certainly differ in form and content from the essay that begins the chapter (ll. 1–28), I have argued in another work that their inner cultivation practices could very well have been followed by the primitivist author.[62] In the first passage, a certain master named Kuang Ch'eng-tzu (廣成子) instructs the Yellow Emperor on how to "cultivate one's person" (*chih-shen,* 治身) and attain longevity as follows.

> The ultimate essence of the Utmost Way
> Is dark, dark, secret, secret.
> The ultimate limit of the Utmost Way
> Is mysterious, mysterious, silent, silent.
> Look at nothing, listen to nothing.
> Embrace the numen by being tranquil
> And your body will be naturally aligned.
> You must be tranquil, you must be pure.
> Do not let your body toil,
> Do not let your vital essence waver.
> By doing this you will enhance your vitality.[63]

In the second narrative, a perplexed ruler named Cloud General (Yün Chiang, 雲將) received instructions about "mind nourishing" (*hsin yang,* 心養) from a teacher named Vast Obscurity (Hung Meng, 鴻蒙):

> Just settle yourself in nonaction
> And things will naturally transform.
> Drop away your body and members.
> Spit out your eyesight and hearing.
> Forget your relationships with things.
> And you will merge in the totality of the boundless.[64]

Both passages contain the technical terminology of inner cultivation practice. In the former the Yellow Emperor is taught to avoid perception and excessive knowledge in order to embrace the numen, preserve the vital essence, and enhance vitality and longevity. The wording of this advice is so similar to ideas in *Inward Training* that it could have been extracted directly from it.

In the latter passage, the further instructions on apophatic practice repeat almost verbatim the techniques and goals of the "sitting and forget-ting" passage analyzed above from the *Chuang Tzu*, chapter 6. "Drop away your body and members" (*tuo ju hsing t'i,* 墮爾形體) in chapter 11 re-sembles "drop away organs and members" (*tuo chih t'i,* 墮肢體) in *Chuang Tzu* 6. "Spit out your eyesight and hearing" (*t'u ju tsung ming,* 吐爾聰明) in *Chuang Tzu* 11 resembles "dismiss eyesight and hearing" (*ch'u ts'ung ming,* 黜聰明) in *Chuang Tzu* 6; and "merge in the totality of the boundless" (*ta-t'ung yü hsing-ming,* 大同於涬溟) in *Chuang Tzu* 11 resembles to "merge with the universal thoroughfare" (*t'ung yü ta-t'ung,* 同於大通) in *Chuang Tzu* 6. These parallels indicate a deliberate attempt to imitate the "sitting and forgetting" passage and show that the authors of both were well versed in the lore of inner cultivation.

Another significant parallel between these passages in the *Chuang Tzu's* chapter 11 and *Inward Training* is that their instructions are given in tetrasyllabic rhymed verse. Other early Taoist texts that embed instruc-tions on inner cultivation practice in this type of rhymed verse include the "Wu-cheng" (Five Regulators, 五正) section of *Shih-liu ching* (Sixteen Canons, 十六經), one of the four Ma-wang-tui *Four Classics,* and essay 14 from the *Huai-nan Tzu,* "Ch'üan-yen" (Inquiring Words, 詮言), which actually uses Kuang Ch'eng-tzu's words from the *Chuang Tzu* and attributes them to him.[65] They offer further evidence of the existence of the distinc-tive early Taoist literary genre identified by Baxter.

Chapters 19–23 of the *Chuang Tzu* are filled with the lore of inner cultivation. Chapter 19, "Ta-sheng" (Fathoming Life, 達生), is a collection of some of the most famous "skill narratives" in the entire book and looks like a direct continuation of the central theme of chapter 3, "Yang-sheng chu" (The Mastery of Nourishing Life, 養生主). Chapter 19 features such unique characters as the cicada-catching hunchback, the trainer of gamecocks, the swimmer at Spinebridge Falls, and the bellstand carver. All exhibit rare skills developed as a result of their inner cultivation prac-tice. For example, the bellstand carver—in allusions to both the "inner chapters" and *Inward Training*—prepares for his work by "fasting in order to make his mind tranquil." After seven days he forgets that he even has his four limbs and body. He can then go into the forest and choose the per-fect tree in which the bellstand just appears to him. The skills of these various masters are described as numinous, and they develop because they have nourished their vitality through inner cultivation.

Chapter 22, "Chih pei-yu" (Knowledge Wanders North, 知北遊) contains the figure of Lao Tan, the reputed author of the *Lao Tzu*, and teachings from his text, sometimes quoted anonymously. It contains several narratives describing inner cultivation techniques, including the one in which the character Wearcoat (Pei I, 被衣) instructs the character Gnaw Gap (Nieh Ch'üeh, 齧缺) as follows:

> You must align your body [*cheng ju hsing,* 正汝形],
> Unify your vision,
> And the heavenly harmony will arrive.
> Gather in your knowledge,
> Unify your attention,[66]
> And the numinous will enter its lodging place [*shen chiang lai she,*
>   神將來舍],
> The inner power will beautify you,
> And the Way will reside in you.
> You will see things with the eyes of a newborn calf
> And will not seek out their precedents.[67]

Although this advice is written in verse of an irregular meter, nevertheless its wording is quite close to that of *Inward Training*.

Chapter 23, "Keng-sang Ch'u" (庚桑楚), contains the longest extended narrative in the work. It is devoted to a quest for inner cultivation in which a character named Nan-jung Chu (南榮趎) first seeks the teaching of the adept Keng-sang Ch'u, who is described as a follower of Lao Tan who partially attained his master's Way. He leaves dissatisfied and goes to seek the advice of the Old Master (Lao Tzu) himself. After ten days of meditation in which he is obsessed by external perceptions and internal thoughts, he goes again to see Lao Tzu and asks him for the "practice for guarding vitality" (*wei-sheng chih ching,* 衛生之經).[68] He receives the following teaching:

衛生之經
The practice for guarding vitality:
能抱一乎。
Can you embrace the One?
能勿失乎。

Can you not lose it?

能無卜筮

Can you not resort to divining by tortoise or milfoil

而知吉凶乎。

Yet know good and bad fortune?

能止乎。能已乎。

Can you be still? Can you cease?

能舍諸人

Can you quit (seeking for) it in others

而求諸己乎。

And seek for within yourself?

Can you be casual?

Can you be naive?

Can you be like a child?

The child howls all day but its throat does not become hoarse.[69]

The teaching continues with a description of further characteristics of this exemplar of the child that are very similar to the *Lao Tzu*, chapter 55. However, what is particularly striking about these instructions is that they are an almost verbatim repetition of the following lines from verse XIX of *Inward Training*:

3 能專，能一乎。

   Can you concentrate? Can you unite with them?

4 能無卜筮

   Can you not resort to divining by tortoise or milfoil

5 而知<吉凶>「凶吉」乎

   Yet know bad and good fortune?

6 能止乎，能已乎。

   Can you stop? Can you cease?

7 能勿求諸人

   Can you not seek it in others,

8 而「得」之己乎。

   Yet attain it within yourself?

Thus it appears that *Inward Training* or a text similar to it was known to the authors of this *Chuang Tzu* chapter. These particular lines were known to the authors of other important early Taoist works (see chapter 5). The inner cultivation instructions given herein by Keng-sang Ch'u and Lao Tan are a blend of teachings from *Inward Training*, the *Lao Tzu*, and the "inner chapters" of the *Chuang Tzu*. Thus it seems clear from this that "Keng-sang Ch'u" was written later than these other three sources and its inclusion in the text indicates that its author was probably someone who considered himself a lineal descendant of Chuang Chou. Furthermore it is apparent that this *Chuang Tzu* author was well steeped in the practice and lore of inner cultivation.

The latest source of inner cultivation material in the *Chuang Tzu* is the Syncretist chapter 15, "K'o-i" (Fixed Ideas, 刻意), which places its mystical teachings in the context of advice to the ruler on effective government. This is an integral essay on how to "nourish the numen" (*yang-shen,* 養神). Its author takes pains to differentiate this practice from "nourishing the body" (*yang-hsing,* 養形), a practice followed by the physical hygiene practitioners of breath control and the "guiding and pulling" gymnastic exercises who regard P'eng-tsu as their founder.[70]

This essay advocates an apophatic inner cultivation practice consistent with the earlier sources: limiting perception, relinquishing emotions, desires, and wisdom, in order to become empty and tranquil and thereby preserve the vital essence and guard the numen—as shown in the following lines.

> Thus it is said,
> Sadness and joy are deviations from inner power.
> Pleasure and anger are transgressions of the Way.
> Likes and dislikes are failings of the mind.[71]
> Thus when the mind does not worry or rejoice
> This is the perfection of inner power.
> When the mind is unified and does not alter
> This is the perfection of tranquility.
> When there is no object that it bumps up against
> This is the perfection of emptiness.[72]

Indeed, the nourishing of the numen and its distinctive vital essence— referred to as the "numinous essence" (*ching-shen,* 精神)—is paramount:

The owner of a valuable sword from Kan or Yüeh keeps it in a case and does not dare to use it. This is because it is extremely precious. The numinous essence flows everywhere throughout the Four Directions and there is nowhere that it does not reach. It "reaches up to the heavens above and coils round the earth below." It transforms and nourishes the myriad things but we cannot even make an image of it. Its name is "merged with the High Lord." The Pure and Unadorned Way is simply to focus on the numen. Focus on it and do not lose it and you will become one with the numen. The Vital Essence of this union flows and unites with the constancies of the heavens.[73]

The author of "Fixed Ideas" thus refers to the apophatic inner cultivation practices enumerated in this essay as the means to nourish the numen. This numen is, further, regarded as something of the utmost value; the very vital essence of which it is constituted is spoken of using locutions similar to those used for the cosmic Way itself. These ideas place this author squarely within the lineage of those who followed and promoted this distinctive Taoist practice, whose oldest extant textual source is *Inward Training*. Incidentally, the lines about the numinous essence "reaching up to the heavens above" are also found in verse XIV of *Inward Training,* where they refer to how people are released from their limited perspectives by the word "Way."

This is only a sample of the most compelling evidence that the authors of most—if not all—of the principal sections of the *Chuang Tzu* were aware of the practice and lore of inner cultivation. (The implications of this are explored in chapter 5.)

The Stages of Meditation in Inner Cultivation Practice

In a recent article, I identify a distinctive rhetorical structure through which a series of stages of apophatic breathing meditation are discussed in a wide variety of early Taoist texts.[74] The oldest extant source for this rhetorical structure, referred to as the "Duodecagonal Jade Tablet Inscription on Breath Circulation," while not a Taoist work itself, is also the oldest extant source in China that discusses breath meditation.

This jade tablet inscription was found on a twelve-sided jade cylindrical object whose use and precise date are now unclear. It may have served as the knob of a staff, the hilt of a weapon, the handle attached to the wooden bar of a scroll painting, or, alternately, as a writing tablet.[75] Kuo Mo-jo thought its style of writing was similar to the style of the characters on a bronze utensil from the state of Han (韓) that was found in a village near Lo-yang and dated to approximately 380 B.C.[76] More recently doubts have been raised that it even came from this tomb site.[77] Joseph Needham thought that its rhetorical structure and technical terminology were very close to the earliest inscription on the Five Phase theory, found on a jade sword hilt from the state of Ch'i that dates back to about 400 B.C.[78] He further suggested that the jade tablet might even be earlier. Gilbert Mattos, however, suggests an origin in the San Chin area during the last part of the fourth century B.C.[79] Even if he is correct, the simplicity of its concepts bespeaks an origin that is earlier than the more complicated ideas on this topic in *Inward Training*. In any case, all scholars agree that this is the earliest epigraphical evidence on the practice of breath meditation in China.

1 行氣：
To circulate the vital breath:

2 <深> [吞] 則蓄；
Swallow it and it will collect.

3 蓄則伸；
When it is collected, it will expand.

4 伸則下；
When it expands, it will descend.

5 下則定；
When it descends, it will become stable.

6 定則固；
When it is stable, it will be firm.

7 固則萌；
When it is firm, it will sprout.

8 萌則長；
When it sprouts, it will grow.

9 長則 <退> [復]；
When it grows, it will return.

10 <退> [復] 則天。

When it returns, it will become heavenly.

11 天機春在上；

The heavenly dynamism is revealed in the ascending [of the breath];

12 地機春在下。

The earthly dynamism is revealed in the descending [of the breath].

13 順則生；

Follow this and you will live;

14 逆則死。

Oppose it and you will die.[80]

The inscription gives instructions on how to move from a stage of mental agitation to one of regular and patterned breathing. This is accomplished by first taking a deep breath and then purposefully cycling through a series of exhalation and inhalation sequences until the breathing becomes stable and regular. Doing so enables one to reach an inherent, natural pattern of breathing in which one need not exert the will any further. This inherent pattern is what "sprouts and grows." When one can accomplish this, one can directly apprehend the heavenly and earthly dynamisms (t'ien-chi, 天機; ti-chi, 地機), which are revealed through the ascending and descending of the breath. If you accord with this practice then your vitality will flourish.

The meaning of "dynamism" here is obscure, but a reference to the "heavenly dynamism" in Chuang Tzu, chaper 6, may be relevant.[81] This chapter contrasts the profound breathing of the Perfected with the shallow breathing of the multitude who are filled with lusts and desires and in whom the "heavenly dynamism" is shallow. Judging from the context of the Chuang Tzu, some kind of profound and perhaps mystical breath cultivation could also be implied in the inscription.

While the reference to mysticism in this inscription is rather vague, it nonetheless contains a distinct rhetorical structure referring to breath meditation and its results that occurs in later Taoist works. This is the sorites argument in lines 2–10 that talks about successive stages of breath cultivation and the denouement in lines 11–14 that discusses the results of this practice. Sorites arguments follow the form "if X then Y; if Y then Z." The Taoist sources then add to this structure a "preamble" containing detail about the apophatic preparations for the stages of meditation that follow and yielding the following structure:

1. A *preamble* in which the practices that prepare for the later stages are discussed.
2. A *sorites*-style argument in which the stages of meditation are presented in a consecutive fashion.
3. A *denouement* that discusses the noetic and practical benefits of having attained these stages.

The Syncretic Taoist essay 25.3 of the *Annals of Mr. Lü* collection, "Yu-tu" (Having Limits, 有度), contains an excellent example of this rhetorical structure. The essay argues that, through inner cultivation practice, a ruler can "hold fast to the One" (*chih-i,* 執一), comprehend the "essentials of our nature and destiny" (*hsing ming chih ch'ing,* 性明之情), and become spontaneously ethical without following Confucian teachings. It quotes the following advice from an unnamed source—possibly *Chuang Tzu's* "Keng-sang Ch'u" chapter—that contains the same words almost verbatim or a common source for both of them.[82]

Preamble
Break through the perturbations of the will,
Release the fetters of the mind,
Cast off the constraints to inner power,
Break through the blockages of the Way.

Honor and wealth, prominence and grandeur, reputation and profit: these six are what perturb the will. Demeanor and bearing, physical beauty and elegant speech, temperament and attitude: these six are what bind up the mind. Hatred and desire, pleasure and anger, grief and joy: these six are what constrain inner power. Wisdom and talent, departing and approaching, taking and relinquishing: these are what block the Way.

Sorites
When these four sets of six do not disturb what is within your chest, then you will become aligned [*cheng,* 正]. When you are aligned you

will become tranquil [*ching,* 靜]. When you are tranquil, you will become clear and lucid. When you are clear and lucid then you will become empty.

Denouement
When you are empty, then you "take no action and yet nothing is left undone."

This passage exhibits familiar aspects of apophatic practice presented in greater detail than seen thus far. In addition to the emotions that must be removed, new things that ensnare the ego must be dispensed with: the lust for power and wealth, concern with how you present yourself to others, and the entire process of acquiring knowledge. The passages suggests that these are all set aside when one is "aligned." In the context of inner cultivation theory, alignment refers here to the alignment of body and breathing. After this alignment is attained and the blockages to mental concentration are removed, one becomes tranquil and thus open to deeper layers of the mind. The preceding of tranquility (*ching*) by alignment (*cheng*) is a characteristic idea of inner cultivation practice.

In this passage the stages of meditation are presented in a sorites chain. They move through alignment to tranquility, from tranquility to clarity and lucidity, and from these finally to emptiness. At this point, when you are completely empty, you can be filled with—or can merge with—the Way. After this, to quote the *Lao Tzu*, "you take no action, and yet nothing is left undone." Your actions have become the same as those of the Way.

A very similar pattern emerges in the other five passages I analyzed. These passages, in addition to the virtually identical "Keng-sang Ch'u" passage, include the following:

The essay "Lun" (Assessment, 論) from the "Ching-fa" (Normative Standards, 經法) text in the *Four Classics*.[83]

"Lun-jen" (The Assessment of Others, 論人), essay 4 in chapter 3 of the *Annals of Mr. Lü*.[84]

Techniques of the Mind I from the *Kuan Tzu*.[85]

"Ching-shen" (The Numinous Essence, 精神), essay 7 in the *Huai-nan Tzu*.[86]

In all except the first in this group, the preamble specifies one or more of these similar apophatic results: restricting or eliminating perception; removing desires; relinquishing "wisdom and scheming," and "cleverness and precedent." *Techniques of the Mind* I collectively symbolizes these results as "cleaning out the abode (of the numen)" (*ch'u-kuan,* 除館). In "The Numinous Essence," the last and most detailed in the group, these results are specifically linked to concentrating the breathing so that it fills the chest and belly and the vital breath circulates in a regular fashion in accordance with its inherent pattern (*li*).

In all but "The Numinous Essence" and *Annals of Mr. Lü,* chapter 3, essay 4 (referred to below as 3.4), this regular pattern of breathing is referred to as "alignment" (*cheng*), a term that also implies the alignment of the mind and body. This begins the second part of the rhetorical structure in which the stages of meditation are indicated in sorites order. In the "Normative Standards" passages in *Annals of Mr. Lü,* chapter 25, essay 3 (referred to below as 25.3), *Chuang Tzu,* chapter 23, and *Techniques of the Mind* I, this alignment is followed by "tranquility (*ching*). While there is some variation among our sources as to the details of the successive stages, most include the attainment of the refined concentration that is the psychological experience associated with the vital essence and then the realization of the numen, or numinous mind. *Annals of Mr. Lü* 3.4 follows this with "attaining the One" (*te-i,* 得一). *Techniques of the Mind* I follows this with "attaining the empty Way" (*te hsü-Tao,* 得虛道). *Annals of Mr. Lü* 25.3 and *Chuang Tzu* 23 ignore the attainment of the numinous and simply speak of attaining emptiness. Regardless of which phrase is employed, they all refer to the experience of merging with the Way, the penultimate introvertive mystical experience. This ends the sorites chain of stages of meditation.

Finally, the denouement of each of these passages delineates the practical results these mystical techniques and experiences confer on those who attain them. *Annals of Mr. Lü* 25.3, which introduces this rhetorical structure as the way to "hold fast to the One," and *Chuang Tzu* 23 use the familiar phrase from the *Lao Tzu,* "take no action and nothing is left undone." *Huai-nan Tzu,* chapter 7, offers a more detailed version of this: "with vision nothing is unseen, with hearing nothing is unheard, with action, nothing is unaccomplished." *Annals of Mr. Lü* 3.4 speaks of being able to respond spontaneously to the alternations and transformations of things among its long list of results. "Assessment" speaks of these results in terms of the unique preoccupation of the authors of the "Normative Standards": "seeing and knowing are never deluded" (*chien chih pu-huo,* 見 知 不 惑). All these results are part of the numinous cognition attained by those who follow inner cultivation practice. They are all the consequence of extrovertive mystical experience similar to those spoken of in the *Lao Tzu* and *Chuang Tzu* mentioned above.

Although this rhetorical structure for communicating inner cultivation practice and its results is completely absent from *Inward Training,* the ideas it contains are most certainly not absent. *Inward Training* speaks of the details of apophatic practice in similar terms: restricting or removing the emotions and limiting perception and thinking are emphasized. The attainment of tranquility is another important idea in *Inward Training* and, just as in the passages containing this distinctive rhetorical structure, it must be preceded by a condition of alignment of body, breathing, and mind. In *Inward Training,* aligned sitting, regular circulation, and a concentration of the vital breath produce the refined vital essence, and, eventually, the numinous "mind within the mind" is attained. *Inward Training* does not speak of emptiness, but this is certainly the result of the practices it commends. And the experience of halting or attaining the Way is also seen as the ultimate introvertive result of inner cultivation practice in all our sources.

Furthermore the results of this practice are similar. In *Inward Training* it enables one to "hold fast to the One" and so "master the myriad things." To do this also enables "one to transform things without expending vital energy and influence events without expending wisdom." This numinous ability to influence events in the world could be one central element in the oft-repeated rhetorical phrase "take no action but nothing is left undone" first enunciated in the *Lao Tzu.* In addition, the clear cognition and perception of the external world that result from inner cultivation practice in *Inward Training* are found in these later texts as well.

Taken together, the evidence of apophatic inner cultivation practice in the *Lao Tzu,* almost the entire *Chuang Tzu,* and the rhetorical structure for stages of meditation in the other five texts is quite extensive. Indeed, if we were to explore more than just the meditative stages passages in these five texts, we would find even more evidence of the same mystical techniques, experiences, and philosophy. This is not to say that all our sources are completely uniform on this topic. They exhibit a considerable amount of variation, as one would expect given the fact that they span almost two centuries. This lack of uniformity indicates that they did not all have the same textual source for their inner cultivation practices. But it does not detract from the considerable evidence that it was the *practice itself*—rather than any one specific text—that the authors of all these early Taoist works followed. *Inward Training* is the oldest extant source for this practice, although it was not the sole source. It was probably part of a body of oral and written texts that grew up surrounding inner cultivation practice as it originated and evolved. Most of the earlier texts were probably written in a form that could be easily memorized: rhymed verse. The distinct literary genre identified by William Baxter could indeed represent the form that much of the early lore of inner cultivation took. This lore would have been transmitted by individual teachers to students, who would then have embellished it and adapted it on the basis of their own experience and circumstances. As discussed in chapter 5, this lore of inner cultivation was most likely the basis of the early Taoist tradition.

Inner Cultivation and Physical Hygiene

The question of the relationship between the inner cultivation practices identified here and the physical and macrobiotic hygiene practices for which we now have considerable textual evidence from Ma-wang-tui and Chang-chia shan deserves a much more complete and thorough analysis than can be undertaken in this book.[87] The bases for comparison are extensive and involve a shared technical vocabulary of breath cultivation including familiar concepts such as the vital energy, the vital essence, and the numen. These bases also involve the sharing of the concern for circulating the vital energy, the common use of a sitting posture in which to do this, and the sharing of certain metaphors, such as the bellows analogy that Donald Harper has pointed out.

These bases for comparison indicate that the practitioners of both inner cultivation and macrobiotic hygiene most likely shared ideas with one another and interacted with one another at local state centers like Chi-hsia in Ch'i (345–260 B.C.), Lü Pu-wei's Ch'in court (250–39 B.C.), Liu An's court at Huai-nan (150–22 B.C.), and other, smaller locations about which history remains silent. The question of whether they came from the same or different social groups is a fascinating one that cannot be resolved without further study. Absent the extensive analysis this question merits, following are a few observations about the topic.

Much of the physical hygiene literature unearthed at Ma-wang-tui and Chang-chia shan is concerned with either physical or macrobiotic goals; that is, attaining health and vitality and extending the term of life. Even though *Inward Training* speaks of the physical benefits of inner cultivation practice and once mentions longevity, its goals are better described as psychological and spiritual. This contrast can best be seen by analyzing specific textual passages.

Among the Ma-wang-tui hygiene literature, perhaps the text that comes closest to *Inward Training* is the "Shih-wen" (Ten Questions, 十問), a work that presents its ideas in the familiar rhetorical frame of a ruler's questions and a master's responses.[88] In this text, the fourth dialogue, between the Yellow Emperor and the character called Jung Ch'eng (容成), contains many close parallels to certain words and phrases in *Inward Training*. Both texts talk of "concentrating the vital breath," yet in the "Ten Questions" it is done in the service of attaining longevity and in *Inward Training*, verse XIX, it is part of apophatic practice aimed at attaining a numinous knowledge of the future and attaining the Way. Both texts speak of the vital essence being like a well spring, but in the "Ten Questions" it is generated by "sucking in vital energy" and making it reach the extremities and in *Inward Training* it is generated by apophatic practices that lead to the attainment of tranquility.[89]

The "Ten Questions" talks about "improving the skin's webbed pattern" (*tso li,* 膝理), as does verse XXVI of *Inward Training*.[90] But in the former it is improved by replenishing the vital essence through sleep. In the latter it is said that the Way as vital essence permeates the channels and pores that constitute this physiological structure.

The "Ten Questions" contains the phrase "carefully maintain it and do not lose it" (*shen-shou wu-shih,* 慎守勿失), which is almost identical to the line in verse II of *Inward Training*, "reverently maintain it and do not lose it" (*ching-shou wu-shih,* 敬守勿失).[91] But in the "Ten Questions" the subject is the practice of mastering life and death by preventing the egress of vital energy, and in *Inward Training* the subject is developing inner power and vital essence through apophatic practice.

Finally, the two texts share the lines "reach up to the heavens above, stretch down to the earth below," yet their contexts are characteristically different.[92] In the "Ten Questions," the subject is the life of longevity in which the numen is preserved and even released from the body. In verse XIV of *Inward Training*, the subject is the person who has been released from his limited individual perspective by attaining the Way through apophatic practice.

Throughout the "Ten Questions" the heart or mind is mentioned only once, and then the context is not that of cultivating the mind through apophatic practice. Alignment and tranquility are absent from this text, and the numen is viewed in the context of attaining longevity, not psychological clarity and spiritual mastery. It seems as if the authors of *Inward Training* were aware of the physical and macrobiotic goals described in texts such as the "Ten Questions," but their focus was elsewhere, on the psychological and spiritual goals that dominate their work.

Raising here the issue of the contrast between these two types of practices should come as no surprise. Clarifying their distinctions was also a problem for the early Taoist tradition, as attested to by two passages in the *Chuang Tzu*. The author of chapter 15, "Fixed Ideas," criticizes five groups of people—among them the followers of macrobiotic hygiene practices—whose attachment to erroneous methods prevent them from achieving their goals.

> To huff and puff, exhale and inhale, blow out the old (breath) and take in the new, do the "bear stride" and the "bird-stretch," and to be interested in nothing more than longevity, these are the methods of those who practice the "guiding and pulling (of the vital breath)" (*tao-yin,* 導引), those who nourish the body (*yang-hsing chih Tao,* 養形之道) and try to attain the longevity of Ancestor P'eng.[93]

These methods are inferior to the apophatic inner cultivation practices that the author refers to as the "Way of nourishing the numen" (*yang-shen chih Tao,* 養神之道), which attain these ends anyway. A similar criticism is made in the "Numinous Essence" essay of the *Huai-nan Tzu*.[94]

The *tao-yin* exercises such as the "bear stride" and "bird-stretch" are now known to us through the excavation of a painting at Ma-wang-tui and a descriptive text for them at Chang-chia shan.[95] *Chuang Tzu*'s Syncretist here has in mind both these gymnastic exercises and others involving breath cultivation that are included in such texts as the "Ten Questions." That he is criticizing these methods here has as much to do with the fact that they were popular and that he thinks his own are superior as it does with the likely existence of confusion on the part of non-Taoists about how Taoist and physical hygiene techniques differed.

Such a confusion appears to be at the basis of another passage that begins chapter 19 of the *Chuang Tzu*, "Fathoming Life."

> It is sad indeed that people of this age should think that nourishing the body [*yang-hsing*] is sufficient to preserve life. Yet in the last analysis it is not sufficient to preserve life, so why does this generation persist in thinking it sufficient? It is because there are people who think they must do this even though it is insufficient and so their actions cannot escape this preoccupation.
>
> Now for those who desire to escape this preoccupation with the body, there is nothing better than abandoning the world. If you abandon the world then there are no attachments. If there are no attachments you can be aligned and balanced. Being aligned and balanced, you can be born together with other things. If you are born together with other things then you are almost there. Why is it that we should abandon worldly affairs and set aside our preoccupation with life? If affairs are abandoned then the body will not toil. If we set aside our preoccupation with life then the vital essence will not diminish.
>
> Now if the body's energies are kept intact and the vital essence is restored then you become one with the heavens. The heavens and the earth are the father and mother of the myriad things. When they unite they complete the physical frame. When they disperse completion begins again. When the bodily energies and vital essence remain undiminished, this is called "being able to shift (to a new level)." Here your vital essence is refined and further refined until you return to being a coequal companion of the heavens.[96]

What may not be apparent on first reading this passage is that it is commending not just abandoning the world but doing so in order to better practice inner cultivation. That these apophatic practices are being implied here is indicated by the phrase "aligned and balanced," which seems to be used in the same technical sense it has in *Inward Training*. In verse XXI, it refers to the balanced and aligned breathing that fills the chest and ultimately confers longevity. It confers longevity precisely because it enables the harmonious uniting of the heavenly vital essence and the earthly body. Verse XXI specifically refers to emotions and sense-desires as the "dual misfortunes" that must be restricted by apophatic inner cultivation practice to attain this balance. The entire discussion of the uniting of heavenly and earthly factors in the last paragraph of the above passage from chapter 19 particularly in this context of balanced and aligned breathing implies an awareness of *Inward Training* or a similar work by the *Chuang Tzu* author.

Moreover, the extrovertive mystical experience that results from this practice in *Inward Training* is also implied here. "To be born together with other things" involves the simultaneous arising of self and other that does not privilege the individual self and enables it to see the other clearly and without bias. In the *Chuang Tzu*'s "Essay on Seeing Things as Equal," this is part of the numinous cognition of the "that's it which goes by circumstance" in the enlightened sage. Perhaps thinking of this parallel, the author of chapter 19 borrows a phrase from this chapter to say that this cognition is "almost there," that is, it is almost united with the Way. Perhaps this union is implied in the phrases "uniting with the heavenly" and "returning to be a coequal companion of the heavens." Perhaps these simply refer to the completely spontaneous action of the numinous sage. Whichever the case, these parallels with *Inward Training* make it clear that the author of "Fathoming Life" is making the effort to differentiate between the inner cultivation practices that nourish the numinous and inferior practices aimed merely at nourishing the body. Interestingly, just as in "Fixed Ideas," the author suggests that psychospiritual cultivation will accomplish the goal of preserving life more effectively than physical cultivation.

These passages suggest that, even as early as the third and second centuries B.C., people were confused about the distinction between inner cultivation and physical cultivation. That the former could best be practiced by abandoning worldly affairs, as in "Fathoming Life," indicates that it involved not just daily breath cultivation as part of a regime that included gymnastics and dietary and sexual practices while living in society, but the sustained practice of breath meditation over a long period of time while removed from such obligations. Eremiticism has been a part of the Chinese world for a long time, and Taoists were involved in such practice throughout their long history.[97] The existence of ascetic groups might also be expected, if we are to judge by mystical practices in other cultures and some of the narratives in the *Chuang Tzu*.[98] Whatever the case, this distinction between the cultivation of the mind and numen, on the one hand, and the cultivation of the body, on the other, might form a promising framework for further research that endeavors to distinguish between these two sets of practices and their practitioners.

CHAPTER FIVE

Inward Training
in the Context of Early Taoism

Of course, these *Kuan-tzu* chapters and the manuscripts from Ma-wang-tui failed to reach the status of "classic" (*ching*), and from a modern point of view, they may seem far less important than the *Lao-tzu*. The *Lao-tzu* is one of the most translated books in the world . . . whereas the other texts have received relatively little attention. But the compilers of these texts cannot have known in advance that the *Lao-tzu* would win out in such spectacular fashion. If we wish to clarify the early history of the genre which the *Lao-tzu* represents, these other texts could turn out to be as useful as the *Lao Tzu* itself.

WILLIAM BAXTER
("Situating the Language of the *Lao-tzu*," pp. 242–43)

This concluding chapter offers a new definition of Warring States and early Han Taoism derived from my earlier work on "Huang-Lao" Taoism and the present work on *Inward Training* and inner cultivation practice. The chapter's central working hypothesis is that, even in the absence of evidence for a "Lao-Chuang" school of philosophical Taoism, a distinct group of people existed who can justifiably be labeled Taoists because they followed and recommended to others an apophatic practice of breathing meditation aimed at the mystical realization of the Way and its integration into their daily lives. These people also created and transmitted a body of doctrinal texts that evolved over time in response to the changing

173

circumstances in which the members of this "distinctive lineage" found themselves.¹ For example, a political dimension gradually developed and employed ideas and methods culled from the other lineages encountered by Taoist thinkers at various state courts during this period.

Thus the inner cultivation program, its experiential results, and the philosophy that developed from it are central to this new definition of Taoism in this early period. Moreover, *Inward Training* is the oldest extant source for this distinctive method of mystical self-cultivation, the evidence for which is found in all the major textual sources of early Taoism. Thus calling particular thinkers "Taoist" means that they followed a regimen of inner cultivation first enunciated in *Inward Training*. Labeling a particular text "Taoist" means that it exhibits evidence of this inner cultivation practice and the distinctive nexus of ideas that developed from it, especially a cosmology based on the Way as the underlying power of the human and natural worlds.

Toward a Definition of Early Taoism

It may surprise the nonspecialist reader that different scholars often define early Taoism differently or that they question the existence of a clearly definable school or philosophical lineage that can be designated by this term. The problem derives in part from the fact that the term "Taoism" is used—and often uncritically so—not just for the sources explored in this book but for the rather complex religion that arose at the end of the second century A.D. and various tangential phenomena related to each. Although in the twentieth century scholars have distinguished between "Tao-chia" (or philosophical Taoism) and "Tao-chiao" (or religious Taoism), and have seen a great gulf between the two, in recent years scholars have realized that these categories obscure the fact that these two aspects of Taoism are related in a variety of complex ways hitherto not well understood. Indeed, when one becomes aware of the religious phenomena associated with the category "philosophical Taoism," many elements that contribute to this "great gulf" melt away. Like the term "mysticism," the term "Taoism" must be carefully defined and its use equally carefully circumscribed, as Nathan Sivin argued in a seminal article written some twenty years ago.²

Another difficulty in arriving at a definition of early Taoism, in light of the absence of evidence for a "Lao-Chuang" school, is the entire problem of precisely what constituted a school of philosophy in the pre-Han period. Before the work of the Han historian Ssu-ma T'an (司馬談), who delineated six "schools" (chia, 家) of thought in about 110 B.C., previous analyses of pre-Han thought were teacher-based. That is, specific thinkers and their ideas were discussed, but little attempt was made to relate them together as followers of a particular school, even when this was obviously the case, as for the Confucians and Mohists. This kind of analysis occurs in the famous chapter 33 of the Chuang Tzu, "T'ien-hsia" (All Under the Heavens, 天下), which discusses the ideas of Mo Tzu and a few followers, Sung Hsing and Yin Wen, P'eng Meng, T'ien P'ien, and Shen Tao, Lao Tan and Kuan Yin, Chuang Tzu himself, and then his friend the terminologist Hui Shih. However, even when several thinkers are grouped together, they are not treated as belonging to one "school." Similar types of "teacher-based" discussions are found in the Hsün Tzu, the Annals of Mr. Lü, and the Huai-nan Tzu.[3] None of the analyses of thinkers before the time of Ssu-ma T'an grouped them into "schools," even when the individual thinkers were quite obviously related to one another intellectually, such as Confucius, Mencius, and Hsün Tzu.

By contrast, Ssu-ma T'an, in his discourse on the essential ideas of the six schools that is now a colophon to the Records of the Grand Historian, delineated six schools of thought, apparently on the basis of their doctrines.[4] These schools were Naturalists (yin-yang), Confucians, Mohists, Terminologists (Ming-chia), Legalists (Fa-chia), and Taoists. Each group contained certain thinkers about whose identity he remained silent, although he certainly knew about them in view of what he and his son, Ssu-ma Ch'ien (司馬遷), say in other sections of their monumental historical work.

In recent years the very nature and existence of the schools distinguished by Ssu-ma T'an have been called into question.[5] Do they actually refer to existing schools with a set series of texts and doctrines, of masters and disciples, and perhaps a specific geographic origin and continuing location? Many have assumed this to be the case. Or was he simply creating a new category into which he could place earlier teachers who themselves had no such category, group membership, or lineage designation?

Edmund Ryden has significantly clarified this question by distinguishing two ways of analyzing philosophical schools.[6] Adapting the definitions of the linguist Ferdinand de Saussure (1857–1913), he distinguishes between "synchronic" analyses and "diachronic" analyses. The former are like cross-sections frozen in time. They define each school in relation to the others at the moment in time that the synchronic analysis is created. Diachronic analyses often focus on one school and attempt to understand it from a developmental perspective as the teachings of generations of masters and disciples. In other words, diachronic analyses are based upon the nature and intellectual content of master-disciple lineages over time; synchronic analyses attempt to identify these lineages by the doctrines to which they subscribed (or by some other common factor) at a given point in time. Ryden argues that in identifying the "six schools" the project of Ssu-ma T'an was *largely* synchronic, although a diachronic element does enter in with the two "clearly identifiable groups" for him, namely, the Confucians and the Mohists.[7] On the other hand, the later project of the Han historical bibliographer Pan Ku, who wrote his ""Bibliographical Monograph" of the *History of Former Han Dynasty* in about A.D. 55, was *purely* synchronic and related to the contents of the imperial library he was cataloguing more than to any extant intellectual lineages. According to Ryden, the problem arises when these two types of analyses are confused. Thus he suggests that, if we employ Ssu-ma T'an's categories to define pre-Han Taoism, we are committing a fundamental "category error"; we are mistaking his synchronic analysis for a diachronic one.

These distinctions are valuable, but the picture is more complicated than they would lead us to believe. Ssu-ma T'an's choice of the word *chia* for his six groups implies that he had a diachronic view as well. *Chia* normally means "home" or "family." This implies that he thought of his six groups as having an important lineage dimension in which masters and disciples functioned according to a family model. Teachers were like parents to their disciples, who in turn were like children to their teachers. This model is very old indeed. This kind of social grouping is seen as early as the *Analects,* in which Confucius serves as the intellectual and spiritual father to his students.

Moreover, a closer look at the Taoists indicates that they, as well as the Confucians and Mohists, had a powerful diachronic element about which Ssu-ma T'an cannot have been unaware. Ssu-ma T'an presents Taoism as decidedly syncretic: It adapts the best teachings of the other five groups of thinkers within a cosmology of the Way and its inner power.[8] This syncretic form is similar to much of the *Huai-nan Tzu* and can justifiably be labeled "Huang-Lao," a term found elsewhere in the *Records of the Grand Historian*. This was the Han term for the particular form of Syncretic Taoism then prevalent. *Records,* chapters 63 and 74, identify thinkers at the Chi-hsia Academy and elsewhere as Huang-Lao students. Furthermore, chapter 80 describes a lineage of Huang-Lao masters stretching for more than a century, down to the lifetime of Ssu-ma T'an.[9] This latter analysis is clearly diachronic and indicates that, while he used the term "Tao-chia" in a synchronic sense in his discussion of the six schools, he was aware that, as in the case of the Confucians and the Mohists, it also had a diachronic basis. Ssu-ma T'an is said to have been a student of a Huang-Lao master, so he evidently gained his knowledge of that tradition directly from someone within it.[10]

So does this mean that we can talk about a Taoist school or that it is perhaps best simply to abandon the concept of philosophical schools and adapt the idea of lineages? But does that mean we should also abandon the term "Taoism"? Does this imply, as Angus Graham says, that most of Ssu-ma T'an's schools were nothing more than "tendencies established retrospectively"?[11] Was there nothing by which these six groups differentiated themselves?

Answering these questions requires that we distinguish two related issues. First, the concept of how a school is defined in the West. Second, the use of "philosophy" as a way to differentiate among groups of pre-Han thinkers.

On the topic of schools, Ryden argues that Robert Kramers and Angus Graham both emphasize the diachronic sense of masters and disciples in a lineage that is maintained over generations.[12] Kramers adds another sense of independent reflection developed in response to historical and social conditions. Both conclude that the Confucians are what Graham—who adds the Mohists as well—calls a "true school."

In the West the word "school" has been defined largely in terms of Greek and medieval European models. Hence the *New Shorter Oxford Dictionary* entry includes three relevant definitions:

1. A body of people who have been taught by a particular philosopher. . . .

2. A group of people who are disciples of the same person or who share some principle, method, or style.

3. Originally, an organized body of teachers and scholars in one of the higher branches of study cultivated in medieval Europe constituting a university.

In the first two definitions, one idea predominates: that schools are defined by particular thinkers and their disciples. They may stretch across generations and so can be diachronic. They may also share some defining principle or method. And they are organized bodies. According to these definitions, Confucians and Mohists can be called schools. Each group had a founder and generations of disciples, and each group enunciated distinctive intellectual principles and methods. They also transmitted foundational texts containing these principles and methods. Furthermore the Mohists were well organized: They even had a system of tithing, in which a school member sent dues to a central authority.[13]

If we restrict ourselves to meeting all three of these criteria, the early Taoists would fall short. Indeed, one of the difficulties in identifying a pre-Han form of Taoism is that its origins are truly obscure. Unlike Confucianism and the Mohism, Taoism does not have a single founder, despite the efforts of late Warring States members of this lineage to establish a founder in the figure of Lao Tan, reputed author of the *Lao Tzu*. Furthermore little is known about early Taoist organization. Although at best we can speculate about their having formed small communities to follow their distinctive inner cultivation practice, there is no clear evidence of a well-established social organization that extended over several generations. Nonetheless, this does not mean that Taoists lacked distinctive principles and methods or a body of texts in which they were transmitted.

The concept of schools of philosophy also needs reexamination. Although each of the groups defined by Ssu-ma T'an has its distinctive ideas, to define them by their ideas alone is to engage in a doctrine-based synchronic analysis that overemphasizes the importance of philosophy. Early Confucians, for example, as Robert Eno demonstrates, did not merely read the *Analects*; they studied it with a teacher in the context of an entire program of learning and practice.[14] It is often said that the Confucians thought about benevolence, the Mohists about universal love, the Taoists about the Way, and so on. Yet this simplistic summary overlooks the other equally—if not more—important element: their distinctive techniques (*shu*, 術).

A closer examination of Ssu-ma T'an's essay shows that his synchronic analysis is based not so much on doctrines as on techniques, practical methods. For example, "the techniques of the Naturalists magnify the importance of omens and proliferate avoidances and taboos, causing people to feel constrained and to fear many things. Nonetheless, one cannot fault how they prioritize the grand compliances of the four seasons." And again,

> The Confucians are erudite, yet they lack the essentials. They labor much but achieve little. That is why their doctrines are difficult to follow completely. Nonetheless, one cannot detract from the way they prioritize the various rituals between ruler and minister and father and son and how they enumerate the various distinctions between husband and wife and elder and younger.[15]

Notice that Ssu-ma T'an talks not about their ethical ideas but, rather, about their ritual practices. His discussions of the other four groups contain a similar emphasis on techniques. Technique is the principal focus of his analysis, not the philosophies that developed along with them and that support them. When the idea of a philosophical school is applied to these groupings, doctrine is emphasized at the expense of methods, thus doing them—and ourselves—a grave disservice.

Moreover, to emphasize ideas at the expense of techniques is to deemphasize the diachronic aspect. We can read ideas in a book, but we can learn techniques only with a teacher. I am no more a Taoist by virtue of reading the *Lao Tzu* than I am a physicist from reading Einstein's *The Meaning of Relativity* (Princeton: Princeton University Press, 1950). As Donald Harper has shown, during the Warring States period medical literature had a widespread circulation that was not limited to physicians. The occupant of Ma-wang-tui tomb number three was not a physician; he was interested in medical works, as well as philosophical and astrological works, for his own edification.[16] Techniques must be seen as a way to define pre-Han intellectual lineages, not just philosophical ideas alone.

Doing so helps solve two related problems in determining pre-Han intellectual lineages. During the latter part of the Warring States period, philosophical ideas began to be exchanged between distinct traditions at state courts throughout what was then China. Intellectual lineages were no longer relatively hermetic traditions but show increasing evidence of the incorporation of ideas from other traditions. If we remain fixated on philosophical concepts as the sole criteria for identifying intellectual traditions, we are left having to demonstrate why, for example, the author of the "Way of Heaven" chapter of the *Chuang Tzu* is not a Confucian because he approves of benevolence and rightness or why Hsün Tzu is not a Taoist because he approves of mental tranquility. The obvious answer in both cases is that these ideas are contained within a greater context shaped primarily by the distinctive techniques each author advocated. If we know these techniques and use them to identify members of a given tradition, when such members incorporate ideas from other traditions we can place them in their proper contexts.

A second problem resolved by this use of techniques to identify lineages is that of change and development within traditions. When we look for diachronic evidence of schools that had a set body of philosophical ideas that did not evolve, as some have done, we are looking for something that did not exist. But if we alter our approach and focus on techniques, then we can be more open to changes in ideas that develop in the continued application over time of a relatively set body of practices. This is what should be done to arrive at an understanding of the nature of early Taoism.

An examination of the various pre-Han groups identified by Ssu-ma T'an as schools demonstrates that each has a primary focus on techniques. Broadly stated, these are: for the Naturalists, coordinating the human polity with the greater patterns of the heavens and the earth; for the Confucians, maintaining proper ritual in the family and the state; for the Mohists, economizing state and family expenditures to maximize the benefit of available resources; for the Legalists, establishing the rule of law and the methods of maintaining adherance to it; for the Terminologists, the rectification of names; and, for the Taoists, the advocacy of mystical cultivation leading to uniting with the Way as the essential element of rulership.

From this perspective, it is to be expected that corollary methods and philosophical concepts will develop and evolve over time to suit different historical circumstances. Thus we should not be concerned that Ssu-ma T'an or the authors of the *Huai-nan Tzu* identified a syncretic program of rulership that integrated elements of Confucian teachings into a Taoist context while the *Lao Tzu* vehemently attacks such teachings. The important link between them is their shared mystical techniques and the insights into the nature of the world derived from them. For this reason, we should also not be concerned that *Inward Training* is virtually silent on the application of its inner cultivation practice to rulership, whereas for the *Lao Tzu* and a wide variety of Syncretic Taoist texts such an application is pivotal.

This analysis indicates that we should rely more heavily on techniques as the defining characteristics for early Chinese groups of thinkers than the philosophies that arose from them. It also indicates that, despite the lack of historical evidence for well-developed social organization, distinctive lineages of thought did develop. These lineages of masters and disciples exhibit a level of organization that justifies the label "school" only for the Confucians and the Mohists. Yet, when these lineages are looked at from the standpoint of shared techniques of mystical self-cultivation, a Taoist group can be distinguished as well. Rather than call the group a school, why not a distinct tradition that consisted of several master-disciple lineages that shared these common techniques?

The "Techniques of the Way"

The labels of the six groups identified by Ssu-ma T'an indicate that he derived them from several different perspectives. Some of these groups are epitomized by a concept central to their distinctive techniques (*shu*), such as the Naturalists (yin-yang), the Legalists (law), the Terminologists (names). The Confucians are epitomized by the term that designated their social group (literati: *ju*, 儒) and the Mohists by the name of their founder, Mo Tzu.

Significantly for our analysis, the Taoists are also epitomized by the central concept in their *shu*: the goal of their distinctive methods of self-realization, the Way. While teachers in each of the other five groups at times spoke of their "way," these, for the most part, designated their programs of education and practice. For the Taoists, their specific inner cultivation techniques were aimed at the direct realization of *the* Way, the unifying power that pervades the entire cosmos. This seems to have been the basis for Ssu-ma T'an calling them the "Tao-chia." But did he simply dream up this term by himself? Was there no basis for this in earlier teachings?

There is no evidence that the early Taoists identified themselves by either of the Han historians' labels, "Tao-chia" or "Huang-Lao," or—for that matter—by the Wei and Chin (third-century A.D.) label of "Lao-Chuang." If we keep this in mind we can avoid much of the confusion and controversy that has troubled traditional understandings of Taoism and recent scholarly attempts to clarify them. However, some evidence indicates that early Taoists may have defined themselves along lines not altogether dissimilar to those used by Ssu-ma T'an: They referred to their distinctive practices as the "techniques of the Way."

Chapter 6 of the *Chuang Tzu*, "Ta-tsung shih" (The Teacher Who Is the Ultimate Ancestor), contains a dialogue between Confucius and his disciple Tzu-kung about three masters who are able to see through life and death and live forgetful of themselves and one another.[17] Having cultivated a high degree of numinous clarity, they symbolize selfless sages who "roam beyond the guidelines" while Confucius and Tzu-kung remain within them, "condemned by the sentence of heaven." Confucius explains that they are able to do this because these extraordinary men forget about one another in the "techniques of the Way" (*Tao-shu*). It thus appears that these techniques are what gives them their numinous abilities, qualities that derive from their talent for forgetting themselves.

This same term is used in the dialogue from *Annals of Mr. Lü* we examined in chapter 1, in which the Chi-hsia Taoist T'ien P'ien[18] teaches the "techniques of the Way" to the king of Ch'i.[19] Although few explicit inner cultivation methods are presented here, their presence is implied when T'ien urges the king to draw resources from within himself and then adds, "There is nothing about governing in my words, yet they can be used to attain [the ability to] govern." The author of this essay continues, "This is what Ancestor P'eng used to be long-lived." Thus the teachings of T'ien P'ien here imply not just an awareness of inner cultivation but a suggestion of its links to early macrobiotic hygiene theories, whose symbol was Ancestor P'eng, and the beginnings of its application to rulership. One can imagine how such an application might have actually occurred through dialogues such as this one.

Another well-known use of the term "techniques of the Way" occurs in *Chuang Tzu* 33, "All Under the Heavens." In this chapter the author contrasts the comprehensive "techniques of the Way" symbolizing the Syncretic Taoist techniques and philosophies that he and his group advocated with the limited "techniques of one corner" (*fang-shu*, 方 術), which retain only a portion of this comprehensive knowledge. The analysis proceeds from here to demonstrate the strengths and weaknesses of each of the six groups of teachers. The "techniques of the Way" advocated here are aimed at developing "inner sageliness and outer kingliness" and so contain an important element of inner cultivation. Chapters 15 and parts of chapters 12–14 are by the same group of thinkers and provide further detail on the specifics of such a practice. (The evidence for inner cultivation in chapter 15 was analyzed here in chapter 4.) While the authors of these Syncretist chapters conceived of their program as following the comprehensive "Way of the heavens and the earth" (t'ien-ti chih Tao, 天地之道), it is clear that they also conceived of its practice as adhering to the "techniques of the Way."

The term "techniques of the Way" is also used in seven passages in the *Huai-nan Tzu*, the Syncretic Taoist text written under the aegis of Liu An, the second king of Huai-nan, and presented to his nephew, the Han emperor Wu, in 139 B.C. Two of these are versions of the passage from the *Chuang Tzu* 6 and *Annals of Mr. Lü* 17.8 already discussed. In these as well as the rest, the "techniques of the Way" refer to inner cultivation practices.

For example, chapter 2, "Ch'u-chen" (The Primeval Reality, 俶真), explains:

> Sages internally cultivate the "techniques of the Way" and do not externally adorn themselves with benevolence and rightness. They do not know what objects are suitable to the eyes and ears and they wander in the harmony of their numen and vital essence.[20]

In chapter 11, "Ch'i-su" (Placing Customs on a Par, 齊俗), the "techniques of the Way" are seen as objective practices that can continue from generation to generation just as can the equally objective measures of the balance beam and water-level. They can continue regardless of whether they are mastered in a given generation and so "we cannot place exclusive dependence on human talents but the 'techniques of the Way' may be impartially practiced."[21] Chapter 13, "Fan-lun" (A Far-reaching Discussion, 氾論), argues that those who have penetrated the Way can empty their minds of emotions and desires because they restrict them according to the "techniques of the Way." And so these "sages have a balanced mind and a relaxed awareness. Their numen and vital essence are maintained internally and there is no thing that is sufficient to delude them."[22] In chapter 14, "Ch'üan-yen" (Inquiring Words, 詮言) we read that:

> the "techniques of the Way" cannot be used to advance and seek fame but can be used to withdraw and cultivate the person. They cannot be

used to attain benefit but can be used to avoid harm. Therefore sages do not seek fame for their conduct nor look for praise for their wisdom. They follow and comply with what is naturally so [tzu-jan] and their selves have nothing to which they are joined.[23]

The final passage in "Inquiring Words" talks about the excellent talents of worthy people that include benevolence, wisdom, courage, and strength but are completely insufficient for ruling the country. For that one must comply with the "techniques of the Way." Details follow in which the aligned circulation of the vital breath is seen as the practice to limit desire and perception and allow one to order the person and nourish the nature.[24] From these examples, it is clear that the "techniques of the Way" for the *Huai-nan Tzu* authors were the apophatic inner cultivation practices advocated first in *Inward Training.*

Of course the Taoists did not have a copyright on the term "techniques of the Way," just as they did not have one on the word "Tao." I have found two uses of this phrase in Confucian sources, one in the *Hsün Tzu* and one in a Confucian essay in the *Annals of Mr. Lü.*[25] But the evidence is strong of a consistent and a predominant use of the "techniques of the Way" in Taoist sources from the *Chuang Tzu* to the *Huai-nan Tzu,* where it refers to the techniques of inner cultivation. When combined with the evidence for the presence of inner cultivation techniques in a wide variety of early Taoist sources, this suggests the strong possibility that their authors were people who all followed the "techniques of the Way." These techniques then become a critical element in a diachronic analysis of early Taoism, from which follow important implications for the synchronic analysis of Ssu-ma T'an.

As mentioned above, when Ssu-ma T'an presented his synchronic analysis of the six schools, he compared them on the basis of their techniques. In view of the possibility that he studied in a Huang-Lao lineage, he was most likely familiar with their distinctive techniques and presented his understanding of them—and their superiority—in his discourse. Since he worked in the imperial archives after the *Huai-nan Tzu* had been presented to the emperor Wu in 139 B.C., he may have read that work. This possibility is enhanced by the closeness of his summary of Taoism to much of the content of the *Huai-nan Tzu*; thus it is likely that he also drew his understanding of distinctive Taoist techniques from this work as well as from his Huang-Lao teachers. It is therefore also possible that he coined the term "Tao-chia" to refer to the broadly conceived intellectual tradition of those who practiced the "techniques of the Way." His use was synchronic, but it was based on the diachronic import of the closely related term "Tao-shu." Therefore, because his synchronic use had a diachronic basis, the term "Taoist" can be used to refer to the people who practiced the "techniques of the Way," and these techniques can justifiably be used as a basis for identifying textual sources of early Taoism.

The relevance of this for determining the significance of *Inward Training* in the early history of Taoism cannot be overemphasized. If the essential defining characteristic in the diachronic analysis of an early Taoist tradition is that its members all practiced the "techniques of the Way"—a term that encompasses apophatic inner cultivation practice aimed at a mystical realization of the Way and its integration into everyday life—then *Inward Training*, which contains the earliest extant expression of this practice, must be regarded as one of the foundations of Taoism. So although this scenario may not represent a social phenomenon clearly definable as a philosophical school with a rigid set of doctrines that remained relatively fixed over time, it suggests strongly that early Taoism was made of a number of closely related master-disciple lineages, all of whom followed a common inner cultivation practice first enunciated in *Inward Training*. This is the most logical way to account for the considerable evidence for inner cultivation practice in early Taoist works and in the classifications of Ssu-ma T'an.

Inward Training AND THE Lao Tzu

One question that emerges from these arguments is how *Inward Training* is related to the *Lao Tzu*. As seen above, this relationship is quite close. According to William Baxter, both are part of a distinctive genre of early Taoist literature, and the present analysis demonstrates a commonality of mystical practice, mystical experience, and mystical philosophy between the two works. The principal difference between the two—in addition to the greater length and metaphysical tendency in the *Lao Tzu*—is that *Inward Training* does not exhibit the interest in political matters that so dominates its more famous companion.

The date of the *Lao Tzu* has been debated vigorously during the twentieth century, and those who insist on the traditional sixth-century B.C. date are now in a clear minority. Based largely on the fact that other thinkers do not seem to be aware of the work before Lao Tzu is mentioned by

Hsün Tzu—who probably first encountered his text during the decade he spent at the Chi-hsia Academy, beginning in about 275 B.C.—the consensus among Western sinologists is to follow Ch'ien Mu's theory that the received recensions of the *Lao Tzu* date from no earlier than about the year 300 B.C.[26]

The approximate date of 300 B.C. for the Kuo-tien *Lao Tzu* parallels seems to support Ch'ien's dating. It is important to remember that their testimony does not necessarily prove the existence of a complete *Lao Tzu* at this time but, rather, attests to the attempt to establish written works similar to the *Lao Tzu* that apply inner cultivation to political life.

Baxter's approximate date of 400 B.C. for the *Lao Tzu* is also not necessarily in conflict with Ch'ien's dating. His conclusions are based on his finding that the *Lao Tzu* preserves some of the rhymes of the *Book of Poetry* that are lost by the time of the *Ch'u Tz'u* and the inner chapters of *Chuang Tzu*. As he concludes, "Given that these texts are generally dated to the late fourth or early third century B.C.E., it is linguistically quite plausible to date the bulk of the *Lao Tzu* to the mid or early fourth century, a view that agrees with traditional scholarship."[27] Taken together with the testimony from Kuo-tien, Baxter's findings suggest that works that we might call "proto-*Lao Tzu*" could have begun to have been compiled around the middle of the fourth century B.C. This is also the case for *Inward Training*. Yet there is also some evidence that they are based upon an even older oral tradition.

Victor Mair has suggested that, because the text is largely in the form of verse, the *Lao Tzu* was probably transmitted orally for some time before being written down, since rhymed and unrhymed metrical verse is recited and memorized more easily than prose.[28] Michael LaFargue agrees and has analyzed how the composers of the written text assembled the independent units of verse to form the work as we now know it. LaFargue asserts that those who created and transmitted the units of verse and later assembled them into a complete composition were probably members of a community, whom he prefers to identify simply as "Laoists," after the lead of A. C. Graham.[29] There is no particular reason to doubt a theory as general as this, but with further research it may become possible to speak with more precision about this community, which, at the very least, amounts to one early Taoist lineage.

With regard to works of this vintage, dating is extremely problematic, especially when we take into account the possibility that they are based upon an earlier oral tradition and may contain strata written at different times. So too is the attempt to specify the geographic region in which they were produced. *Lao Tzu* has been linked to both Ch'u, the traditional ascription that started with Ssu-ma Ch'ien (and now supported by the Kuo-tien find from the old Ch'u capital region), and Ch'i by recent scholars such as Ch'ien Mu. These are also the two possible locations for *Inward Training*. The closeness in philosophy and literary form of these two works and the significance of *Inward Training* as the earliest extant statement of inner cultivation theory—the "techniques of the Way"—invite a comparison of their relative dates, even though this comparison cannot yield conclusions, only hypotheses.

Nevertheless, for many reasons *Inward Training* should be considered an earlier work than the *Lao Tzu*. These reasons can be grouped under three headings: literary, logical, and philosophical. As for the literary reasons, while both works are characteristic of a distinct genre of anonymous Taoist philosophical verse, the *Lao Tzu* is a much more sophisticated compilation (as seen in chapter 1). Virtually all of the verses of *Inward Training* are simply verses, with few of the additional compositional devices found in the *Lao Tzu* that weave together independent verses and aphorisms, as identified by LaFargue. For this reason, it seems clear that the compilation of *Inward Training* represents an earlier attempt at compiling and arranging independent units of verse from an oral tradition.

The second group of reasons emerge from the logical priority of inner cultivation practice, which is shared by both works. The cultivation of mystical states of consciousness is the priority in *Inward Training*; their application to governing is the priority in the *Lao Tzu*. It seems logical that the cultivation of these states must precede their application to government for the proponents of the *Lao Tzu*. If the master-disciple lineage(s) that produced these works were not primarily able to achieve these states, then how could they teach them to others, especially rulers who might be extremely unhappy if these practices proved less rewarding than promised?

The Kuo-tien *Lao Tzu* parallels seem to confirm such a movement from inner cultivation to politics. Compared to the received *Lao Tzu*, a significantly higher percentage of the passages in the Kuo-tien *Lao Tzu* parallels are devoted to self-cultivation. LaFargue groups together all the *Lao Tzu* chapters on this topic, assigning sixteen of the eighty-one (almost 20 percent) to this group.[30] Yet the Kuo-tien parallels include eight of LaFargue's self-cultivation passages in their total of twenty-nine parallels (almost 28 percent) with the *Lao Tzu*.[31] Moreover, LaFargue's total ignores a significant grouping of verses in the Kuo-tien material, those commending inner cultivation to the ruler as part of the arts of rulership. Since the first ten passages of the first bundle of *Lao Tzu* parallels from Kuo-tien all do this and none of these are in LaFargue's self-cultivation list, these comparative percentages are extremely conservative. Now, if these Kuo-tien parallels are interpreted not as extracts from a complete *Lao Tzu* but as a kind of "proto-*Lao Tzu*," then they represent an interim state between the pure inner cultivation practice of *Inward Training* and the more heavily politicized inner cultivation of the received *Lao Tzu*.[32]

Furthermore, *Inward Training* contains none of the polemical attacks on other non-Taoist lineages that are found in the *Lao Tzu*. For example, verses 18, 19, and 38 contain strong criticisms of the Confucians, and verse 75 takes a swipe at the Yangists, "who value life" (*kuei-sheng*, 貴生) but are inferior to those who do not act for the purpose of living.[33] This suggests that the *Lao Tzu* took shape—or at least these verses did—at a time of contention between its proponents and the followers of Confucius and Yang Chu, when its creators were beginning to define their ideas in contradistinction to those of other thinkers. Little evidence of such contention appears before the second half of the fourth century B.C., when advocates of different lineages began to compete for government sanction at local courts or debated one another at Chi-hsia. The absence of such polemical ideas in *Inward Training* is further indication of its greater antiquity.

The third group of reasons to consider *Inward Training* an earlier work than the *Lao Tzu* is philosophical. When the key ideas of the two works are compared, it is clear, first, that *Inward Training* speaks of both the Way and inner power (Tao and Te) and links the two together in verse XVII. These ideas are so important to the *Lao Tzu* that the text has also been called the *Tao Te ching* and has traditionally been divided into Tao and Te sections. The occurrence of these two terms together often indicates a source's debt to the *Lao Tzu*, but it is also possible that the *Lao Tzu* itself drew these defining terms from *Inward Training*. Without presuming which work is earlier, all that can be said here is that authors of one of these works must have been familiar with the other, or at least with its key ideas, if the borrowing occurred before orally transmitted verses in each of them was composed into a written text.

If the *Lao Tzu* were the basis for *Inward Training*, then a comparison of the two would yield several features that seem rather odd. First, *Inward*

Training is devoid of any of the distinctive metaphors of the *Lao Tzu,* such as the empty vessel, the Profound Mirror, the valley spirit, the Unadorned, and the Unhewn. It is clear from prior analyses that both texts have similar ideas about the Way and about spiritual cultivation, which are encoded in these metaphors. If *Inward Training* were derivative, then why would it omit such important metaphors? We cannot fall back on such "school-based" explanations as Fung Yu-lan's that *Inward Training* and the other "Techniques of the Mind" texts are a combination of "Lao-Chuang" and "Huang-Lao."[34]

In addition, although *Inward Training* exhorts the apophatic mystical practice of emptying out the mind, it never uses the term "emptiness" (*hsü*) to refer to it. This suggests that it has not yet been influenced by the distinct locutions and rhetoric of the *Lao Tzu,* as the absence of the latter's distinctive metaphors also does. Further, the fact that *Lao Tzu*'s idea of nonaction is also not found in *Inward Training,* but is suggested—at least in part—by the idea of numinous transformation in verse IX, provides further evidence that *Inward Training* was written before the important ideas of the *Lao Tzu* were crystallized. This is suggested yet again by the general observation that the concepts of the Way and inner power in *Inward Training* are much less abstract than in the *Lao Tzu.* All these factors lead to the conjecture that *Inward Training* was not based on the *Lao Tzu* but contains an earlier formulation of ideas that became the core teachings of the latter, such as the Way, inner power, emptiness, nonaction, tranquility, and so on.

Furthermore, while *Inward Training* does not use the term "emptiness," it refers to its underlying meditative experience by its own unique metaphor of "cleaning out the lodging place of the numinous." Such a metaphor is a most interesting image, for it suggests an external temple that is being cleansed in preparation for the descent of some divinity to receive a sacrifice or perhaps the purification of a shaman in preparation for serving as a medium for some divinity. This provides evidence, as Graham has succinctly put it, "that the meditation practiced privately and recommended to rulers as an arcanum of government descends directly from the trance of the professional shaman."[35] Scholars including Kristopher Schipper and Isabelle Robinet have suggested shamanistic origins for early Taoist religious experience, and Jordan Paper has developed a theory as to how early Taoist mysticism may have evolved from shamanistic roots.[36] Although surviving evidence is insufficient to arrive at a definitive conclusion about this hypothesis, metaphors such as this one from *Inward Training* strongly suggest that such a process occurred. If it did, it would furnish further evidence of the chronological priority of inner cultivation practice and, hence, of *Inward Training*.

That this distinctive metaphor of sweeping clean the lodging place of the numinous—the only one in *Inward Training*—is not found in the *Lao Tzu* shows that the latter was not based directly on the former. *Techniques of the Mind* I does contain it, a strong reason for concluding that it was based directly on *Inward Training*. But our identification of inner cultivation as the critical core of early Taoism indicates that texts containing this practice need not include identical formulations to show influence on one another. The commonality of mystical techniques and mystical ideas offers strong evidence that the two works are closely related, and the absence of just one metaphor is not terribly significant. However, the absence in *Inward Training* of an entire set of metaphors and distinctive locutions from the *Lao Tzu* makes it more likely that it is the earlier of the two works. And their many parallels suggest that both are likely to have come from the same master-disciple lineage or, at least, from two closely related ones.

The presence of strong indications that both works were based on earlier oral traditions makes the problem of textual priority particularly difficult to resolve. Perhaps the intellectual parallels between the two derived more from their common practice and from their having descended from a shared lineage of master and disciples that conceived of this practice according to the ideas in both works. Perhaps this common lineage split into many regional branches, each associated with one of these texts. However, even if this is the case, it does not substantially change the fact that the ideas contained in the *Lao Tzu* appear to constitute an elaboration of those contained in *Inward Training*. Therefore, *Inward Training* brings us closer to the very origins of the philosophy and practice that defines Taoism in its formative period.

Inward Training AND THE "LORE OF THE WAY"

Up to this point, the present discussion has focused on two types of influences within early Taoism, technical and textual. In the case of *Inward Training*, the former predominates. As mentioned above, the distinctive mystical techniques presented in *Inward Training* exerted a powerful influence throughout early Taoism. This is not to say that this influence came directly from the text of *Inward Training* but, rather, that it came from the transmission from master to disciples of the inner cultivation practice found in *Inward Training*. Nonetheless, the text of *Inward Training* is not without its own influence as well.

The first place to look for signs of this influence is in the three other "Techniques of the Mind" works. Signs of this influence are most extensive in *Techniques of the Mind* I but are present in *Techniques of the Mind* II as well. In addition, sections from two verses of *Inward Training* are reproduced almost verbatim in early Taoist works of the third and second centuries B.C.

As already seen, lines 3–8 of verse XIX are repeated in *Chuang Tzu* 23, "Keng-sang Ch'u." They are also found, with a number of variants, in the section "Ming hsing" (Names and Forms, 名 刑) in the *Sixteen Canons* of the Ma-wang-tui *Four Classics*, as well as in *Techniques of the Mind* I.[37] The lines in question refer to concentrating and unifying: mental concentration on one thing, which is an essential element of inner cultivation practice. In the *Sixteen Canons* and *Techniques of the Mind* I, such a concentration is recommended to the ruler as an important aspect of the arts of governing.

Another related and important aspect of the arts of governing is the application of the idea of maintaining or holding fast to the One, or the Way. Verse XIV in *Inward Training* talks about how the Way, which interfuses the heavens and the earth, is realized through an awareness that precedes words deep within the "mind within the mind" that yields a release from the limited individual perspective. Lines 4–9 from this verse, which speak of this release, are repeated almost verbatim (in whole or in part) in five other sources: the "Ch'eng-fa" (Perfecting Standards, 成 法) essay in the *Ching-fa* of the *Four Classics*; *Techniques of the Mind* I; *Chuang Tzu* 15 ("Fixed Ideas"); *Huai-nan Tzu* 1 ("The Original Way"); and the "Tao-yüan" (Source That Is the Way, 道 原) essay of the *Wen Tzu*.[38] In all these contexts except the *Chuang Tzu*, the subject is similar: the implications for rulership of attaining the One and then holding fast to it.[39] In other words, these passages demonstrate how the mystical experience of attaining the One yields practical benefits for the ruler. For example, in "Perfecting Standards," Li Hei advises the Yellow Emperor that "maintaining the One" (*shou-i*) is the foundation of rulership because "the traces of the One reach throughout the heavens and the earth and the guiding principles (*li*) of the One stretch throughout the four seas." This is based on the idea that all things have the Way within them as their essential guiding principle and so "to grasp the One is to understand the many." This application of the mystical "techniques of the Way" to the arts of rulership is an important development in the early Taoist tradition and is one of the essential defining characterics of Syncretic Taoism.

Combining this with the evidence that a great deal of inner cultivation practice was transmitted through the literary form of tetrasyllabic verse leads to further insights into the nature of the early Taoist tradition. The verses of *Inward Training* were part of this genre of "Taoist wisdom poetry," which could be transmitted orally, quoted imperfectly, and inserted into different literary and historical contexts. This genre is governed by certain rhetorical structures—such as that used for stages of meditation (mentioned in chapter 4) and the ones identified by Baxter in his analysis of the *Lao Tzu*—and contains certain characteristic locutions—such as the "maintaining the One" pattern in the *Lao Tzu* and *Inward Training*. With further research it may be possible to find more examples of this genre (for example, the teachings of Kuan-yin in *Chuang Tzu* 33) and to further specify its distinctive literary features.[40] This effort promises a clearer understanding of the *Lao Tzu*, *Inward Training*, and the very origins of Taoism. Indeed, William Baxter concludes:

> The existence of other texts with similar characteristics, such as certain chapters of the *Kuan Tzu*, has been recognized for some time; but the canonical status of the *Lao Tzu* may have tended to hide the importance of these similarities. Study of these sometimes obscure texts may clarify the history of the *Lao Tzu* more than comparison with other texts which happen to have been recognized as classics. Certainly, the development of the genre which the *Lao Tzu* represents cannot be studied from the *Lao Tzu* alone. A reasonable conjecture would be that the *Lao Tzu* and similar texts emerged from a distinctive tradition of philosophical verse with strong oral elements and little concept of individual authorship.[41]

This distinctive Taoist wisdom poetry and the "techniques of the Way" it transmitted together constitute what might be called the "lore of the Way." This lore probably also included stories of early Taoist adepts with numinous characteristics such as those in the *Chuang Tzu* and incisive comments from early teachers in this tradition, at times remembered imperfectly. Thus many of the figures who appear in the most narrative-filled of the early Taoist texts, the *Chuang Tzu*, may have been real or legendary personages about whom stories arose that were included in this lore. This would include the figures touched upon in this book such as Kuang Ch'eng-tzu, Keng-sang Ch'u, Nan-kuo Tzu-ch'i, Nan-jung Chu, and T'ien P'ien. This distinctive lore was transmitted widely throughout China in the fourth, third, and second centuries B.C. and formed the basis for the variations and political applications of Taoism that developed during these centuries.

This techniques-based definition of an early Taoist tradition and its literary genre now allows us to offer a broader perspective with political as well as mystical aspects, always keeping in mind the role in it of *Inward Training*.

A NEW APPROACH TO THE EVOLUTION OF EARLY TAOISM

Having moved into a "post-Lao-Chuang" world in which we can no longer use the *Lao Tzu* and the "inner chapters" of *Chuang Tzu* as the basis from which to evaluate other early Taoist textual sources, a world in which we can no longer talk with our former confidence about the six "schools" of early Chinese philosophy, how are we to sort through and organize the wide variety of these early Taoist texts and determine their intellectual filiations? If "Lao-Chuang" is a Wei-Chin (third-century A.D.) label and "Huang-Lao" is a Han dynasty (second-century B.C.) label, what are the intellectual filiations of the *Lao Tzu*, the *Chuang Tzu*, and the *Kuan Tzu*? Having concluded that to label the *Four Classics* as the product of a "Tao-Fa" school presupposes the existence of a Taoist (Lao-Chuang) school and a Legalist school, both of which have been recently challenged, how are we to categorize this important work whose discovery at Ma-wang-tui a quarter of a century ago began the profound questioning of our assumptions about early Taoism that have left us in this predicament?

As seen in earlier chapters, despite the absence of organized schools of Lao-Chuang and Huang-Lao philosophy, there is incontrovertible evidence of a pre-Han Taoist textual tradition that has heretofore been categorized according to these labels. In their absence, some scholars refer to a variety of separate lineages that produced each of the textual sources of early Taoism, calling them "Laoists," "Chuangists," "Huang-Laoists," and so forth. But this severely underplays the clear connections that pervade this literature. Edmund Ryden suggests another alternative, which seems reasonable (except for the apparent equation of Taoism and Huang-Lao):

Rather than assign *Laozi* to one school and the *Huangdi sijing* [Huang-ti ssu-ching, the Four Classics] to another because they do not have exactly the same philosophy, it is truer to their historical origins to describe both as early Daoism or *Huanglao*. Instead of creating a bewildering array of schools it is better to talk of one lineage with distinct voices.[42]

The way to best accomplish this is to focus on shared techniques, not just doctrines. It is possible to identify a distinct practice of self-cultivation common to all the authors of the textual sources of early Taoism and to use this as the basis for developing a minimal definition of the essential characteristics of this tradition in order to classify each of its sources.

If we lacked historical information on any of the foundational figures of the Confucian tradition but had its texts—the *Analects*, the *Mencius*, the *Hsün Tzu*, the *Li chi* (Record of Rites), and so forth—how could we establish that they were related to one another and formed part of the same intellectual tradition?

First, by identifying key concepts, isolating the important technical terms of each text and seeing whether they were repeated in any of the others. Doing so would show that such notions as benevolence, rightness, wisdom, and ritual are found—and play important roles—in all these works. It would also show that the concept of human nature was a central concern in the *Mencius* and the *Hsün Tzu*, but that there was considerable disagreement between them on just what human nature consisted of. But the fact of these disagreements would not lead to the conclusion that these texts were not related. Evidence would reveal that the practice of the proper performance of rituals, both in the state and the family, was critical to all these works and that the five human relationships as the field in which these rituals could be practiced were also central. Finally, it would become clear that a common concern for the cultivation of the ethical qualities developed through the process of attempting to fulfill our deepest inner tendencies and motivations.

We would also pay attention to which of the texts quoted material from which others. We would then come to see that the *Analects* seemed to be the earliest because the others quote it and it does not quote the others.

This process would lead to the conclusion that such a tradition did, in fact, exist. It developed and evolved over time and any given text produced within it would not completely agree with any other on a particular topic. But their provenance from one and the same tradition would be proved because a significant number of ideas, themes, and practices persisted in all the texts and formed a defining pattern that could be used to confirm their relationships to one another.

Such an analysis comprises identifying a "semantic core" within the texts of this tradition. It consists of the central ideas, themes, and—most important—the practices attested to in all the texts of this tradition. This is precisely what I have been doing with early Taoism.

In a recent article I argued that the categories used by several scholars of the *Chuang Tzu* to identify its distinct philosophical voices and determine their filiation can be expanded to form a basis for developing a broad, yet precise conceptualization of all of early Taoism. Kuan Feng (關鋒), Angus Graham, and Liu Hsiao-kan (劉笑敢) have all developed similar schemes to analyze the *Chuang Tzu*, although they have disagreements especially about how to date and classify certain of its chapters.[43] The methodology they use to identify the various strata of the *Chuang Tzu* represents a type of literary criticism in which shared technical terms, parallel or identical phrases, and common grammatical structures are the criteria for the inclusion of material in their distinct categories of authorial voices or ideologies.[44] In addition, all three scholars develop arguments about the relationships between these strata and other early Taoist sources, and a careful reading of their works shows that they do so by simply extending this methodology. Thus, for example, all identify a distinct stratum of the *Chuang Tzu* in chapters 8–11 and then demonstrate how its basic viewpoint is close to that of the *Lao Tzu*. Their basic assumption is that the repeated occurrence of certain groupings of technical terms in several different texts has a significance for identifying important philosophical relationships among these texts.

Drawing from them and adding a few observations of my own, I propose the theory of three aspects of early Taoism mentioned in the Introduction to this book: Individualist, Primitivist, and Syncretist. All three aspects share a common cosmology of the Way and its inner power and a common inner cultivation practice. Where they differ is in the area of political thought. The Individualist sources have little or none, the Primitivist sources advocate a minimalist government of "nonaction" within small agrarian communities, and the Syncretist sources favor a complex, hierarchically organized government that attempts to establish its political institutions to parallel the greater patterns of the heavens and the earth. It should be clear from these definitions that the one thing all three aspects have in common is the "techniques of the Way" and the philosophical insights that developed from their practice. Placing these techniques in a political context or recommending them as an "arcanum of government," as Graham has put it, in no way entails that the resultant philosophy be categorized as anything *other* than Taoist.[45]

The theory of these aspects is, in turn, based on identifying a "semantic pattern" of technical terms that form three distinctive categories: cosmology, inner cultivation, and political thought. These can now be refined further based on the evidence for inner cultivation practice presented in this book.

The category of cosmology includes such familiar mystical ideas as Tao and Te, nonaction (*wu-wei,* 無為), formlessness (*wu-hsing,* 無形), the vital essence (*ching,* 精), the Way of the heavens (*t'ien chih Tao,* 天之道), and the Way of the heavens and the earth (*t'ien-ti chih Tao,* 天地之道).

Under the category of inner cultivation can be added such mystical goals as attaining tranquility (*ching,* 靜), cultivating emptiness (*hsü,* 虛), achieving desirelessness (*wu-yü,* 無欲) and selflessness (*wu-ssu,* 無私), and merging with the Way (*t'ung yü Tao,* 同於道), and related phrases such as "attaining the One" (*te Tao,* 得道) and attaining the empty Way (*te hsü Tao,* 得虛道). These goals are based on such apophatic practices as circulating the vital breath (*hsing ch'i,* 行氣), eliminating desires and emotions, restricting thought and perception, "maintaining the One" (*shou-i,* 守一), and related phrases in this distinct locution, developing inner power, and refining the vital essence. These practices are included under such rubric terms as nourishing the numen/numinous (*yang-shen,* 養神) and nourishing the innate nature (*yang-hsing,* 養性).

The final category of political thought is dominated by the technical terminology of the early Han Syncretists. It includes such concepts as nonaction (*wu-wei,* 無為), which they share with the Primitivists and Individualists, spontaneous response (*ying,* 應), adaptation (*yin,* 因), compliance (*hsü,* 循), suitability (*i,* 宜), and, for certain texts, the use of elements of Legalist and Confucian political and social thought. These latter ideas are unique to the Syncretists.

These categories of ideas and practices are not meant to be inclusive, and they are in need of further refinement. They are presented to begin the process through which this might occur. Furthermore, it is important to remember that it is not the random occurrence of one or several of these ideas in a given work that merits identifying it as a Taoist text of whatever aspect but, rather, the presence of a distinctive pattern of these ideas grounded in inner cultivation practice. Indeed, inner cultivation is the basis for the other two categories. The application of the "techniques of the Way" in order to "nourish the numinous" and "merge with the Great Pervader" is fundamental to all of pre- and early Han Taoism, both its apolitical and political forms. In this light, the significance of *Inward Training* as the earliest extant expression of these distinctive mystical techniques can no longer be overlooked.

This theory does not mean to suggest that some actual intellectual lineages referred to themselves by these labels of Individualist, Primitivist, and Syncretist. These labels are essentially heuristic devices to organize the panoply of early Taoist texts and viewpoints in as flexible a way as possible. However, the central role of the technical terminology of inner cultivation practice in these three general categories can best be explained by theorizing that the texts that contain it must have been produced in a series of related master-disciple lineages that all followed and promulgated this central practice. Thus these three general philosophical orientations must have had a basis in social groupings of teachers and students who pursued this practice and transmitted the "lore of the Way" that developed along with it.

This way of defining early Taoism is specific enough to differentiate this tradition from the others mentioned by Ssu-ma T'an and yet flexible enough to accommodate the differences among textual sources without losing sight of their larger context. It can both provide a basis for synchronic analyses as well as help identify the presence of a diachronic basis for the tradition. It can help us stay clear of retrospectively projecting later categories such as "Lao-Chuang" and "Huang-Lao" onto earlier texts and thinkers yet still account for why such terms gained currency. It can serve as the basis for identifying lineage groups within these aspects by locating specific combinations of technical terms that are consistent within them. Using this basis, it may be possible in the future to distinguish Ch'i Taoists from Ch'u Taoists or to determine which group the Taoist authors in the *Annals of Mr. Lü* were part of. Finally, it can demonstrate contrasts between early Taoists and the practitioners of macrobiotic hygiene with whom they shared technical terminology and an interest in breath cultivation practice.

In this new picture of the history of early Taoism, *Inward Training* assumes a significance that has not heretofore been appreciated: It is the oldest extant expression of the distinctive mystical practice and philosophy that is the basis of the entire tradition from its obscure origins to the time of the *Huai-nan Tzu* in the mid-second century B.C. But if this is the case, why is so little known about this work and so much about the text that has stood for over two millenia as the foundational text of Taoism, the *Lao Tzu?* In the process of answering this question, I hope to clarify some of the historical and social circumstances in which this tradition developed. This answer is somewhat provisional and is thus not a conclusion but, rather, a set of hypotheses that, in the future, can lead to more definitive conclusions.

The process of answering to the question why the *Lao Tzu*, among all the early texts of Taoism, gained ascendency has benefited greatly from the insights of A. C. Graham in his article exploring the origins and development of the legend that Lao Tan, a historical figure in the biography of Confucius, was also the author of the *Lao Tzu*.[46] Graham argues that the legend originated with the Confucian story that Confucius received instruction in proper ritual forms from a Chou archivist named Lao Tan. The book that came to be known as the *Lao Tzu* began circulating early in the third century B.C. Hsün Tzu is the first to cite one of its key doctrines under the name of Lao Tzu, and, as mentioned above, it is likely that he encountered the work at Chi-hsia by about 275 B.C. The earliest datable testimony that associates Lao Tan with the *Lao Tzu* appears in the Syncretic Taoist essay from *Annals of Mr. Lü* 17.7, "Pu-erh" (Not Two, 不 二). It states that "Lao Tan valued yielding" and places him immediately before Confucius at the head of a line of mainly Taoist teachers that includes Kuan Yin, Lieh Tzu, and T'ien P'ien.[47] It is only after this time that Lao Tan and Lao Tzu become, in the narratives of the *Chuang Tzu*, spokesmen for the ideas now found in the text of the *Lao Tzu*. This occurs particularly in the *Chuang Tzu*, chapters 21–23 and 27. The mainly Syncretist chapters 12–14 also contain some vexed evidence of this in the dialogues between Confucius and Lao Tan.[48]

Although it is clear from this evidence that the linking of Lao Tan with the *Lao Tzu* occurred by the middle of the third century B.C., Graham argues that this linkage was put to polemical use only in the Han dynasty.

He believes that the Taoists of the early Han, who were then vying with the Confucians, created this legend as an act of "one-upmanship" demonstrating the superiority of their own founder over that of their main rivals:

> The writing of the *Lao Tzu* in his [Lao Tan's] name would consolidate his status as a Taoist sage. By the 2nd century B.C., when the Taoist school took shape among the Six Schools as the strongest rival of the Confucians, in urgent need of providing itself retrospectively with a founder, Lao Tan would present himself as a very suitable candidate. On this hypothesis, it would hardly matter whether the obscure instructor in the rites was a historical person or a Confucian invention to point to the lesson that even the greatest must be willing to learn. The importance of Lao Tan would begin with his transformation by Taoist legend.[49]

As seen in the present analysis of the concept of an early Taoist "school," the early Taoists—unlike the Confucians, Mohists, and Yangists—did not originally have one person who could serve as the historical founder of their tradition. Hence they were at a disadvantage in an era when argumentation from historical precedent was one of the primary proofs for the veracity of any position advocated at a local court. Identifying their founder with the man who taught Confucius accomplished this purpose. However, contra Graham, there is no evidence that this attribution was *not* put to polemical use at the time of its first appearance, in the debates among the retainers of the Ch'in prime minister Lü Pu-wei that led to the writing of the *Annals of Mr. Lü* in about 239 B.C.

Although space limitations prevent us from going into detail here, if the categories of Taoist thought and practice developed here are applied to the *Annals of Mr. Lü*, it is possible to identify some of its chapters—including chapter 17—as the products of a Syncretic Taoist lineage.[50] Thus there were Taoists at the court of Lü Pu-wei. Moreover, Graham provides additional evidence linking the legend of Lao Tan to Ch'in: the story of the Chou historiographer Tan, who is said to have predicted the rise of the Ch'in in about 350 B.C. He suggests that this linking was made by "admirers of the *Lao Tzu*" who wished to win it the favor of the Ch'in state, which, after 239 B.C., became increasingly hostile to philosophers.[51] This provides further testimony connecting the creation of the legend of Lao Tan as the author of the *Lao Tzu* with Taoists in the state of Ch'in, perhaps those who had survived the dispersal of the intellectual academy of Prime Minister Lü Pu-wei.

This gives us an important date in the history of early Taoism. C. 239 B.C. is when we find concrete evidence of the Taoists' attempt to create a lineage rivaling that of the Confucians. This has many important implications.

The attempt to establish Lao Tan as the author of the *Lao Tzu* implies the development of a distinctive self-identity as the tradition that began with this teacher and this work. From this point on, while other minor lineages may have still persisted, the main tradition of the Taoists is carried forth by the people who believe in this founding legend. This self-identity carries over strongly into the Syncretic Taoism of the early Han that is found in the *Huai-nan Tzu* and from this point on continues into the later Han origins of the institutionalized Taoist religion. The entire self-understanding of early Han Huang-Lao teachers is based strongly on the teachings of Lao Tan found in the *Lao Tzu*. This can be seen by the frequent quotation of this text throughout the *Huai-nan Tzu* introduced by the phrase "Lao Tzu said." It is a canonical text for the *Huai-nan Tzu;* canon implies a school in all senses of the word that were explored above, a school that can truly rival the Confucians. It should come as no surprise then that evidence of the importance of the *Lao Tzu* emerges in the depiction of Taoism by Ssu-ma T'an.

Thus one principal reason that the *Lao Tzu* gained ascendency as the foundational work of Taoism was for this polemical purpose. However, this does not answer the question of why this work, among all other extant texts in this tradition, was exalted. Although this question cannot be answered with complete certainty because we know so little about the historical contexts in which other early Taoist sources on rulership were created, it is apparent that the *Lao Tzu* gained ascendency because it applied mystical teachings to the arena of politics. To survive in the intellectual world of late Warring States China, texts and their proponents needed to have a pervasive political dimension, particularly relevant to the concerns of ruling. Thus *Inward Training* survived not as a separate work but in a collection devoted mainly to political and economic thought, the *Kuan Tzu*. And it is ironic that the *Chuang Tzu*, filled with some of the most wonderful mystical and apolitical narratives ever created by human beings, survived, not because of these but because of the political teachings of its final, Syncretist stratum. This is not intended to denigrate the renowned beauty of the mystical poetry of the *Lao Tzu*, only to say that *Inward Training* contains mystical poetry every bit as beautiful as that in the *Lao Tzu*. That it did not gain the fame of the *Lao Tzu* is due primarily to the historical circumstances of late Warring States China rather than the inherent importance of both works in the early Taoist tradition.

Thus the origin of a self-conscious Taoist "school" can be traced in both the synchronic and diachronic senses to this legend of Lao Tan established by at least 239 B.C. Before this point, several relatively closely related lineage groups were based on the mystical techniques of inner cultivation enunciated in *Inward Training*. The origins of this practice remain obscure. As Graham and others have asserted, there is good reason to see them as developing from the trances of early shamans, but where and when remain a mystery. There is, however, a reasonable amount of circumstantial evidence to locate an earlier focal point for them in Ch'i. *Inward Training* is included in the *Kuan Tzu* collection, which originated there. Chuang Tzu is said to have visited Ch'i and the most important of the "inner chapters" of the work that bears his name, the "Essay on Seeing Things as Equal," shows possible influence of the Chi-hsia teacher T'ien P'ien, if the testimony to his ideas in chapter 33 of this work is to be believed.[52] Ch'ien Mu and others have argued that the *Lao Tzu* first affects the intellectual world of early China in Ch'i. And the basic intellectual framework of the inner cultivation practice in *Inward Training* shares much with the ideas of the early Chinese physicians who were well represented in Ch'i.

The Ch'u origins of Taoist mysticism cannot be discounted either. In addition to the legend that associates the *Lao Tzu* with Ch'u, Allyn Rickett has argued that many of the early Taoist textual sources contain distinctive rhyme patterns that some think can be associated with Ch'u. Furthermore, the recently discovered Kuo-tien tomb that yielded the *Lao Tzu* parallels discussed above is located in the part of Hupei province that once was home to the capital of the state of Ch'u, which existed until its conquest by Ch'in in 278 B.C. And then there is the collection of poetry with shamanistic and mystical content associated with this area, the *Elegies of Ch'u*.[53] All these point to Ch'u origins of Taoist mysticism. If the four "Techniques of the Mind" texts included in the Ch'i collection *Kuan Tzu* contain distinctive Ch'u rhyme patterns, this could suggest that the origins or early development of the Taoist tradition in Ch'i owes much to Ch'u adepts who came there during the fourth century B.C. to attend the courts of the early Ch'i kings.

The fact that a distinctive literary genre within the early Taoist tradition can now be identified has further implications for its historical origins. The transmission of the practices and philosophy of inner cultivation in regular, often tetrasyllabic and rhymed metrical verse that formed distinct units suggests that, before early Taoist texts like *Inward Training* and the *Lao Tzu* were written down, they were transmitted orally within lineages of masters and disciples. Thus this early "lore of the Way" may reach back in time well before it was recorded in written form in the mid-fourth century B.C. That it remained in this distinct form indicates that a certain amount of oral transmission occurred after the first written texts were created. This lore—both oral and written—was probably taught by a master to students and constituted a core of the teachings they carried with them when they finished their study and went elsewhere to teach on their own. In their new situations, they could apply their teachings on mystical self-cultivation, and they often did so in the intellectual context demanded by the times—advice to local rulers on how to govern effectively. Hence the later developments of Primitivist and Syncretist aspects to early Taoism incorporate inner cultivation teachings. These teachings appear in various forms, sometimes in tetrasyllabic verse, sometimes in prose explications, sometimes in set rhetorical structures. Sometimes they are attributed to Taoist masters, both legendary and historical. Sometimes they remain apocryphal. What is surprising is the evidence as to how widespread their influence was, occurring in works from *Inward Training* to the *Huai-nan Tzu* and spanning over two centuries.

Much work is yet to be done to complete our tentative picture of early Taoism in this "post-Lao-Chuang" world. Further research is needed to clarify the close relationship between the early Taoists and the practitioners of physical and macrobiotic hygiene. More work is also needed to see how the "cult of immortality" relates to these groupings, although the historical testimony regarding such a cult does not appear particularly strong.[54] Further research should explore the possible historical relevance of the many narratives from the "lore of the Way" within the *Chuang Tzu*.[55] Yet further research should examine the nature of the mystical practices and mystical experiences in the Taoist religion, which seem—at first glance—to have striking parallels with those in *Inward Training* and other sources of early Taoism examined in this book. Finally, further research is needed into how the theories presented herein affect the attempt to find possible historical connections between the early Taoist tradition identified here and the origins of the institutionalized Taoist religion at the end of the Han.

If this book prompts all or even some of this research to be undertaken, then it may result in our finally gaining a more complete picture of the origins and development of a unified Taoist tradition encompassing both its early and later forms, and this experiment in "textual archaeology" will have been worthwhile. Regardless of whether this takes place, the past quarter century of research and debate about the origins of Taoism ensures that we can never again see Taoist philosophy in the same way. In this new era of understanding of the origins of Taoism, the pivotal role of this beautiful and simple collection of Taoist poetic verse entitled *Inward Training* must now be acknowledged.

NOTES

INTRODUCTION

1. Ma-wang-tui is a small village near the major south-central Chinese city of Ch'ang-sha, capital of Hunan province. In 1973 a major cache of texts was found there in a tomb dated to 168 B.C., among which were two manuscripts of the *Lao Tzu*, also known as the *Tao Te ching* (The Way and Its Inner Power). For a summary of this find and the first translation of the *Lao Tzu* manuscripts found there, see Robert Henricks, *Lao Tzu Te Tao Ching* (New York: Ballantine Books, 1989). Lao Tzu literally means "Master Lao." The term *tzu* (master, 子) was an honorific title given to certain major teachers whose ideas were presumably compiled into texts that now bear their honorific names such as *Chuang Tzu, Han-fei Tzu, Hsün Tzu,* and *Huai-nan Tzu*. However, in spite of their titles, many of these early texts were composite works containing the ideas of not just their namesakes but other authors who were in some way associated with them. Even though the *Lao Tzu* is attributed to one man, it is likely an apochryphal collection of poetic verses compiled within an early Taoist master-disciple lineage.

2. For English studies, see R. P. Peerenboom, *Law and Morality in Ancient China: The Silk Manuscripts of Huang-Lao* (Albany: State University of New York Press, 1992); and Edmund Ryden, *The Yellow Emperor's Four Canons* (Taipei: Ricci Institute, 1997). For new critical editions, see Ch'en Ku-ying [陳鼓應], *Huang-ti ssu-ching chin-chu chin-i* [黃帝四經今註今譯] (Taipei: Taiwan Commercial Press, 1995); and Ryden, *Yellow Emperor*, pp. 273–430 (which also contains an

invaluable concordance, pp. 431–79). For a complete English translation, see Robin D. S. Yates, *Five Lost Classics: Tao, Huang-Lao, and Yin-yang in Han China* (New York: Ballantine Books, 1997). Despite the considerable scholarly controversy generated by the debate over whether the four Ma-wang-tui Yellow Emperor manuscripts can, in the last analysis, be identified with the work by this title listed in the *Han-shu i-wen chih*, I follow Ch'en and Ryden in choosing this as a "title of convenience" until conclusive proof is established one way or the other. For summaries of this controversy about the proper title, see Peerenboom, *Law and Morality*, pp. 7–9; and Ryden, *Yellow Emperor*, pp. 1–3.

3. For a translation and analysis of these texts, see Donald Harper, *Early Chinese Medical Literature: The Mawangdui Medical Manuscripts* (London: Kegan Paul International, 1998). I thank Professor Harper for sending me copies of the page proofs of this book.

4. For a new translation of the *Lü-shih ch'un-ch'iu*, see John Knoblock and Jeffrey Riegel, *The Almanac of Lü Buwei* (Stanford: Stanford University Press, in press); for new translations of chapters of the *Huai-nan Tzu*, see John S. Major, *Heaven and Earth in Early Han Thought: Chapters Three, Four, and Five of the Huainanzi* (Albany: State University of New York Press, 1993); for a new study of the *Ho-kuan Tzu*, see Carine Defoort, *The Pheasant Cap Master (He guan zi): A Rhetorical Reading* (Albany: State University of New York Press, 1997); for a new translation of the *Kuan Tzu*, see W. Allyn Rickett, *Guanzi: Political, Economic, and Philosophical Essays from Early China*, 2 vols. (Princeton: Princeton University Press, 1985 and 1998).

5. See, for example, such works as Wu Kuang [吳光], *Huang-Lao che-hsüeh t'ung-lun* [黃老哲學通論] (Hangchou: Chekiang People's Press, 1985); Yü Ming-kuang [余明光], *Huang-ti ssu-ching yü Huang-Lao ssu-hsiang* [黃帝四經 與黃老思想] (Harbin: Heilungchiang People's Press, 1989); Peerenboom, *Law and Morality*; Ryden, *Yellow Emperor*.

6. A. C. Graham, *Disputers of the Tao* (LaSalle, IL: Open Court Press, 1989), p. 100.

7. Harper, *Early Chinese Medical Literature*, pp. 6–7. The *Han-shu i-wen chih* (Taipei: Hua-lien, 1973) classifies this literature under the category of medical literature (*fang chi*, 方技) and the two subcategories of "Within the Bedchamber" (*fang-chung*, 方中) and "Numinous Transcendence" (*shen hsien*, 神仙).

8. Harper discusses this in his *Early Chinese Medical Literature* and in his article "The Bellows Analogy in *Laozi* V and Warring States Macrobiotic Hygiene," *Early China* 20 (1995): 381–92.

9. Rickett's excellent translation of the entire work has finally been completed. For a thorough discussion of origins and intellectual filiations of the

Kuan Tzu, see Rickett, Guanzi, 1: 3–47. This two-volume translation supercedes an earlier partial translation by the same author, Kuan Tzu: A Repository of Early Chinese Thought (Hong Kong: Hong Kong University Press, 1965).

10. Michael LaFargue has attempted a similar project with the Tao Te ching and has provided a detailed discussion of the underlying philosophy of historical hermeneutics with which I am in general agreement. While it has become fashionable in scholarly circles to say that the interpretation is the meaning, I believe it is still possible to retrieve the original meaning of a text through a careful study of its ideas, their manner of presentation, and the historical context in which it was written. That is what I am attempting to do in this book. For LaFargue's excellent discussion of historical hermeneutics, see Michael LaFargue, Tao and Method: A Reasoned Approach to the Tao Te Ching (Albany: State University of New York Press, 1994), pp. 5–21.

11. A. C. Graham, The Book of Lieh-tzu: A Classic of the Way, 2d ed. (New York: Columbia University Press, 1990), p. xi.

12. An excellent example of this now-superceded position is the famous article of H. G. Creel, "What Is Taoism?" Journal of the American Oriental Society 76 (1956): 139–52, reprinted in H. G. Creel, What Is Taoism? and Other Studies in Chinese Cultural History (Chicago: University of Chicago Press, 1970), pp. 1–24.

13. The Lao Tzu parallels found there will be analyzed below. See Ching-men shih po-wu kuan [荆門市博物館], Kuo-tien Ch'u mu chu-chien [郭店楚墓竹簡] (Peking: Wen-wu, 1998). For an early report on the Lao Tzu parallels, see P'eng Hao [彭浩], "Lun Kuo-tien Ch'u chien chung de Lao-hsüeh chu-tso" [論郭店楚簡中的老學著作], manuscript of an article submitted to Wen-wu, 1996.

14. Graham conclusively proved this about the Lieh Tzu in his 1961 article recently reprinted as "The Date and Composition of Lieh Tzu," in Studies in Chinese Philosophy and Philosophical Literature (Albany: State University of New York Press, 1990), pp. 216–82. The situation with the Wen Tzu is more complex. For the past century, it has been suspected by many East Asian scholars to be a fourth-century forgery. However, a manuscript of the Wen Tzu was recently discovered at the excavation of a tomb in Ting-hsien, along with what is believed to be the long-lost Ch'i version of the Confucian Analects. This called into question the issue of the forgery of the received recension of the Wen Tzu. However, when the text of this manuscript was finally published, only about 15 percent of it corresponded to material in the received Wen Tzu. See Ho-pei-sheng wen-wu yen-chiu-so Ting-chou Han-chien cheng-li hsiao-tsu [河北省文物研究所定洲漢簡整理小組], "Ting-chou hsi-Han Chung-shan Huai-Wang-mu chu-chien Wen Tzu chiao-kan chi" [定洲西漢中山懷王墓竹簡文子校勘記], Wen Wu [文物] 12

(1995): 35–38. Thus the theory that the *Wen Tzu* is a fourth-century forgery based on some authentic material remains a distinct possibility.

15. For this theory, see A. C. Graham, "How Much of *Chuang Tzu* Did Chuang Tzu Write?" in *Studies in Chinese Philosophy and Philosophical Literature* (Albany: State University of New York Press, 1990), pp. 283–321; and Harold Roth, "Who Compiled the *Chuang Tzu?*" in Henry Rosemont, Jr., ed., *Chinese Texts and Philosophical Contexts: Essays Dedicated to Angus C. Graham* (LaSalle, IL: Open Court, 1991), pp. 79–128.

16. For excellent summaries of scholarly opinion about the intellectual filiation of these texts, see Peerenboom, *Law and Morality,* pp. 1–12, and Ryden, *Yellow Emperor*, pp. 1–13, 262–72.

17. For a detailed discussion of these categories of ideas derived from early Taoist texts, see Harold D. Roth, "Psychology and Self-Cultivation in Early Taoistic Thought," *Harvard Journal of Asiatic Studies* 51.2 (1991): 599–650; and Roth, "Who Compiled the *Chuang Tzu?*" pp. 84–114, which focuses on applying these categories to the Syncretist author in the *Chuang Tzu*.

18. Benjamin Schwartz, *The World of Thought in Ancient China* (Cambridge: Belknap Press of Harvard University Press, 1985), p. 193. In his chapter on Taoism, Schwartz provides a superb analysis of the mystical dimensions of early Taoist thought.

19. Ibid., pp. 205–25; A. C. Graham, *Chuang Tzu: The Seven Inner Chapters and Other Writings from the Chuang Tzu* (London: George Allen and Unwin, 1981), pp. 197–99; and idem, *Disputers of the Tao*, pp. 306–11.

20. For Graham's ideas on the Syncretist stratum in the *Chuang Tzu*, see his *Disputers of the Tao*, pp. 171–73; and *Chuang Tzu: The Seven Inner Chapters*, pp. 257–58. The fullest presentation of his ideas on the strata in the *Chuang Tzu* is found in his "How Much of *Chuang Tzu* Did Chuang Tzu Write?" in his *Studies in Chinese Philosophy*, pp. 283–321.

21. See, for example, Schwartz, *The World of Thought,* pp. 237 ff. For a fuller argument about the Syncretist phase as the source for Ssu-ma T'an's presentation of "Tao-chia," see Roth, "Psychology and Self-Cultivation," especially pp. 604–8.

1. THE TEXT OF *Inward Training*

1. Axel Schuessler, *A Dictionary of Early Zhou Chinese* (Honolulu: University of Hawaii Press, 1987), p. 724.

2. Jeffrey Riegel, "The Four 'Tzu Ssu' Chapters of the *Li Chi*" (Ph.D. diss., Stanford University, 1978), p. 143; Rickett, *Guanzi*, 2:15.

3. Chao Shou-cheng, *Kuan Tzu t'ung-chieh* [管子通解], 2 vols. (Peking:

Peking Institute for Studies in Economics, 1989), 2:121 (hereafter cited as Chao, *KTTC*).

4. Riegel, "The Four 'Tzu Ssu' Chapters," pp. 143–69. In an appendix to this work, Riegel presents a critical text of *Inward Training* based on the manuscript of Gustav Haloun, given to him by Denis Twitchett. This critical text is divided into eighteen verses, of which four are further subdivided, thus yielding twenty-two. However, the twenty-two verses of this critical text differ somewhat from my own arrangement. Hereafter references to the critical text of Riegel based upon Haloun's work are cited as "Riegel/Haloun."

5. Rickett, *Guanzi*, 2:39–55, divides the text into fifteen sections. Within these he finds an additional eighteen subsections, thus totaling thirty-three distinct verses. His divisions are based on the arrangement found in Ma Fei-pai (also known as Ma Yüan-tsai [馬元材]), "*Kuan Tzu Nei-yeh* p'ien chi-chu" [管子內業篇集注], Kuan Tzu hsüeh-k'an [管子學刊] 1 (1990): 6–13; 2 (1990): 14–21; 3 (1990): 12–21 (hereafter cited as Ma, *KTNY*). Chao Shou-cheng (*Kuan Tzu t'ung-chieh*) divides the text into seventeen sections.

6. Riegel, "The Four Tzu Ssu Chapters," p. 148.

7. LaFargue, *Tao and Method*, pp. 180–99.

8. Henricks, *Lao Tzu*, pp. xvii–xviii. The Ma-wang-tui manuscripts of the *Lao Tzu* are still the oldest complete versions of this work since the Kuo-tien *Lao Tzu* material is far from complete.

9. Harold D. Roth, *The Textual History of the Huai-nan Tzu* (Ann Arbor: Association for Asian Studies, Monograph no. 46, 1992), p. 40.

10. William H. Baxter, "Situating the Language of the *Lao Tzu*: The Probable Date of the *Tao Te Ching*," in Michael LaFargue and Livia Kohn, eds., *Lao-Tzu and the Tao-Te-Ching* (Albany: State University of New York Press, 1998), pp. 231–53. I thank Professors Kohn and LaFargue for calling my attention to this article.

11. Baxter, "Situating the Language of *Lao Tzu*," pp. 240–43.

12. Ibid., pp. 243–49.

13. Ibid., pp. 234–40.

14. Ibid., p. 237.

15. Ibid., p. 242.

16. Ibid., p. 249.

17. Rickett, *Guanzi*, 2:24–27. Rickett defines "irregular rhymes" as those that do not fit the the twenty or so rhyme categories that Chinese and Western scholars have derived from the *Shih ching* (pp. 6–7). They are often found in fourth- to first-century B.C. texts that are thought to come from the area of the old state of Ch'u. These texts are a group often categorized as "Taoist" and include, in addition, the *Huang-ti ssu-ching*, *Chuang Tzu*, and *Huai-nan Tzu*.

18. LaFargue, *Tao and Method*, especially pp. 301–36.

19. For a more succinct statement of his methodology and results, see Michael LaFargue, *The Tao of the Tao Te Ching* (Albany: State University of New York Press, 1992), especially pp. 196–214.

20. Eighty-six chapter titles have survived, but ten of these chapters, mostly those at the ends of silk scrolls (*chüan*), have been lost. See Rickett, *Guanzi*, 1:4, 15. The introduction to this work by Rickett contains an excellent summary of the textual history of the *Kuan Tzu*, as does a later article by Rickett, "*Kuan Tzu*," in Michael Loewe, ed., *Early Chinese Texts: A Bibliographical Guide* (Berkeley: Institute for East Asian Studies and Society for the Study of Early China, Early China Special Monograph Series no. 2, 1993), pp. 244–51.

21. The only exception to this appears to be the "Light and Heavy" chapters (*p'ien* 80–86), which taken together seem to constitute one whole and distinct text devoted to monetary policy within the *Kuan Tzu* collection.

22. Hu Chia-ts'ung, *Kuan Tzu hsin-t'an* [管子新探] (Peking: Chinese Academy of Social Sciences, 1995).

23. Kanaya Osamu, *Kanshi no kenkyū* [管子の研究] (Tokyo: Iwanami Shoten, 1987). For a brilliant discussion of this problem, see especially the final chapter on the position of *Kuan Tzu* in the history of Chinese thought, pp. 301–60. For a very brief summary of his analysis, see Kanaya Osamu, "Taoist Thought in the *Kuan Tzu*," in Koichi Shinohara and Gregory Schopen, eds., *From Benares to Beijing: Essays on Buddhism and Chinese Religion in Honor of Professor Jan Yün-hua* (Oakville, ON: Mosaic Press, 1991), pp. 35–40.

24. Graham, *Disputers of the Tao*, pp. 2–3.

25. One exception to this lack of appreciation of the importance of techniques within early Chinese intellectual lineages is the insightful and controversial book by Robert Eno, *The Confucian Creation of Heaven: Philosophy and the Defense of Ritual Mastery* (Albany: State University of New York Press, 1990).

26. My summary of the Chi-hsia Academy is taken from the following sources: Ch'ien Mu [錢穆], *Hsien-Ch'in chu-tzu hsi-nien* [先秦諸子繫年], 2 vols. (1st ed., 1935; rev. ed., 1956; repr., Peking: Chung-hua, 1985), pp. 231–35, 540–74; Fung Yu-lan [馮友蘭], *Chung-kuo che-hsüeh shih hsin-pien* [中國哲學史新編], 6 vols. (1964; rev. ed., People's Press, 1983), 2:197–98; Fung's earlier work, *A History of Chinese Philosophy*, trans. Derk Bodde (Princeton: Princeton University Press, 1937/1952), pp. 132–33; and Rickett, *Guanzi*, 1:14–19.

27. *Shih chi* [史記] (Peking: Chung-hua, 1959), *chüan* 46 ("The Hereditary House of the T'ien Ruling Family of Ch'i"), p. 1895 (henceforth cited in the form 46:1895), and 74 ("Biography of Mencius and Hsün Tzu"):2346–47.

28. *Shih chi*, 46:1895. All dates are from Ch'ien Mu, *Hsien-Ch'in chu-tzu hsi-nien*, pp. 618–19, and represent his approximations.

29. See Harper, *Early Chinese Medical Literature,* pp. 22–35, for an overview of the Ma-wang-tui medical corpus and other related excavated texts that are all representative of what he calls the "*fang*-literature" of this time. For a fuller overview of these techniques based on later sources, see Kenneth J. DeWoskin, *Doctors, Diviners, and Magicians of Ancient China: Biographies of Fang-shih* (New York: Columbia University Press, 1983), pp. 23–25.

30. Harper, *Early Chinese Medical Literature*, p. 42.

31. *Shih chi*, 28:1368–79. See Harper, *Early Chinese Medical Literature*, pp. 50–52, for an astute discussion of the *Shih chi* as a "hostile witness" to this group.

32. See, for example, Rickett, *Guanzi,* 1:15, and Kanaya, *Kanshi no kenkyū,* p. 328.

33. Rickett, *Guanzi,* 1:14–16; and "*Kuan Tzu,*" pp. 245–49.

34. Kanaya, *Kanshi no kenkyū*, pp. 328–29.

35. "The Purified Mind" is a mostly prose essay on applying the techniques of inner cultivation to the government of the sage. It follows the general orientation of *Techniques of the Mind* I and II toward the Syncretist Taoist synthesis of the best ideas of earlier schools within a Taoist cosmological and self-cultivation framework. Kanaya Osamu has recognized that, while the three other texts are extremely close in technical vocabulary, metaphors, and explicit textual parallels, "The Purified Mind" differs from them to such an extent that he would not consider them together in the absence of a long-standing scholarly tradition of doing so. See Kanaya, *Kanshi no kenkyū*, p. 265. I concur with his assessment. Most scholars conclude that it is also the latest work in the group. For these reasons, despite being an important source for early Syncretic Taoism, it has little to add to the question of determining the dating and authorship of *Inward Training*.

36. Roth, "Who Compiled the *Chuang Tzu?*" pp. 91–92, 96–98. The use of *Inward Training*'s distinctive metaphor for this program, "sweeping out the lodging place so the numinous mind will enter" is concrete evidence of its debt to this text and to the group of practitioners who transmitted it. For this metaphor see *Inward Training*, verse XIII, and *Techniques of the Mind* I, *Ssu-pu tsung-kan* (四部叢刊) ed., 13/1a11, 2b8 and 1b8, 3b8 (*chüan* 13, p. 1a [recto], col. 11). All textual references to the *Kuan Tzu* are to this edition.

37. Kuo Mo-jo [郭沫若], "Sung Hsing Yin Wen i-chu k'ao" [宋鈃尹文遺著考], in Kuo, ed., *Ch'ing-t'ung shih-dai* [青銅時代] (Shanghai: Hsin-wen, 1951), pp. 245–71. The intellectual filiations of these philosophers are the subject of controversy, since many sources label them as Mohists. Sung Hsing's writings

are lost, and the work that passes as Yin Wen's is generally regarded as a late Han forgery. Their ideas are now known mostly through criticisms of them in the writings of others, where they are most often listed as Mohists. In the *Han-fei Tzu* and *Hsün Tzu*, Sung is listed as a Mohist and criticized for his pacifistic doctrines and his failure to understand human psychology. However, the early sources are not uniform. While ignored in the *Records of the Grand Historian*, Sung is said by Pan Ku (班 古) to have been a Huang-Lao thinker in the *Han-shu*, and Yin is therein listed as a Terminologist (*ming chia*, 名 家). A comprehensive analysis of the ideas and intellectual filiations of Sung Hsing and Yin Wen is found in Ch'ien Mu, *Hsien-Ch'in chu-tzu hsi-nien*, pp. 374–80. For an excellent English summary of the philosophical positions attributed to Sung and Yin, see Fung Yu-lan, *A History of Chinese Philosophy*, pp. 148–53. *Han-fei Tzu*, chap. 50, criticizes Sung for his opposition to warfare and his teaching that "to be insulted is not a disgrace." Hsün Tzu criticizes him in several places for some of his doctrines. In chap. 18, "Cheng-lun" (Rectifying Theses), he argues against the latter thesis saying that, while being insulted may not be a disgrace, it is still human nature to dislike being insulted. See John Knoblock, *Xunzi: A Translation and Study of the Complete Works*, 3 vols. (Stanford: Stanford University Press, 1988–94), 3:45.

38. Kuo Mo-jo, "Sung Hsing Yin Wen i-chu k'ao," pp. 251–55.

39. Machida Saburo [町 田 三 郎], *Kin Kan shisho shi no kenkyū* [秦漢思想 史 の 研 究] (Tokyo: Sōbunsha, 1985), pp. 361–80; Kanaya, *Kanshi no kenkyū*, pp. 347–51; Fung Yu-lan, *Chung-kuo che-hsüeh shih hsin-pien*, 2:198–99; Hu Chia-tsung, *Kuan Tzu hsin-t'an*, pp. 92–97; Rickett, *Guanzi*, 2:49–58. Machida is reluctant to use the term "Huang-Lao" because it is a later appellation from the Han dynasty. He prefers the more neutral label of the Chi-hsia Taoist-Legalist school, as does Kanaya. Fung and Hu identify them as products of Huang-Lao thinkers who gave a materialist interpretation to the idealistic theories of Lao Tzu and Chuang Tzu. Fung Yu-lan, *Chung-kuo che-hsüeh shih hsin-pien*, 2:198–99; Hu Chia-tsung, *Kuan Tzu hsin-t'an*, pp. 92–97.

40. Rickett, *Guanzi*, 2:24–27, 56–58, 69–70.

41. Ch'iu sees them as a synthesis of Taoist and Legalist ideas that he prefers not to call "Huang-Lao" because it is a Han dynasty appellation. Ch'iu Hsi-kuei, "Ma-wang-tui *Lao Tzu* chia i pen chüan-ch'ien-hou i-shu yü 'Tao-Fa chia'" [馬 王 堆老子甲乙本卷前后佚書與道法家], *Chung-kuo che-hsüeh* 2 (1980): 68–84. Ch'iu concentrates his arguments on only two of our four texts, *Techniques of the Mind* I and "The Purified Mind," and says nothing about the other two.

42. Kanaya, *Kanshi no kenkyū*, pp. 348–49.

43. To be more precise, Kanaya argues that *Inward Training* was derived from an earlier version of *Techniques of the Mind* II now lost (thus accounting for the

parallels between the two works) and from *Techniques of the Mind* I. The latter dates from about 320 B.C.; and the former from about 265. Kanaya, *Kanshi no kenkyū*, pp. 263–65 and 334–46.

44. Li Ts'un-shan, "*Nei-yeh* teng ssu-p'ien de hsieh-tso shih-chien ho tso-che" [內業等四篇的寫作時間和作者], *Kuan Tzu hsüeh-k'an* 1 (1987): 31–37.

45. Harold D. Roth, "Redaction Criticism and the Early History of Taoism," *Early China* 19 (1994): 1–46, especially pp. 14–16. Some linguistic features indicate an early date for *Inward Training*: 1. Its exclusive use of *ju* (如), the postverbal preposition *yü* (於) and the prohibitive *wu⁴* (勿) mark it as a fourth—century B.C. work, along with the *Tso chuan* and *Mencius*. 2. Its failure to confuse the prohibitive *wu³* (毋) and the verb *wu³* (無) is also an indicator of its antiquity. According to Edwin Pulleyblank, these two characters originally represented two distinct morphemes that were already homophonous in late Chou times and were confused in many texts including the *Mencius*. (See Edwin G. Pulleyblank, *Outline of Classical Chinese Grammar* [Vancouver: University of British Columbia Press, 1995], p. 107); 3. The clear distinction among negative particles found in *Inward Training* is another indicator of its early date. As the Warring States period was drawing to a close, distinctions among negatives gradually came to blur.

46. Bernhard Karlgren states that about three-fourths of the *Lao Tzu* consists of rhymed verse. See his *The Poetical Parts in Lao-Tsï* (Goteborg: Elanders Boktryckeri Aktiebolag, 1932), p. 4.

47. For a discussion of the literary form of the *Lao Tzu* as evidence of its antiquity, see Victor Mair, *Tao Te Ching: The Classic Book of Integrity and the Way* (New York: Bantam, 1990), pp. 119–26. Bruce and Taeko Brooks provide an approximate date for the transition from an oral to a literate culture from evidence in the *Analects* and place this date in the mid-fourth century B.C. See E. Bruce Brooks and Taeko Brooks, *The Original Analects: Sayings of Confucius and His Successors* (New York: Columbia University Press, 1998), p. 256.

48. Ching-men shih po-wu kuan, *Kuo-tien Ch'u-mu chu-chien*; for photographs of the bamboo strips containing the *Lao Tzu* parallels, see pp. 1–14; for an edited transcription, see pp. 109–26.

49. The dating of the tomb is made from tomb artifacts and from the known date of a nearby tomb at Pao-shan whose date can be fixed at 316 B.C. from texts buried in it. In his early overview, Ts'ui Jen-i gave a wide range of 377 (the death date of Duke Mu of Lu, who appears in a heretofore unknown text included in the find) to 278 B.C. (when this area was conquered by Ch'in). See Ts'ui Jen-i [崔仁義], "Ching-men Ch'u-mu ch'u-t'u teh chu-chien *Lao Tzu* ch'u-t'an" [荊門楚墓出土的竹簡老子初探], *Ching-men she-hui k'o-hsüeh* [荊門社會

科學] 5 (1997): 31–35. However, most scholars now think that the 377 B.C. date cannot be justified by archaeological testimony. Bruce Brooks, in a posting to the Warring States Working Group electronic bulletin board dated May 29, 1998, has suggested the range 308–293 B.C. for the date the tomb was sealed. For an overview of the tomb and its contents, see Hu-pei sheng Ching-men shih po-wu kuan [湖北省荆門市博物館], "Ching-men Kuo-tien i-hao Ch'u-mu" [荆門郭店一號楚墓], Wen-wu 7 (1997): 35–48. On p. 47, the authors approximate the tomb's date as mid-fourth to early third century B.C.

50. For example, the following important political and military passages from the received Lao Tzu are not found in the Kuo-tien parallels: 36, 50, 58, 60, 61, 65, 67, 68, 69, 74, 76, 78, and 80. However, chaps. 30, 31, and 57, which deal with the military matters, are in the Kuo-tien corpus.

51. For this opinion, see Harold D. Roth, "Some Methodological Issues in the Study of the Kuo-tien Lao Tzu Parallels," in Sarah Allan and Robert Henricks, ed., Proceedings of the International Conference on the Guodian Laozi (forthcoming). Each of the three bundles may have had a different compiler. Because of stylistic similarities in the form of the characters between the first and second bundles, they might have had the same compiler although the length of their bamboo strips is different. The third bundle differs from the first two in the length of strips and in the form of characters and is clearly by a different hand. For details, see Ts'ui Jen-i, "Ching-men Ch'u-mu ch'u-t'u ti chu-chien Lao Tzu ch'u-t'an," p. 32.

52. Allyn Ricket proposes a somewhat different dating for these texts. While agreeing on a fourth-century date for Inward Training, he proposes that Techniques of the Mind II was written c. 140 B.C. at the court of Liu An at Huai-nan. It was at that time the much older verses in the first part of Techniques of the Mind I were gathered together and the second, commentarial part was written. Rickett, Guanzi, 2:70.

53. William Baxter suggests that research on Old Chinese pronunciation in general, which was based on the pioneering efforts of Ch'ing philologists (and based upon the rhymes of the Shih ching), must be updated as modern scholars continue to refine the understanding of the pronunciation of Old Chinese. He advises caution when basing work on the rhyme categories constructed by Ch'ing scholars, for not all are accurate (Baxter, "Situating the Language of the Lao Tzu," pp. 244–49). Scholars who identify a Ch'u dialect often include rhymes that do not conform to the categories of these Ch'ing scholars. However, if these very categories themselves need refinement, so too does the notion of "irregular rhymes."

54. His related assertion that the other companion texts to Inward Training were entered into the Kuan Tzu collection by Liu Hsiang from the Huai-nan

library's surviving holdings might also be doubtful. See Rickett, *Guanzi*, 2:57–58, 70. In addition to these doubts about independent Ch'u authorship of these texts, there is no apparent reason why Liu Hsiang would have added them to the Ch'i *Kuan Tzu* collection if he had found them from a Ch'u source.

55. This point has been made by many scholars, including, Machida, *Kin Kan shisho shi no kenkyū*, pp. 358–61; Kanaya, *Kanshi no kenkyū*, pp. 259–61; Hu, *Kuan Tzu hsin-t'an*, pp. 299–300; and Rickett, *Guanzi*, 2:32–35. A recent but unconvincing attempt to revive Kuo's theory is Li Hsüeh-ch'in [李學勤], "Kuan Tzu Hsin-shu teng p'ien te tsai k'ao-ch'a" [管子心術等篇的再考察], *Kuan Tzu hsüeh-k'an* [管子學刊] 1 (1991): 12–16. Herein Li argues that Sung and Yin were not Mohists, as most early sources indicate, but, rather, Huang-Lao thinkers who influenced the later Mohists.

56. Kuo Mo-jo, "Sung Hsing Yin Wen i-chu k'ao," pp. 265–68.

57. Graham, "How Much of *Chuang Tzu* Did Chuang Tzu Write?" p. 317. The phrase is found in *Chuang Tzu yin-te* (Peking: Harvard-Yenching Institute Sinological Index Series no. 20, 1947), p. 92, chap. 33, l. 34 (hereafter cited in the style 92/33/34, the standard method of citations in this series; only the last two numbers are cited below). For a translation, see Graham, *Chuang Tzu: The Seven Inner Chapters*, p. 278.

58. The superb critical edition of fragments from the writings of Shen Tao established by Paul Thompson have almost no passages from Shen with mystical content. Instead his ideas seem focussed almost exclusively on various aspects of political thought. See Paul Mulligan Thompson, *The Shen Tzu Fragments* (Oxford: Oxford University Press, 1979).

59. Kanaya, *Kanshi no kenkyū*, pp. 348–49.

60. For the *Chuang Tzu* summary of the ideas of Shen Tao and T'ien P'ien, see *Chuang Tzu yin-te*, 33/41–54; and Graham, *Chuang Tzu: The Seven Inner Chapters*, pp. 279–81. For further details, see Fung Yu-lan, *A History of Chinese Philosophy*, 1:155.

61. Kanaya, *Kanshi no kenkyū*, p. 349.

62. D. C. Lau and Chen Fong Ching, eds., *A Concordance to the Lüshi chunqiu* (Hong Kong: Commercial Press, Institute of Chinese Studies Ancient Chinese Texts Concordance Series, Philosophical Works no. 12, 1994), chap. 17, essay 8, ll. 23–26, p. 107 (hereafter cited in the style 17.8/23–26/107).

63. His comments contain several technical terms I associate with Syncretic Taoism: adaptation to the underlying patterns and innate natures of things (*yin*) and assigning tasks to people that are suitable (*i*) to their innate talents and abilities. For details, see Roth, "Who Compiled the *Chuang Tzu*?" pp. 106–8. That the author of this essay might have been a lineal descendant of T'ien is

possible because of the inner cultivation concepts embedded in the essay and because he refers to T'ien by his personal name of P'ien.

64. For a list of these central concepts of Syncretist Taoism, see Roth, "Who Compiled the *Chuang Tzu?*" pp. 106–8.

65. Dates are from Ch'ien Mu, *Hsien-Ch'in chu-tzu hsi-nien*, p. 618.

66. *Han-shu i-wen chih*, p. 22.

67. Bernhard Karlgren, *The Authenticity and Nature of the Tso Chuan* (Goteborg: Elanders Boktryckeri Aktiebolag, 1926), pp. 35–38 and 63–64. The only other occurrence of *jo* in this sense is found in verse XX: 10–11, where it appears to be a later interpolation.

68. The only other mention of Confucian concepts in the entire text occurs in verse XI and is widely recognized as a gloss that destroys the rhyme and meter. For details, see chapter 2, n. 59.

69. The concept of innate nature is completely absent from the Inner Chapters of the *Chuang Tzu* and from the *Lao Tzu*. Its first occurrence in Taoist sources is in the roughly contemporaneous "Primitivist" chapters of the *Chuang Tzu* (8-11/28) and the Taoist essays in chaps. 3, 5, 17, and 25 of the *Lü-shih ch'un-ch'iu*. For an insightful analysis of these four chapters, see Andrew S. Meyer, "Late Warring States Daoism and the Origins of Huang-Lao: Evidence from the *Lüshi chunqiu*" (unpublished manuscript, 1996). Since in both sources the majority of ocurrences of *hsing* are in the phrase *hsing-ming chih-ch'ing* (the essentials of our nature and destiny)—a phrase that also occurs in the Yangist chapters of the *Lü-shih ch'un-ch'iu*—the occurrences of this concept in both sources could be related not just to each other but to these Yangist essays and to the debates that may have occurred at the Ch'in court under the patronage of Lü Pu-wei.

70. See, for example, the eleventh essay, "Ch'i-su" (齊俗) and its translation in Benjamin Wallacker, *The Huai-nan Tzu, Book Eleven: Behavior, Culture, and Cosmos* (New Haven: American Oriental Society, 1962). For an analysis of the concept of *hsing* in the *Huai-nan Tzu*, see Harold D. Roth, "The Concept of Human Nature in the *Huai-nan Tzu*," *Journal of Chinese Philosophy* 12 (1985): 1–22.

71. Roth, "Who Compiled the *Chuang Tzu?*" pp. 102–3.

72. Riegel, "The Four Tzu Ssu Chapters," pp. 107, 143–44.

73. P'ang P'u [龐樸], *Po-shu wu-hsing p'ien yen-chiu* [帛書五行篇研究] (N.p: Ch'i-Lu shu-she, 1980).

74. Ching-men shih po-wu kuan, *Kuo-tien Ch'u-mu chu-chien*, pp. 147–54. The translation of *wu-hsing* as "five conducts" is taken from Sarah A. Queen, "A Translation of the Jingmen Guodian Five Conducts Manuscript" (paper presented at the International Conference on the Guodian *Laozi*, Dartmouth College, May 1998).

75. For an interesting initial assessment of the moral thought in this essay, see Mark Csikszentmihalyi, "Fivefold Virtue: Reformulating Mencian Moral Psychology in Han Dynasty China," *Religion* 28 (1998): 77–89.

76. Wang Hsien-ch'ien [王先謙], *Hsün Tzu chi-chieh* [荀子集解], *Hsin-pien Chu-tzu chi-ch'eng* [新編諸子集成] ed., 2 vols. (1891; repr. Peking: Chung-hua, 1988), 1:26–7. Translation from Knoblock, *Xunzi,* 1:154.

2. A Critical Edition and Translation of *Inward Training*

1. See, for example, Harold D. Roth, "Text and Edition in Early Chinese Philosophical Literature," *Journal of the American Oriental Society* 113.2 (1993): 214–27.

2. Gustav Haloun, "Legalist Fragments: Part I: *Kuan-tsï* 55 and Related Texts," *Asia Major,* n.s. 2.1 (April 1951): 85–120; Piet van der Loon, "On the Transmission of the *Kuan-Tzu,*" *T'oung Pao* 41.1–3 (1952): 357–91.

3. Kuo Mo-jo [郭沫若], Hsü Wei-yü [許維遹], Wen I-to [聞一多], *Kuan Tzu chi-chiao* [官子集校] (Peking: Chung-hua shu chü, 1955) (hereafter cited as Kuo/Hsü/Wen, *KTCC*); Kanaya Osamu, *Kanshi no kenkyū,* pp. 23–47.

4. Rickett, *Guanzi,* 1:31–40; and *"Kuan Tzu,"* pp. 244–51.

5. Roth, "Text and Edition," p. 216.

6. Filiation analysis is a method I developed in which we identify all extant editions of a text, determine their publication dates, direct ancestors and descendants, and then organize them into lineages headed by an "ancestral redaction." These ancestral redactions are what then needs to be consulted in order to establish a critical text based on the minimum number of editions that contain the maximum number of possibly authentic textual variants. For details, see Harold D. Roth, "Filiation Analysis and the Textual History of the *Huai-nan Tzu,*" *Transactions of the International Conference of Orientalists in Japan* 28 (1982): 60–81; and idem, *The Textual History of the Huai-nan Tzu,* pt. II.

7. Kuo/Hsü/Wen, *KTCC,* pp. 2 and 13.

8. For details on this *Huai-nan Tzu* edition and its provenance, see Roth, *The Textual History of the Huai-nan Tzu,* pp. 125–42, especially pp. 132–37, for this question. For a fascinating examination of how we owe the very existence of this *Ssu-pu ts'ung-k'an Huai-nan Tzu* edition to irresponsible book borrowing, see Harold D. Roth, "The Strange Case of the Overdue Book: A Study in the Fortuity of Textual Transmission," in Shinohara and Schopen, eds., *From Benares to Beijing,* pp. 161–86.

9. Kuo/Hsü/Wen, *KTCC,* pp. 2–4 and 13–14.

10. Kanaya, *Kanshi no kenkyū,* pp. 28–32; Roth, *The Textual History of the Huai-nan Tzu,* p. 165.

11. Kuo/Hsü/Wen, *KTCC*, pp. 4 and 14–15.

12. For Chu's *Huai-nan Tzu* edition, its characteristics and the circumstances of its creation that are the same as those for his *Kuan Tzu* edition, see Roth, *The Textual History of the Huai-nan Tzu*, pp. 203–24.

13. Kuo/Hsü/Wen, *KTCC*, pp. 4 and 14.

14. On the renowned An-cheng T'ang publishing house and its edition of the *Huai-nan Tzu*, see Roth, *The Textual History of the Huai-nan Tzu*, pp. 154–55.

15. Kuo/Hsü/Wen, *KTCC*, pp. 5–6, 15.

16. These textual variations are found in Kuo/Hsü/Wen, *KTCC*, pp. 784–86, 788, 790–91, 793, 795.

17. Based on this small sample from the *Kuan Tzu*, if I had to recommend a text-critical procedure for those with access to only a small Chinese library, I would say that the *redactio* stage could be accomplished by simply collating the *Ssu-pu ts'ung-k'an* facsmile of the Yang Chen redaction and the *Ssu-pu pei-yao* edition of the Chao Yung-hsien redaction.

18. I follow Allyn Rickett's lead (*Guanzi*, 2:7) in using Chou. See Chou Fa-kao [周法高], *Han-tz'u ku chin yin-hui* [漢字古今音彙] (Hong Kong: Chinese University of Hong Kong Press, 1973).

19. Ma, *KTNY*, 1:9, n. 1; Chao, *KTTC*, p. 123, n. 1.

20. Willard Peterson, "Making Connections: 'Commentary on the Attached Verbalizations' of the *Book Of Change*," *Harvard Journal of Asiatic Studies* 42.1 (1982): 67–122.

21. D. C. Lau and Chen Fong Ching, eds., *A Concordance to the Zhouyi* (Hong Kong: Commercial Press, Institute of Chinese Studies Ancient Chinese Texts Concordance Series, Classical Works no. 8, 1995), sec. 65, p. 78, l. 1.

22. W. K. Liao, trans., *The Complete Works of Han Fei Tzu*, 2 vols. (London: Probsthain, 1939 and 1959).

23. For Graham's defense of his translation of *shen* as "daemonic," see Graham, *Chuang Tzu: The Seven Inner Chapters*, p. 35 n. 72.

24. To examine the extraordinary detail of the observations of the heavens made by the early Chinese, one need only look to John Major's meticulously annotated translation of this *Huai-nan Tzu* essay in Major, *Heaven and Earth*, pp. 55–139. Many Western scholars have translated the term *t'ien* as "Heaven," which is misleading because of Western religious connotations. "*T'ien*" is not a paradise where souls go after they die, nor is it the home of a singular, anthropomorphic, all-powerful God. While it may have originally represented some kind of deity to the early Chou and may have retained an aura of the divine—or numinous—to early Taoist thinkers, *t'ien* is not a deity or divine realm to them. The translation as "heaven," which others prefer, is an improvement but still retains some of

these connotations, so I have experimented with a more naturalistic translation, "the heavens."

25. Haloun (Riegel/Haloun, p. 159) deletes line 2, which he thinks entered from the Yin commentary, but to do this disrupts the parallel structure of lines 1–4 and removes the rhyme between 生 (sreng) and 星 (seng). I have rejected the different suggestions by several scholars to emend the first character of line 2 as semantically unnecessary.

26. Haloun (Riegel/Haloun, p. 159) deletes these two characters in order to preserve the meter of the four-character line. Haloun is very systematic about preserving the meter throughout *Inward Training* and, while like him I favor this approach, I recognize that texts are frequently not this orderly and so recognize the tentativeness of such emendations.

27. "This vital energy" of lines 1 and 6 refers to the vital essence that is the subject of verse I. The vital essence is a concentrated and ethereal form of the vital energy (*ch'i*) and is so defined in verse VIII.

28. Lines 6–14 recall Mencius's admonition in 2A:2 to not follow the man of Sung in trying to subject the vital breath to excessive conscious control. In this verse the vital essence is secured through developing the "inner power" that comes from the mental concentration attained through breathing meditation.

29. Emendations by Ting (Kuo/Hsü/Wen, *KTCC*, p. 781) and Chao (Chao, *KTTC*, 2:121) of a similar-form corruption. This also preserves a semantic and syntactic parallel with line 6. "Similar-form corruptions" occur when a copyist writes an erroneous character that is similar in written form to the original character, which he cannot clearly discern.

30. This is a semantic emendation of homophonous characters suggested by Ting (Kuo/Hsü/Wen, *KTCC*, p. 781). By "semantic emendation" I mean one that better suits the meaning of a line, sentence, or phrase. Context is often a primary determinant of such an emendation as here, in line 4, where the problematic character means "gentle" and the preferred reading means "vast."

31. I follow Igai's emendation of *tsu* (卒) to *ts'u* (苹) and Kuo's of *chi* (己) to *ch'i* (屺) to preserve the meaning of the line and the parallel with line 4. (Kuo/Hsü/Wen, *KTCC*, pp. 781–82).

32. This is an emendation by Yasui and Wang Nien-sun of *yin* (音) to *i* (意), a variant in the late Ming edition of Chang Pang [張榜] (Kuo/Hsü/Wen, *KTCC*, p. 782). Wang argues that in early texts the two are often substituted for each other. This also occurs in verse XIII.

33. Wang Nien-sun emends *kuo* (果) to *pi* (畢) because of similar-form corruption (Kuo/Hsü/Wen, *KTCC*, p. 782).

34. Ma Fei-pai interprets the "forms of the mind" to refer to the various

exemplary mental states that are mentioned throughout the text: the excellent mind, the stable mind, and so forth (*KTNY* 1:8). Chao Shou-cheng thinks it refers to the physical structure of the heart/mind (*KTTC*, 2:122). I think, rather, that it refers to states of consciousness in general. For further information, see verse VIII and chapter 3.

35. Haloun thinks this list of four emotions is an erroneous contamination from verse XXII (Riegel/Haloun, p. 153). However, because the order of the emotions is different in that verse and "happiness" is replaced by "anxiety," I see no need to make this emendation.

36. Haloun's emendation of homophonous characters better suits the semantic context (ibid.).

37. An emendation of phonetic loan characters by Ting Shih-han (Kuo/Hsü/Wen, *KTCC*, p. 782).

38. Haloun deletes these two grammatical particles to preserve the meter (Riegel/Haloun, p. 154). A literal translation would be "The Way is that with which the physical form is infused."

39. Wang Nien-sun makes this emendation because of a similar-form corruption, not between these characters as they are now written, but between a rare alternate form of 寂 cited in the *Shuo-wen* and 謀 (Kuo/Hsü/Wen, *KTCC*, p. 783).

40. Chang Ping-lin (Kuo/Hsü/Wen, *KTCC*, p. 783), Ma (*KTNY*, 1:10), and Chao (*KTTC*, 2:124) all suggest the phonetic loan of *an* to *yen*. Chang defines this as 於是: "within this." Wang, T'ao, and Kuo emend *ai* to *ch'u*, suggesting it is a similar-form corruption (Kuo/Hsü/Wen, *KTCC*, pp. 783–84). The emendation restores the rhyme.

41. Ma Fei-pai makes this emendation here and in line 8 because he sees the error created by post-T'ang editors who thought that *min* had been changed to *jen* to observe a T'ang taboo (*KTNY*, 1:7, 10).

42. Kuo makes this emendation to restore the rhyme between 和 (gwa) and 離 (lia) (Kuo/Hsü/Wen, *KTCC*, p. 784). It looks like a similar-form corruption.

43. Haloun deletes *shih ku* to preserve the meter, but I think this connective conjunction should be retained (Riegel/Haloun, p. 155). Hsü Wei-yü (Kuo/Hsü/Wen, *KTCC*, p. 784) and Riegel (Riegel/Haloun, p. 155) double the character *ts'u* to preserve the meter and the parallel syntax with line 10. Here I read *ts'u* as *ts'ui* (萃, thick or dense grass; gathered), which recalls the gathering of the Way in the emptiness that is the fasting of the mind in the *Chuang Tzu* 4 (*Chuang-tzu yin te*, 4/28).

44. Ma Fei-pai's emendation here for consistency with verse III, line 3, makes better sense (*KTNY*, 1:11). It essentially consists in a shift in meaning from "minute, subtle" (眇) to "vast, boundless" (渺).

45. Kuo Mo-jo makes this emendation from all other editions of the *Kuan Tzu* that he consulted (Kuo/Hsü/Wen, *KTCC*, p. 784). Chang P'ei-lun and Hsü Wei-yü also make it.

46. This emendation by Chang P'ei-lun is a semantic emendation of a similar-form corruption (Kuo/Hsü/Wen, *KTCC*, p. 784). Ma concurs (*KTNY*, 1:11).

47. This semantic emendation of a similar-form corruption is made by many scholars, including Igai and Kuo (Kuo/Hsü/Wen, *KTCC*, pp. 784–85), Ma (*KTNY*, 1:11), and Chao (*KTTC*, 2:124).

48. To align the body means to sit squarely and firmly in one place and har-monize the flow of the vital energy within the body's five systems. This idea is also spoken of in verse XI and is analyzed in chapter 3.

49. I follow Chao Shou-cheng's interpretation of line 6 (*KTTC*, 2:124).

50. Hsü deletes 安 to preserve the parallel structure of the first three sen-tences (Kuo/Hsü/Wen, *KTCC*, p. 785). He thinks the error arose because of textual contamination from the Yin commentary.

51. Wang Nien-sun (Kuo/Hsü/Wen, *KTCC*, p. 785) makes this emendation to preserve rhyme: 材 (dzəɣ), 時 (djiəɣ) 謀 (mjwəɣ). He supports this with analogous passages from other essays in the *Kuan Tzu* and other early works. Riegel (Riegel/Haloun, 156), Ma (*KTNY* 1: 12), and Chao (*KTTC*, 2:124) all concur.

52. Hsü makes this emendation from the reading in the Yin commentary to preserve the parallel structure with the previous line (Kuo/Hsü/Wen, *KTCC*, pp. 785–86).

53. Riegel (Riegel/Haloun, p. 157) would emend *tao* to *t'ung* (通) because of similar-form corruption. While this is possible, I think that Chao Shou-cheng's emendation (*KTTC*, 2:125) better suits the semantic context here. His sugges-tion of *tao* (導) is the *tao* of the *tao-yin* (導引), the "guiding and pulling" exer-cises to circulate the vital breath that are referred to in both the *Chuang Tzu* 15 and *Huai-nan Tzu* 7 and in texts excavated from Ma-wang-tui and Chang-chia-shan. While I do not think that these physical exercises are being suggested here, I do think that the guiding of the vital breath while seated is what this line, and the entire verse is talking about.

54. "Holding fast to the One" (*chih-i*) and several variations on this phrase that have similar meaning are found in the *Lao Tzu*, chaps. 10, 14, 15, 22, 32, and 52. The One in all these passages is the Way.

55. Verse XIV clarifies that this "one word" is "Way." There it resides within the calm and well-ordered mind in a special place called "the mind within the mind."

56. Wang Nien-sun makes this ementation of a similar-form corruption,

restored based on semantic context: "This is what I mean (by 'When a well-ordered mind lies within.')" This is the understanding of the Yin commentary, which says, 治心之謂 (This is the meaning of a 'well-ordered mind') (Kuo/Hsü/Wen, *KTCC*, p. 786). However, given the Yin commentary, Igai Hikohiro suggests a different similar-form corruption, from the character *hsin* (心) (Endō Tetsuō, *Kanshi* [Tokyo: Meiji Shoin, 1989–93], 2:829). Whichever we choose, the meaning is the same.

57. This is the verse used by the compiler of *Techniques of the Mind* II to begin this latter text.

58. I follow Ma Fei-pai's interpretation of *yin* as "to gradually soak in" based on the definition in the *Shuo-wen* (*KTNY*, 1:10).

59. I consider this a gloss inserted into the text by an unknown commentator or possibly a conjectural reconstruction of a damaged original. Riegel follows Haloun in deleting this clause for disrupting the rhyme pattern (Riegel/Haloun, p. 158). Furthermore it represents an intrusion of Confucian concepts into a text that is, with one very suspicious exception, totally devoid of them. For the exception, see verse XXI. Also, the version of this passage in *Techniques of the Mind* II (13.4b6) omits this clause. Finally, the text makes perfect sense without it.

60. Riegel follows Haloun in emending 至 to 來 to preserve the rhyme (德 tək; 至 tjier; 來 ləy) and because the parallel line in *Techniques of the Mind* II 13.4b7 also contains 來 (Riegel/Haloun, p. 158).

61. I have translated *chao* (usually, "illumination") as "intuitively." It has this meaning in the *Chuang Tzu*, chapter 2, where it is contrasted with the normal dualistic knowing of the intellect that the author is criticizing. Our modern term "intuition" captures the sense of a nonrational, nonintentional, and spontaneous knowing that is an essential characteristic of the type of cognition associated with the *shen*.

62. Riegel makes this emendation of homophonous characters from the parallel line in *Techniques of the Mind* II (Riegel/Haloun, p. 159). Further evidence in support of it is that the phrase *shen ming* does not occur anywhere else in *Inward Training*, whereas the character *shen* by itself occurs often.

63. Wang Nien-sun (Kuo/Hsü/Wen, *KTCC*, p. 787), Haloun (Riegel/Haloun, p. 159), and Chao (*KTTC*, 2:126) delete the character, which is also absent from the Yin commentary.

64. The metaphor of cleaning out the lodging place is also found in *Techniques of the Mind* I (13.2b2).

65. For this meaning of *t'u*, see the quotation from the *Chan-kuo ts'e* found in the *Han-yü ta tz'u-tien* [漢語大詞典] (Peking: Han-yu ta tz'u-tien Publishing Company, 1995), 3:665, definition 8.

66. Literally, "they will attain their due measure." In other words, with a properly aligned mind you will be able to objectively perceive all things you encounter in their true relationships to one another.

67. Kuo Mo-jo deletes *shen* (身) because it breaks the rhyme and meter of the three consecutive four-character lines. The line will then end with *tsai* (在, dzəγ) and will rhyme with *lai* (來, lag) and *ssu* (思, sjiəγ) (Kuo/Hsü/Wen, *KTCC*, p. 787).

68. Kuo (Kuo/Hsü/Wen, *KTCC*, p. 787) and Riegel (Riegel/Haloun, p. 159) emend *ching* (精) to *ching* (靜) because of homophonous corruption.

69. Wang Nien-sun emends *chih* (至) to *tzu* (自) because of the parallel in line 7 (Kuo/Hsü/Wen, *KTCC*, p. 787).

70. For this meaning of *chieh* in a roughly contemporaneous work, see the *Chuang Tzu* (6/53), where Master Lai says of embracing death as a natural process, "This is what of old was called 'being loosed from the bonds'; and whoever cannot loose himself, other things bind still tighter" (Graham, *Chuang Tzu: The Seven Inner Chapters*, p. 88). A similar use is found in *Huai-nan Tzu* 1 (D. C. Lau and Chen Fong Ching, eds., *A Concordance to the Huainanzi* [Hong Kong: Commercial Press, Institute of Chinese Studies Ancient Chinese Texts Concordance Series, 1992], chap. 1, p. 4, l. 26 [hereafter cited in the style 1/4/26]):

> Therefore [sages] exhaust the inexhaustible,
> Reach the limit of the infinite,
> Illuminate things without bedazzling them,
> And spontaneously respond without cease like an echo.
> This is what we call "being released (*chieh*) by heaven."

71. Lines 4–9 are repeated in whole or in part in five later sources: the "Ch'eng-fa" (Perfecting Standards, 成法) essay in the *Ching-fa* of the *Huang-ti ssu-ching*; *Techniques of the Mind* II; the "Fixed Ideas" essay in the *Chuang Tzu*; the "Yüan Tao" (Original Way, 原道) essay in *Huai-nan Tzu*; and the "Tao-yüan" (Source That Is the Way, 道原) essay in the *Wen Tzu*. For details, see chapter 5, n. 26.

72. I have restored this similar-form corruption from semantic context.

73. Wang Nien-sun emends *yin* to *yi* in lines 16 and 17, thus restoring similar-form corruptions from the semantic context (Kuo/Hsü/Wen, *KTCC*, pp. 658, 788).

74. "Floodlike" (*hao-jan*) is here used to describe the vital essence; in *Mencius* 2A:2, it is used to describe the vital energy of moral sages.

75. The nine apertures are the seven sense organs (two eyes, two ears, two nostrils, and one mouth) and the anus and penis or vagina. Through these nine, vital energy flows in and out of the human organism.

76. Wang Nien-sun emends this similar-form corruption to preserve the rhyme between 竭 (giat) and 達 (dat) (Kuo/Hsü/Wen, *KTCC*, p. 789).

77. The Great Circle of the Heavens and the Great Square of the Earth probably refer to the cosmology later enunciated as the *kai-t'ien* (Canopy Heaven) theory that the heavens were a great dome carrying the constellations and planets that rotated daily over a square earth. For details, see Major, *Heaven and Earth*, pp. 38–39, 270–71.

78. Lines 5–8 describe the cognitive abilities of enlightened sages. These four lines are embedded in a poem in *Huai-nan Tzu* 2 that extoll the abilities of sages who have "attained the Way and do not lose it":

> Therefore, those who are able to hold up the Great Circle
> Tread firmly over the Great Square.
> Those who mirror things with great purity,
> Perceive things with great clarity.
> Those who establish Great Peace (*t'ai-p'ing*)
> Reside in the Great Hall (of rulership).
> Those who are able to roam in the Obscure,
> Have the same luminescence as the sun and moon.

See Lau and Chen, *A Concordance to the Huainanzi*, 2/12/2.

79. According to Tai Wang (戴望), *hsin* is an archaic form of *shen* (Kuo/Hsü/Wen, *KTCC*, p. 789).

80. I take coiling/contracting and uncoiling/expanding to refer to breathing and the entire passage to refer to a practice of meditation in which one pays careful attention to breathing. Although veiled in technical language, this is one of the earliest references to regularized breathing meditation in the extant literature. I surmise that the text is not more specific because it was originally intended as an oral instruction given by masters to disciples.

81. The excessive (*yin*): this adjective is frequently used with perception, as in verse XIX, line 18, but can also include emotions and other excesses, as Ma Fei-pai has noted. The trivial (*po*) could refer to trivial thoughts or emotions. Ma Fei-pai sees the contrast here as between the excessive and the constrained (*KTNY*, 2:20).

82. Here I read *tse* (澤) as *shih* (釋), the variant in the Liu Chi edition.

83. This is my conjectural emendation because 知 (tieɣ) and 致 (tier) are virtually homophonous and because the latter word better fits my understanding of the passage.

84. Liu Chi and Wang Nien-sun restore this similar-form corruption from *Techniques of the Mind* II, 13.6a1 (Kuo/Hsü/Wen, *KTCC*, p. 790).

85. Kuo restores this similar-form corruption to preserve the rhyme: *wu* (惡) (·ak); *ku* (鼓) (kwaɣ); *mu* (母) (maɣ) (Kuo/Hsü/Wen, *KTCC*, p. 790). This emendation also agrees with the variant in the parallel line from *Techniques of the Mind* II 13.6a6.

86. Chang Wei-lun's emendation of *i* (意) to *i* (壹) because of similar-form corruption better fits the semantic context (Kuo/Hsü/Wen, *KTCC*, p. 790).

87. All or part of these first eight lines are also found in the "Hsing-ming" (Performance and Title) section of the *Sixteen Canons* text in the *Huang-ti ssu-ching* from Ma-wang-tui, in the *Chuang Tzu*, chap. 23, "Keng-sang Ch'u," and in *Techniques of the Mind* II. See Ch'en Ku-ying, *Huang-ti ssu-ching*, p. 401; *Chuang Tzu yin-te*, 23/34–35; *Techniques of the Mind* II, 13.5a2–7.

88. Kuo Mo-jo restores this similar-form corruption from the readings in the Liu Chi and Chu Tung-kuang editions (Kuo/Hsü/Wen, *KTCC*, p. 790). The same emendation occurs in line 16.

89. This is a graphic inversion, emended to preserve the rhyme between *i* (一, ·jiet) and *chi* (吉, kjiet) by Wang Nien-sun. It is also paralleled in *Techniques of the Mind* II, 13.5a4 (Kuo/Hsü/Wen, *KTCC*, p. 791).

90. Only the *Ssu-pu ts'ung-k'an* and Chao editions preserve this line (Kuo/Hsü/Wen, *KTCC*, p. 791).

91. *Te* (得) is absent from the *Ssu-pu ts'ung-k'an* edition, but present in the Liu Chi and all other major editions (Kuo/Hsü/Wen, *KTCC*, p. 791).

92. These two lines disrupt the four-syllable meter and the six prior lines of rhyme. In addition, they contain one of only two uses of *jo* in the sense of "like, as" in the entire text; the other use in verse XXII is likely to be a later Confucian interpolation. These lines begin a new line of reasoning in this verse, introducing the topic of eating. For these reasons, I suspect that they too are a later interpolation, a piece of commentary that found its way into the text during early transmission.

93. I have deleted *i* in order to preserve the meter of the four-syllable line.

94. Yasui, Tai Wang, and Kuo Mo-jo make this emendation of a similar-form corruption based on the Yin commentary (Kuo/Hsü/Wen, *KTCC*, p. 792).

95. Kuo makes this emendation because of similar-form corruption (Kuo/Hsü/Wen, *KTCC*, p. 792). Chao concurs (*KTTC*, 2:130).

96. Ting Shih-han emends 怣 to 喜 based on the parallel in line 17 (Kuo/Hsü/Wen, *KTCC*, pp. 792–93). Ma concurs (*KTNY* 3:15). Haloun deletes 之 to preserve the meter.

97. Riegel (Riegel/Haloun, p. 167) emends *huan* to *yüeh* (樂) because of similar-form corruption ("graphic error" in Riegel's terminology), but supplies no further justification for it. Undoubtedly, the parallel line in *Techniques of the*

Mind II 13.6a7, which contains the character 樂, is one factor. Another factor could be the appearance of 樂 in lines 6 and 7. However, there is no compelling phonological, semantic, or syntactic reason to make this emendation, so I have decided against it.

98. I am suspicious of the originality of most or all of this passage, especially lines 5–12. To begin with, the first four lines are a summary of the previous verse. Second, lines 6–8 do not rhyme. Third, lines 6–10 contain virtually the only use of *jo* in the text. Fourth, lines 5–12 contain one of the only two instances of Confucian technical terms in the entire text. I suspect, therefore, that most or all of these lines represent material added to the original text of *Inward Training*. The identity of this commentator remains a subject for speculation that is beyond the parameters of the present study.

99. The philosophy of eating in *Inward Training* is to avoid extremes in order to nourish the vital energy and vital essence. It is an integral part of the spiritual practice advocated by the authors, and its presence here reiterates their concern for the integration of the whole person, including physical, psychological, and spiritual aspects. A similar passage on the philosophy of eating is found in the *Lü-shih ch'un-ch'iu* essay entitled "Chin-shu" (Fulfilling Your Lifespan). It reads: "For all, the Way of eating is to neither starve nor to overeat. This is called the treasure of the Five Orbs." See Lau, *A Concordance to the Lüshi chunqiu*, 3.2/13/15.

100. I have followed the suggestions of Li Che-ming (Kuo/Hsü/Wen, *KTCC*, p. 793) and Riegel (Riegel/Haloun, p. 163) to add *ch'i*. Doing so reestablishes the parallel syntactical structure between the two pairs, lines 2–3 and lines 4–5.

101. Hsü Wei-yü deletes *pu* (不) to preserve the parallel with line 5 and emends *tsang* (藏) to *ch'iang* (牂) because of similar-form corruption. The variant *tsang* (藏) in the Liu Chi and Chu Tung-kuang editions is graphically possible as a similar-form corruption, but semantically less likely.

102. Haloun makes this deletion to restore the meter (Riegel/Haloun, p. 168).

103. Haloun makes this deletion to restore the meter (ibid.).

104. Chang P'ei-lun makes this emendation because of a similar-form corruption (Kuo/Hsü/Wen, *KTCC*, p. 793). Chao concurs (*KTTC*, 2:132).

105. Kuo Mo-jo makes this semantic emendation of the similar-form corruption, *chang* (長) to *wang* (忘) both here and in line 19 (Kuo/Hsü/Wen, *KTCC*, pp. 793–94).

106. These two characters are deleted by Haloun to restore the meter (Riegel/Haloun, p. 168).

107. Tai Wang makes these semantic emendation of *pao* (飽) to *ch'ih* (食) and *fa* (廢) to *chih* (止) (Kuo/Hsü/Wen, *KTCC*, p. 794).

108. Ma Fei-pai (*KTNY,* 3:17) and Chao Shou-cheng (*KTTC,* 2:132) make this emendation because of a similar-form corruption from the old form of *yüan,* which is written as 囧 and is found in the *Shuo-wen chieh-tzu.* According to them, the "fount" this refers to is the fount of vital energy within the individual discussed in verse XIV.

109. The phrase "maintain the One" (*shou-i*) in line 4 is the first mention in the extant literature of this practice, which later became central in the meditation traditions of both the Taoist and Buddhist religions. For a further discussion of this phrase, see Livia Kohn, "Guarding the One: Concentrative Meditation in Taoism," in Kohn, ed., *Taoist Meditation and Longevity Techniques* (Ann Arbor: University of Michigan Center for Chinese Studies, Michigan Monographs in Chinese Studies, vol. 61, 1989), pp. 125–58.

110. To have "your thoughts and deeds seem heavenly" means that you act in a completely natural and spontaneous fashion, as do all things within the great vault of the heavens.

111. Ting Shih-han and Kuo Mo-jo make this emendation of a similar-form corruption to restore the rhyme (Kuo/Hsü/Wen, *KTCC,* p. 794).

112. Ma Fei-pai (*KTNY,* 3:19) says that to be "relaxed and unwound" is what the modern *ch'i-kung* masters mean when they talk about the condition of having the mind and feelings totally relaxed. It is a feeling of great contentment. He understands *jen* here as indicating the condition in which the person is acutely sensitive to his perceptions and body. This use of *jen* is found in the *Huang-ti nei-ching su-wen* [黃帝內經素問] (see *Han-yü ta tz'u-tien,* 1:1096).

113. This emendation of a similar-form corruption is made by Yasui Kō and Kuo Mo-jo (Kuo/Hsü/Wen, *KTCC,* p. 794). Chao (*KTTC,* 2:132) concurs.

114. Chang Ping-lin and Yasui Kō say that *yü* (遇) should be read as its homonym *yü* (愚) (Kuo/Hsü/Wen, *KTCC,* p. 795). Hsü Wei-yü, Riegel (Riegel/Haloun, p. 169), and Chao (*KTTC,* 2:133) concur.

115. What I have translated as "pores" is literally "the skin's webbed pattern" (*tso li,* 腠理). According to Donald Harper, in early macrobiotic hygiene literature it is "another important physiological structure in connection with vapor (*ch'i*) circulation. Circulation is complete when vapor permeates the webbed pattern." See Harper, "The Bellows Analogy, p. 387.

116. Wang Yin-chih says that *ch'eng* (丞) should be read as its homonym *cheng* (烝) (Kuo/Hsü/Wen, *KTCC,* p. 795). Haloun deletes *erh* (而) to preserve the four-syllable meter (Riegel/Haloun, p. 169). Wang Yin-chih sees *tun* (屯) as a similar-form corruption for *mao* (毛) (ibid.).

3. The Teachings of *Inward Training*

1. Here and throughout the remainder of the book I insert bracketed ideas to indicate my interpretations of the meaning of given lines, whenever necessary.

2. These pathways are called *mo* (脈, vessel) or *ching* (經, conduits) in the earliest medical texts from Ma-wang-tui and in the *Huang-ti nei-ching*. For details, see Paul U. Unschuld, *Medicine in China: A History of Ideas* (Berkeley: University of California Press, 1985), pp. 73–83. Since *Inward Training* is an earlier work, it is uncertain whether these later ideas were also possessed by its authors.

3. Graham, *Disputers of the Tao*, p. 101.

4. See chapter 2, n. 21.

5. For a fuller discussion of the concept of *shen* in the *Huai-nan Tzu*, see Roth, "The Ghost in the Machine" and "Psychology and Self-Cultivation."

6. For information on this posture, see Harper, "The Bellows Analogy," pp. 381–92.

7. *Chuang Tzu yin-te*, 2/35.

8. I thank Andrew S. Meyer of North Central College in Illinois for pointing out this symbolism to me.

9. Isabelle Robinet, *Taoism, Growth of a Religion*, trans. Phyllis Brooks (Stanford: Stanford University Press, 1997), p. 91.

4. *Inward Training* in the Context of Early Taoist Mysticism

1. Here the term "apophatic" is used in its more general and original sense: "of knowledge of God: obtained through negation." It is usually contrasted with the term "cataphatic": "of knowledge of God: obtained through affirmation." See *The New Shorter Oxford English Dictionary*, 4th ed. (Oxford: Oxford University Press, 1993), pp. 95, 351. "Apophatic" has come to be associated with a particular mode of approach to the nature of God in the writings of Christian mystics, the so-called *via negativa*, in which God is described using negative language. I consider this a subset of "apophasis" and use the term more broadly to indicate a method of negating the self in order to facilitate an experience of the Absolute, however conceived. While A. H. Armstrong's use is more culturally specific than mine, he argues for this more general meaning of apophasis in *Plotinian and Christian Studies* (London: Variorum, 1979), especially in essays 24 and 23. I thank Janet Williams of the University of Bath for this reference. For a pioneering application of these contrasting terms to Indian Buddhist texts, see Luis Gomez, "Proto Mâdhyamika in the Pali Canon," *Philosophy East and West* 26.2 (1976): 137–65.

2. William James, *The Varieties of Religious Experience* (1st ed., 1902; repr. New York: Penguin Books, 1982).

3. Ibid., p. 379.

4. Ibid., pp. 380–81.

5. Robert Gimello, "Mysticism and Meditation," in Steven Katz, ed., *Mysticism and Philosophical Analysis* (Oxford and New York: Oxford University Press, 1978), p. 178.

6. Peter Moore, "Mystical Experience, Mystical Doctrine, Mystical Technique," in Katz, ed., *Mysticism and Philosophical Analysis*, p. 101.

7. Walter Stace, *Mysticism and Philosophy* (1st ed., 1960; repr. Los Angeles: Jeremy P. Tarcher, Inc., n.d.), pp. 67–87.

8. The name usually associated with cosmic consciousness and the person who apparently coined the term is the Canadian psychiatrist R. M. Bucke. See Stace, *Mysticism and Philosophy*, pp. 25–26, 78; and James, *The Varieties of Religious Experience*, pp. 398–99, for a description of Bucke's mystical experience.

9. See Robert K. C. Forman, ed., *The Problem of Pure Consciousness, Mysticism and Philosophy* (New York: Oxford University Press, 1990).

10. Stace, *Mysticism and Philosophy*, p. 78.

11. Steven Katz, "Language, Epistemology, and Mysticism," in Katz, ed., *Mysticism and Philosophical Analysis*, pp. 22–74.

12. Robert Forman, "Mysticism, Constructivism, and Forgetting," in Forman, ed., *The Problem of Pure Consciousness*, pp. 3–49; and Donald Rothberg, "Contemporary Epistemology and the Study of Mysticism," in Forman, ed., *The Problem of Pure Consciousness*, pp. 163–210.

13. Stace, *Mysticism and Philosophy*, chap. 3 (pp. 134–206), considers the problem of the objective referent of mystical experience in detail.

14. Carl A. Keller, "Mystical Literature," in Katz, ed., *Mysticism and Philosophical Analysis*, p. 77.

15. Keller, "Mystical Literature," p. 79.

16. LaFargue argues persuasively that the chapters of the *Tao Te ching* are made up of deliberately composed "sayings collages" that exhibit a number of literary genres including "polemic aphorisms," comments inserted by the composers, and instructions on self-cultivation, among others (*The Tao of the Tao Te ching*, pp. 196–212).

17. Moore, "Mystical Experience, Mystical Doctrine," p. 103.

18. Ibid.

19. Ibid., p. 113.

20. Ibid.

21. Forman, "Mysticism, Constructivism, and Forgetting," pp. 3–49, especially, pp. 3–9 and 30–43.

22. Rothberg, "Contemporary Epistemology," p. 184.

23. Ibid., p. 186.

24. Daniel Brown, "The Stages of Meditation in Cross-Cultural Perspective," in Ken Wilber, Jack Engler, and Daniel Brown, ed., *Transformations of Consciousness and Contemplative Perspectives on Development* (Boston: Shambala, 1986), pp. 263–64. In his analysis of the results of this study, Brown states that he has discovered "a clear underlying structure to meditation stages, a structure highly consistent across traditions," which, despite the "vastly different ways they are conceptualized . . . is believed to represent natural human development available to anyone who practices" (p. 223).

25. Rothberg, "Contemporary Epistemology," p. 186.

26. Forman, "Mysticism, Constructivism, and Forgetting," p. 8. This is a deliberate strategy by Forman, who recognizes that this extrovertive form can be a more permanent mystical state that is typically thought of as a more advanced stage in the mystical journey. He omits it not out of disregard but in order to limit the focus of his collection of essays.

27. Harold D. Roth, "Some Issues in the Study of Chinese Mysticism: A Review Essay," *China Review International* 2.1 (spring 1995): 154–73.

28. Ibid., pp. 159–61. See also n. 14, which calls for further research to clarify various types in a continuum of extrovertive mystical experience.

29. Brown, "The Stages of Meditation," pp. 221–22.

30. LaFargue, *The Tao of the Tao Te Ching*, p. 61.

31. *Chuang Tzu yin-te,* 6/92–93.

32. Rudolph Otto, *The Idea of the Holy*, trans. John W. Harvey (Oxford: Oxford University Press, 1925).

33. Graham, *Chuang Tzu: The Seven Inner Chapters*, p. 35, n. 72.

34. These texts are the Hindu *Yogasūtras* by Patañjali, the Theravāda *Visudhimagga* by Buddhaghosa, and the Tibetan *Mahâmudrâ, Nges don...zla.zer* by Bkra'shih rnam rgyal (Brown, "The Stages of Meditation," p. 222).

35. This summary is derived from ibid., pp. 226–84, especially from the tables on pp. 272–84.

36. See the argument by Victor Mair that meditation entered China from India in his *Tao Te Ching*, pp. 140–48 and 155–61.

37. Sarvepalli Radhakrishnan and Charles A. Moore, *A Sourcebook in Indian Philosophy* (Princeton: Princeton University Press, 1957), pp. 37–39. See p. 49 for their earliest reference to yoga practice, taken from the eighth or seventh century B.C. *Katha Upanisad.*

38. Mair, *Tao Te Ching*, p. 157.

39. See, for example, Arthur J. Deikman, "Deautomatization and the Mystic Experience," in Charles Tart, ed., *Altered States of Consciousness* (New York: John Wiley, 1972), pp. 23–44; and Roland Fischer, "A Cartography of Ecstatic and Mystical States," in Richard Woods, ed., *Understanding Mysticism* (Garden City, NY: Doubleday, 1980), pp. 270–85.

40. See Lau and Chen, *A Concordance to the Huainanzi*, 9/68/10–12. For a translation, see Roger T. Ames, *The Art of Rulership* (1st ed., Honolulu: University of Hawaii Press, 1983; 2d ed., Albany: State University of New York Press, 1994), p. 171.

41. Evelyn Underhill, *Mysticism* (1st ed., 1911; 12th ed., New York: E. P Dutton, 1961), pp. 413–43.

42. Katsuki Sekida, *Zen Training: Methods and Philosophy* (New York: Weatherhill, 1975), p. 95.

43. I refer to the 81 *chang* of the *Lao Tzu* as "verses" and not the standard "chapters" to reflect more accurately their literary style as distinct units of verse. The *Lao Tzu* is a collection of poetic verses, not a book with chapters like the present volume.

44. All references are to Henricks's translation of the *Lao Tzu* (*Lao Tzu Te Tao ching*), with rare exceptions, usually to make consistent translations of technical terms.

45. See Harold D. Roth, "*Laozi* in the Context of Early Daoist Mystical Praxis," in Mark Csikszentmihalyi and P. J. Ivanhoe, eds., *Essays on the Religious and Philosophical Aspects of the Laozi* (Albany: State University of New York Press, 1999), pp. 59–96. This article contains a fuller discussion of mystical practice in the *Lao Tzu* than is included here.

46. Kohn, "Guarding the One," pp. 125–58.

47. The phrase *tai ying p'o* (戴營魄) is extremely problematic and has puzzled commentators since Ho-shang kung (河上公), a mysterious figure whose work probably dates from the Han dynasty (for further information, see Allan Chan, *Two Visions of the Way* [Albany: State University of New York Press, 1991]). The *p'o* is the "bodily soul," associated with *yin*, and the counterpart of the "spiritual soul" (*hun*, 魂), associated with *yang*. The former governs the body; the latter governs the mind. They work harmoniously together during life, but separate after death, the *p'o* returning to earth and the *hun* to heaven. According to Yü Ying-shih, the former concept developed first; there are a few references in the oracle bones. The concept of *hun* seems to have been derived from it and intended to represent the locus of daily conscious activities, somewhat akin to our modern notion of the conscious mind. Along these lines, the *p'o* can be thought of as akin

to our modern notion of the unconscious mind; that is, the mental phenomena now associated with the conscious and unconscious minds were explained in early China by the concepts of the *hun* and *p'o*. Eduard Erkes follows the Ho-shang kung commentary by taking the term *ying* as the functional equivalent of *hun*; he suggests that it was a variant of *ling* (靈) in Ch'u dialect. Thus a literal translation of this phrase would be "to sustain the conscious and unconscious souls." Here it is rendered more freely because the constant activity of these two aspects of the mind does constitute "the daily activity of the psyche." For more information, see Yü Ying-shih, "'O Soul, Come Back!' A Study of the Changing Conceptions of the Soul and Afterlife in Pre-Buddhist China," *Harvard Journal of Asiatic Studies* 47.2 (December 1987): 363–95; and Eduard Erkes, trans., *Ho-Shang-Kung's Commentary on Lao-Tse* (Ascona, Switzerland: Artibus Asiae, 1950), pp. 141–42.

48. *Kuan Tzu*, 13.1a11.

49. D. C. Lau, trans., *Chinese Classics: Tao Te Ching* (Hong Kong: Chinese University Press, 1982), p. 15.

50. For further details, see the brilliant pioneering study by Paul Demiéville, "Le miroir spirituel," *Sinologica* 1.2 (1948): 112–37 (for an English translation, see Neal Donner, trans., "The Mirror of the Mind," in Peter Gregory, ed., *Sudden and Gradual: Approaches to Enlightenment in Chinese Thought* [Honolulu: University of Hawaii Press, 1987], pp. 13–38).

51. *Chuang Tzu yin-te*, 5/9; Graham, *Chuang Tzu: The Seven Inner Chapters*, p. 77. For a modern study of the putative verses of Shen-hsiu on the mind as a mirror in the *Platform Sutra* and a study of this metaphor in the Northern School of Ch'an, see John R. McRae, *The Northern School and the Formation of Early Ch'an Ideology* (Honolulu: University of Hawaii Press, 1986), pp. 1–5, 140–47, 231–38, 246–50.

52. For an excellent discussion of these contrasting models, see Lee H. Yearley, *Mencius and Aquinas: Theories of Virtue and Conceptions of Courage* (Albany: State University of New York Press, 1990), pp. 59–62.

53. For these distinctions, see Graham, "How Much of *Chuang Tzu?*" pp. 283–321; and Roth, "Who Compiled the *Chuang Tzu?*" pp. 79–128.

54. Harold D. Roth, "Bimodal Mystical Experience in the 'Qiwulun' Chapter of the *Zhuangzi*" (paper presented at the annual meeting of the Association for Asian Studies, Chicago, March 1997).

55. *Chuang Tzu yin-te*, 6/92–93; Graham, *Chuang Tzu: The Seven Inner Chapters*, p. 92. I deviate only in translating *t'ung* (同) as "merge" instead of "go along."

56. I follow Graham in understanding *chih t'i* as the four limbs or members and the five orbs or visceral organs that are the physical manifestations of the

five basic systems of vital energy in the human body. This is preferable to the alternative "drop off limbs and body" because two lines later the text refers to parting from the body (*li-hsing*), which would be redundant if the second interpretation were used. For the associations of the emotions with the various internal organs or "orbs," see Manfred Porkert, *The Theoretical Foundations of Chinese Medicine* (Cambridge, MA, and London, UK: MIT Press, 1974), pp. 115–46.

57. Here I follow the emendation of Yü Yüeh (俞越), who reverses *t'ing* and *erh* to retain a parallel syntactical structure with the surrounding lines. See Ch'en Ku-ying [陳鼓應], *Chuang Tzu chin-chu chin-i* [莊子今注今譯] (Peking: Chung-hua, 1983), p. 118. "The ears stop at listening" is the literal translation, but the implication is that it listens only to its objects, namely, sounds. However, the Way is not such an object and so, in order to apprehend it, one must concentrate attention on the breathing.

58. The literal translation of this line is that "the mind stops at what tallies with it." What tallies with it are its various objects. However, the Way is not an object and cannot be apprehended as an object of the mind.

59. *Chuang Tzu yin-te*, 4/26–28.

60. This meaning of *chi* is found in the *Book of Odes,* where it is used when a flock of birds alights onto a group of trees. For this and other similar useages, see Schuessler, *A Dictionary of Early Zhou Chinese*, pp. 269–70.

61. For a fascinating discussion of the meaning of this title, see D. C. Lau, "On the Expression Zai You 在宥," in Rosemont, ed., *Chinese Texts and Philosophical Contexts*, pp. 5–20, and Graham's reply, pp. 267–72. Graham's argument is more persuasive, but his translation is rather cumbersome, so I use a translation that is more concise. The innate nature of human beings must be "preserved and circumscribed," according to the author, to prevent its being damaged and ultimately destroyed by the seductive and destructive forces of civilization.

62. Harold D. Roth, "The Yellow Emperor's Guru: A Narrative Analysis from *Chuang Tzu* 11," *Taoist Resources* 7.1 (April 1997): 43–60. This article also analyzes the narrative structure of these passages and explain their significance.

63. *Chuang Tzu yin-te*, 11/35–38.

64. Ibid., 11/53–54.

65. *Ma-wang-tui Han-mu po-shu* [馬王堆漢墓帛書], 5 vols. (Peking: Wen-wu Press, 1980), vol. 1, sec. 3, p. 65; *A Concordance to the Huainanzi*, 14/134/2. There is considerable debate on which characters should be included in the title of this text from the *Huang-ti ssu-ching*. Robin Yates concludes that it should simply be called *The Canon* (*ching*, 經). See Yates, *The Five Lost Classics*, p. 21.

66. The Sung commentator Lin Hsi-i (林希逸, ?1200–1273) interprets the character *tu* (度, consider, guess) to mean *i tu* (意度, imagine). See Ch'en

Ku-ying, *Chuang Tzu chin-chu chin-i*, p. 566. Whichever we choose, what is implied is focusing the attention on one thing.

67. *Chuang Tzu yin-te*, 22/22–23. Victor Mair's translation of this passage is particularly good and mine is based on his. See his *Wandering on the Way: Early Taoist Tales and Parables from Chuang Tzu* (New York: Bantam Books, 1994), pp. 213–14.

68. For this meaning of *ching*, see Schuessler, *A Dictionary of Early Zhou Chinese*, p. 319.

69. *Chuang Tzu yin-te*, 23/34–38. My translation is based on Mair, *Wandering on the Way*, pp. 229–30.

70. I consider this one of the last additions to the *Chuang Tzu* for several reasons. First, its technical language and logic of argumentation are extremely close to the "Ching-shen" (Numinous Essence, 精神) essay of the *Huai-nan Tzu*. Second, it shares many phrases with other important early sources of Taoist inner cultivation theory, including the *Inward Training* and *Techniques of the Mind* texts from the *Kuan Tzu* and the "Ch'üan-yen" (Inquiring Words) essay from the *Huai-nan Tzu*. Third, it quotes several sentences from the Syncretist chapter 13 of the *Chuang Tzu* (See *Chuang Tzu yin-te*, 13/7 and 15/8). Finally, it contains two sentences used by Ssu-ma T'an in his presentation of the ideas of the Taoist lineage (See *Chuang Tzu yin-te*, 15/16; *Shih chi*, 130.3289).

71. Here I emend *te* (inner power) to *hsin* (mind) after Wang Shu-min (王叔岷) (Ch'en Ku-ying, *Chuang Tzu chin-chu chin-i*, p. 398).

72. *Chuang Tzu yin-te*, 15/14–15. My translation is based on Graham, *Chuang Tzu: The Seven Inner Chapters*, p. 266.

73. *Chuang Tzu yin-te*, 15/18–20.

74. Harold D. Roth, "Evidence for Stages of Meditation in Early Taoism," *Bulletin of the School of Oriental and African Studies* 60.2 (June 1997): 295–314.

75. For an excellent critical analysis of these possible uses, see Li Ling [李零], *Chung-kuo fang-shu k'ao* [中國方術考] (Peking: People's China Press, 1993), pp. 319–22.

76. Kuo Mo-jo, "Ku-tai wen-tzu chih pien-cheng de fa-chan" [古代文字之辨證的發展], *K'ao-ku* [考古] 5 (1972): 9.

77. Li Ling, *Chung-kuo fang-shu k'ao*, p. 322.

78. Joseph Needham, *Science and Civilization in China*, vol. 2 (Cambridge: Cambridge University Press, 1956), p. 242. The inscription is translated and briefly discussed on p. 143.

79. Gilbert L. Mattos, "Notes on a Warring States Period Jade Inscription: The Xing Qi Yu Inscription" (notes for a talk presented at a meeting of the Warring

States Working Group, April 25, 1998). I thank Professor Mattos for making this manuscript available.

80. Kuo Mo-jo, "Ku-tai wen-tzu," p. 9. The style of the characters makes them difficult to decipher. Li Ling reads five of them differently: line 2: he reads *t'un* (吞, swallow) for *shen* (深, deeply) and *hsü* (畜, nurture) for *hsü* (蓄, collect); lines 9 and 10: he reads *fu* (复, return) for *t'ui* (退, recede); line 11: he reads *ch'i* (其, its) for *chi* (機, dynamism) and *pen* (本, foundation) for *ch'ung* (舂, to pound grain to remove the husk and reveal the kernals). I have used two of his readings for semantic reasons, as indicated in the text. Only the readings in line 11 imply a substantial difference in the meaning. For Li, the foundation that lies above refers to the upper cinnabar field of later Taoist meditation and the foundation that lies below refers to the lower cinnabar field. However, despite his learned attempts to justify what would be extremely early references to concepts related to these two much later terms, I do not find his arguments convincing and so have retained Kuo's readings. See Li Ling, *Chung-kuo fang-shu k'ao*, pp. 322–24.

81. *Chuang Tzu yin-te*, 6/6–7.

82. Lau and Chen, *A Concordance to the Lüshi chunqiu*, 162/15–23; and *Chuang Tzu yin-te*, 23/66–70.

83. *Ma-wang-tui Han-mu po-shu*, 1:53.

84. Lau and Chen, *A Concordance to the Lüshi chunqiu*, 15/5–11.

85. *Kuan Tzu*, 13/1a10 and 13/2b5.

86. Lau and Chen, *A Concordance to the Huainanzi*, 7/19–24.

87. For a thorough and insightful analysis of these sources, see Li Ling, *Chung-kuo fang-shu k'ao,* and Harper, *Early Chinese Medical Literature.*

88. *Ma-wang-tui Han-mu po-shu,* 4:145–49. For a lucid, scholarly translation, see Harper, *Early Chinese Medical Literature*, pp. 393–99. In this translation of this text, Harper follows Ch'iu Hsi-kuei in transposing strips 52–59 from the sixth dialogue to the end of our fourth dialogue at line 39. See pp. 396–97, n. 8.

89. These two parallels are pointed out by Harper (*Early Chinese Medical Literature*, p. 394, nn. 1 and 2).

90. *Ma-wang-tui Han-mu po-shu*, 4:148; Harper, *Early Chinese Medical Literature*, pp. 396–97.

91. *Ma-wang-tui Han-mu po-shu*, 4:148; Harper, *Early Chinese Medical Literature*, p. 398.

92. Ibid.

93. *Chuang Tzu yin-te*, 15/5–6.

94. Lau and Chen, *A Concordance to the Huainanzi*, 7/58/4.

95. Li Ling presents a comprehensive analysis of the early textual evidence for the various gymnastic postures, which often linked to characteristic activities of animals (*Chung-kuo fang-shu k'ao*, pp. 346–54).

96. *Chuang Tzu yin-te*, 19/3–7. My translation is based on Mair, *Wandering on the Way*, pp. 174–75.

97. For an interesting study of Chinese eremeticism, see Aat Vervoorn, *Men of the Cliffs and Caves* (Hong Kong: Chinese University Press, 1990), especially pp. 40–73. Despite the pioneering work contained here, I do not agree with the author's conclusions about the frequent rejection of withdrawal from society in the book.

98. I am thinking, for example, of the long retinue of students who follow the cripple Wang T'ai in chapter 5, whose disciples were as numerous as those of Confucius (*Chuang Tzu yin-te*, 5/1–2), and of the extended quest narrative discussed above in the "Keng-sang ch'u" chapter of the *Chuang Tzu*.

5. *Inward Training* IN THE CONTEXT OF EARLY TAOISM

1. The term "lineage" is used here to describe the social organization of these practitioners for reasons that will become clear.

2. Nathan Sivin, "On the Word 'Taoist' as a Source of Perplexity," *History of Religions* 17.3, 4 (1978): 303–30.

3. Wang Hsien-ch'ien [王先謙], *Hsün Tzu chi-chieh*, pp. 89–105 (translated in Knoblock, *Xunzi*, 1:212–29); Lau and Ch'en, *A Concordance to the Lüshi chunqiu*, 17.7/107/3–5; idem, *A Concordance to the Huainanzi*, 21/227/6–228/26.

4. *Shih chi*, 130.3288–92.

5. See, for example, Kidder Smith, Jr., "Sima Tan's Creation of Daoism *et cetera*" (paper presented at a workshop on "Intellectual Lineages in Ancient China, University of Pennsylvania, September 1997).

6. Edmund Ryden, "Was Confucius a Confucian? Confusion over the Use of the Term 'School' in Chinese Philosophy," *Early China News* 9 (1996): 5–9, 28–29.

7. Ibid., pp. 7–8. While I admire his insightful treatment of Ssu-ma T'an's analysis, I cannot agree that the term *chia* was reserved exclusively for the groups that he determined synchronically. After all, as Ryden points out, the entire analysis is introduced by calling the groups that follow the "six *chia*."

8. Roth, "Psychology and Self-Cultivation in Early Taoistic Thought," pp. 604–8.

9. *Shih chi*, 63.2147, 74.2347, and 80.2436. I am not sure what to call the identification of the wide variety of thinkers who the *Shih chi* says studied Huang-Lao. It is a diverse group including Shen Pu-hai and Han Fei, Shen Tao and T'ien P'ien. It looks as if the identification was made on the basis of a retrospective analysis of their thought by comparing it to extant Han dynasty Huang-Lao philos-

ophy. If this is so, then we have a perfect example of the kind of category error that Ryden warns about.

10. This information is given in an introduction to the colophon apparently written by Ssu-ma Ch'ien (*Shih chi*, 130.3288).

11. Graham, *Disputers of the Tao*, p. 31.

12. Ryden, "Was Confucius a Confucian?" p. 5.

13. Graham, *Disputers of the Tao*, pp. 33–36. Could it have been because evidence for their founders and organization was so much more concrete that Ssu-ma T'an refers to them in the body of his colophon as Ju *che* (者) and Mo *che* rather than *chia*, as Ryden observes?

14. Eno, *The Confucian Creation of Heaven*, chap. 2, especially pp. 55–60, details the "Ruist syllabus," which consisted of four elements: study of the gymnastic arts of war, the study and interpretation of texts, the study of rituals, and the study of relevant aesthetic forms such as music and dance. Thus textual study was an element of a total practice aimed at the achievement of sagehood.

15. *Shih chi*, 130.3289. This translation is from H. D. Roth and S. A. Queen, "On the Six Lineages of Thought by Sima Tan," in Wm. Theodore deBary and Irene Bloom, eds., *Sources of Chinese Tradition*, rev. ed. (New York: Columbia University Press, 1999), p. 278.

16. Harper, *Early Chinese Medical Literature*, p. 8.

17. *Chuang Tzu yin-te*, 6/60–74.

18. Recall that T'ien is credited with teachings quite similar to those of Chuang Tzu's "Ch'i-wu lun" essay in *Chuang Tzu* 33 and is linked to "Huang-Lao techniques of the Way and its inner power," in *Shih chi* 74.

19. Lau and Chen, *A Concordance to the Lüshi chunqiu*, 17.8/23–26/107. See above, chapter 1, pp. 28–30.

20. Lau and Ch'en, *A Concordance to the Huainanzi*, 2/14/20.

21. Ibid., 11/102/5–10. For an excellent English translation, see Wallacker, *The Huai-nan Tzu, Book Eleven*, pp. 44–45.

22. Lau and Ch'en, *A Concordance to the Huainanzi*, 13/130/2–10.

23. Ibid., 14/135/16.

24. Ibid., 14/137/13–29.

25. See *Hsün Tzu yin te* (荀子引得) (Peking: Harvard-Yenching Institute, 1949), 31/9, translated in Knoblock, *Xunzi*, 3:260; and Lau and Chen, *A Concordance to the Lüshi chunqiu*, 20/4.4/24 ff.

26. John Knoblock thinks Hsün Tzu first encountered the *Lao Tzu* during his time at Chi-hsia (Knoblock, *Xunzi*, 1:11). This is consonant with the theories of Ch'ien Mu, who as early as 1935 went against tradition in concluding for this c. 300 B.C. date. See Ch'ien Mu, *Hsien-Ch'in chu-tzu hsi-nien*, pp. 202–26.

27. Baxter, "Situating the Language," p. 249.

28. Mair, *Tao Te Ching*, pp. 120–24.

29. LaFargue, *Tao and Method*, pp. 48–49.

30. Ibid., pp. 396–427. The chapters are as follows: 4, 6, 10, 14, 16, 21, 25, 33, 39, 40, 42, 48, 52, 55, 56, and 59.

31. The following passages whose subject, according to LaFargue, is self-cultivation are found in the Kuo-tien *Lao Tzu* parallels: 16, 25, 40, 48, 52, 55, 56, 59.

32. H. D. Roth, "Early Taoist Wisdom Poetry: The Evidence from Kuo-tien" (paper presented at the International Convention of Asia Scholars, Leiden, June 1998).

33. I thank Andrew Meyer of North Central College for pointing out this criticism of the Yangists, for whom "valuing life" was an essential tenet. It is interesting to note that, in the version of *Lao Tzu* 19 found at Kuo-tien, such direct attacks on the Confucians are missing. In place of the opening line "exterminate sagehood, discard wisdom," the Kuo-tien parallel reads "exterminate knowing and discard disputation." In place of the third line that reads "exterminate benevolence and discard righteousness," the Kuo-tien parallel reads "exterminate cleverness and discard profit." These variants make it appear that the Yangists (benefit) and perhaps the Terminologists or the Mohists (knowing, disputation, cleverness) might be the target of the criticism in this chapter instead of the Confucians. However, lest we think that the Confucians escaped criticism in the entire corpus of *Lao Tzu* parallels, the third bundle contains a version of chapter 18, which begins "unless the Great Tao has declined, how would there be talk of benevolence and righteousness?" See Ching-men shih po-wu kuan, *Kuo-tien Ch'u-mu shih-chien*, pp. 111 and 121.

34. Fung Yu-lan, *Chung-kuo che-hsüeh shih hsin-pien*, 2:198–99.

35. Graham, *Disputers of the Tao*, p. 100.

36. Kristofer Schipper, *The Taoist Body*, trans. Karen C. Duval (Berkeley: University of California Press, 1993), p. 6; Robinet, *Taoism, Growth of a Religion*, pp. 35–40; Jordan Paper, *The Spirits Are Drunk: Comparative Approaches to Chinese Religion* (Albany: State University of New York Press, 1995), pp. 125–56.

37. This is some disagreement about the title of this final section of the *Shih-liu ching* (Sixteen Canons). It is untitled in the Chinese original, but Ch'en Ku-ying gives it this title after the key topics in its first sentence. See his *Huang-ti ssu-ching chin-chu chin-i*, p. 401. Ryden cites two other theories but leaves it untitled (*Yellow Emperor*, pp. 405–6).

38. "Ch'eng-fa" (Perfecting Standards): Ch'en Ku-ying, *Huang-ti ssu-ching chin-chu chin-i*, p. 352; *Hsin-shu, hsia: Kuan Tzu*, 13/6b3; "Original Way": Lau

and Ch'en, *A Concordance to the Huainanzi*, 1/6/25; "The Source That Is the Way": D. C. Lau and Chen Fong Ching, eds., *A Concordance to the Wenzi* (Hong Kong: Commercial Press, 1992), 1/3/21–2. It looks as if both "Perfecting Standards" and *Techniques of the Mind* II draw directly on *Inward Training* for their lines. The *Wen Tzu* draws on the *Huai-nan Tzu* and, because the meaning of the paragraph in which these lines are found in the *Huai-nan Tzu* is quite close to the larger context of "Perfecting Standards" (namely, a cosmology of the One), it is likely that the *Huai-nan Tzu* drew on this text for its lines.

39. In the *Chuang Tzu* (*Chuang Tzu yin-te*, 41/15/20) the subject is the numinous essence. However, in the inner cultivation tradition this is the essential vital essence of the numen, cultivated by merging with the Way. So the Way is involved here as well; it is the Way as realized by a sage.

40. *Chuang Tzu yin-te*, 33/56–8.

41. Baxter, "Situating the Language," pp. 231–54.

42. Ryden, *Yellow Emperor*, p. 270.

43. Kuan Feng, "*Chuang Tzu* wai tsa-p'ien ch'u-t'an" [莊子外雜篇初談], in *Chuang Tzu che-hsüeh t'ao-lun chi* [莊子哲學討論集] (Peking: Chung-hua, 1962), pp. 61–98; Graham, "How Much of *Chuang Tzu*?" pp. 283–321; Liu Hsiao-kan, *Chuang Tzu che-hsüeh chi ch'i yen-pien* [莊子哲學及其演變] (Peking: Chinese Social Sciences Press, 1987), p. 84. Part of this latter work has been translated as Liu Xiaogan, *Classifying the Zhuangzi Chapters*, trans. William Savage (Ann Arbor: Center for Chinese Studies, University of Michigan, 1994). Although all three are in general agreement as to the chapters of the different strata of the text, Liu disagrees with Kuan and Graham on issues of dating, preferring to see the entire collection as being completed before 240 B.C.

44. Roth, "Redaction Criticism," pp. 4–6.

45. Graham, *Disputers of the Tao*, p. 100.

46. A. C. Graham, "The Origins of the Legend of Lao Tan," in his *Studies in Chinese Philosophy and Philosophical Literature*, pp. 111–24.

47. Lau and Ch'en, *A Concordance to the Lüshi chunqiu*, 17.7/107/3–5.

48. I say "vexed" for two reasons: Only one of the five dialogues between Confucius and Lao Tan in these three chapters contains phrases that can be definitively linked to the *Lao Tzu* (*Chuang Tzu yin-te*, 14/56–60); and these chapters are not, by any means, uniformly Syncretist in content. This particular dialogue seems closer to the Primitivist chapters.

49. Graham, "The Origins of the Legend of Lao Tan," pp. 114–15.

50. This is, in essence, what Andrew Meyer has done in his article "Late Warring States Daoism." Meyer further identifies chaps. 3, 5, and 25 as the products of this Taoist lineage.

51. Graham, "The Origins of the Legend of Lao Tan," pp. 119–20.

52. For the theory that T'ien's ideas—not those of Shen Tao and P'eng Meng—are the basis of the *Chuang Tzu* 33 description of their teachings, see Kanaya, *Kanshi no kenkyū*, pp. 348–49.

53. For a new and definitive translation of perhaps the most mystical of the poems in this collection, "Yüan-yu" (Far Roaming, 遠遊), see Paul W. Kroll, "On 'Far Roaming,'" *Journal of the American Oriental Society* 116.4 (1996): 653–69.

54. Scholars often speak of such a "cult" without a great deal of precision. It is, in general, associated with the *fang-shih*, but there is little historical evidence that anything like the sociological phenomenon of a cult was organized in pre-Han times. That there are stories of individual *fang shih*, such as those who led the first emperor on a futile search for immortals and their Isles of P'eng-lai in the *Shih chi,* does not prove it, for these stories contain no evidence of cultic organization. Certainly, immortality was a desired goal before the Han, but there is little evidence of a cult devoted to its practice. Although there is a category of writings in the *Han shu* bibliography devoted to the teachings of spirits and immortals, given the synchronic nature of Pan Ku's classifications here, this is hardly evidence for the existence of such a cult. The topic warrants a much more extensive examination than can be undertaken here. A good place to begin is Yü Ying-shih, "Life and Immortality in the Mind of Han China," *Harvard Journal of Asiatic Studies* 25 (1965): 80–122.

55. I have made one attempt to do this in my article "The Yellow Emperor's Guru."

BIBLIOGRAPHY

Ames, Roger T. *The Art of Rulership*. 1st ed., Honolulu: University of Hawaii Press, 1983. 2d ed., Albany: State University of New York Press, 1994.

Armstrong, A. H. *Plotinian and Christian Studies*. London: Variorum, 1979.

Baxter, William H. "Situating the Language of the *Lao Tzu*: The Probable Date of the *Tao Te Ching*." In Michael LaFargue and Livia Kohn, eds., *Lao-Tzu and the Tao-Te-Ching*, pp. 231–53.

Boltz, William. "The Religious and Philosophical Significance of the 'Hsiang erh' *Lao Tzu* in the Light of the Ma-wang-tui Silk Manuscripts." *Bulletin of the School of Oriental and African Studies* 45.1 (1982): 95–117.

Brooks, E. Bruce, and Taeko Brooks. *The Original Analects: Sayings of Confucius and His Successors*. New York: Columbia University Press, 1998.

Brown, Daniel. "The Stages of Meditation in Cross-Cultural Perspective." In Ken Wilber, Jack Engler, and Daniel Brown, ed., *Transformations of Consciousness and Contemplative Perspectives on Development*, pp. 219–84.

Chan, Allan. *Two Visions of the Way*. Albany: State University of New York Press, 1991.

Chao, Shou-cheng [趙守正]. *Kuan Tzu t'ung-chieh* [管子通解]. 2 vols. Peking: Peking Institute for Studies in Economics, 1989.

Che-hsüeh yen-chiu [哲學研究] editorial staff. *Chuang Tzu che-hsüeh t'ao-lun chi* [莊子哲學討論集]. Peking: Chung-hua, 1962.

Ch'en, Ku-ying [陳鼓應]. *Chuang Tzu chin-chu chin-i* [莊子今注今譯]. Peking: Chung-hua, 1983.

———. *Huang-ti ssu-ching chin-chu chin-i* [黃帝四經今註今譯].Taipei:Taiwan Commercial Press, 1995.

Ch'ien, Mu [錢穆]. *Hsien-Ch'in chu-tzu hsi-nien* [先秦諸子繫年]. 2 vols. 1st ed., 1935. Rev. ed., 1956; repr., Peking: Chung-hua, 1985.

Ching-men shih po-wu kuan [荊門市博物官]. *Kuo-tien Ch'u mu chu-chien* [郭店楚墓竹簡]. Peking: Wen-wu, 1998.

Ch'iu, Hsi-kuei [裘錫圭]. "Ma-wang-tui *Lao Tzu* chia i pen chüan-ch'ien-hou i-shu yü 'Tao-Fa chia'" [馬王堆老子甲乙本卷前后佚書與道法家]. *Chung-kuo che-hsüeh* 2 (1980): 68–84.

Chou, Fa-kao [周法高]. *Han-tz'u ku chin yin-hui* [漢字古今音彙] . Hong Kong: Chinese University of Hong Kong Press, 1973.

Chuang-tzu yin te. Peking: Harvard-Yenching Institute Sinological Index Series no. 20, 1947.

Creel, H. G. *What Is Taoism? And Other Studies in Chinese Cultural History.* Chicago: University of Chicago Press, 1970.

Csikszentmihalyi, Mark. "Fivefold Virtue: Reformulating Mencian Moral Psychology in Han Dynasty China." *Religion* 28 (1998): 77–89.

Csikszentmihalyi, Mark, and P. J. Ivanhoe, eds. *Essays on the Religious and Philosophical Aspects of the Laozi.* Albany: State University of New York Press, 1999.

Defoort, Carine. *The Pheasant Cap Master (He guan zi):A Rhetorical Reading.* Albany: State University of New York Press, 1997.

Deikman, Arthur J. "Deautomatization and the Mystic Experience." In Charles Tart, ed., *Altered States of Consciousness,* pp. 23–44.

Demiéville, Paul. "Le miroir spirituel." *Sinologica* 1.2 (1948): 112–37. Translated by Neal Donner as "The Mirror of the Mind," in Peter Gregory, ed., *Sudden and Gradual,* pp. 13–38.

Despeux, Catherine. "Gymnastics: The Ancient Tradition." In Kohn, ed., *Taoist Meditation and Longevity Techniques,* pp. 225–62.

DeWoskin, Kenneth J. *Doctors, Diviners, and Magicians of Ancient China: Biographies of Fang-shih.* New York: Columbia University Press, 1983.

Endō, Tetsuō. 遠藤哲夫. *Kanshi* 3 vols. *Shinshaku kambun taikei* series, nos. 42, 43, 52. Tokyo: Meiji Shoin, 1989–1993.

Eno, Robert. *The Confucian Creation of Heaven: Philosophy and the Defense of Ritual Mastery.* Albany: State University of New York Press, 1990.

Erkes, Eduard, trans. *Ho-Shang-Kung's Commentary on Lao-Tse.* Ascona, Switzerland: Artibus Asiae, 1950.

Fischer, Roland. "A Cartography of Ecstatic and Mystical States." In Richard Woods, ed., *Understanding Mysticism,* pp. 270–85.

Forman, Robert K. C., ed. *The Problem of Pure Consciousnes*. New York: Oxford University Press, 1990.

————. "Introduction: Mysticism, Constructivism, and Forgetting." In Forman, ed., *Problem of Pure Consciousness*, pp. 3–49.

Fung, Yu-lan. *A History of Chinese Philosophy*. Translated by Derk Bodde. 2 vols. Princeton: Princeton University Press, 1937, 1952.

———— [馮友蘭]. *Chung-kuo che-hsüeh shih hsin-pien* [中國哲學史新編]. 6 vols. 1st ed., 1964. Rev. ed., Peking: People's Press, 1983.

Gimello, Robert. "Mysticism and Meditation." In Steven Katz, ed., *Mysticism and Philosophical Analysis*, pp. 170–99.

Gomez, Luis. "Proto Mâdhyamika in the Pali Canon." *Philosophy East and West* 26.2 (1976): 137–65.

Graham, A. C. "Chuang Tzu's Essay on Seeing All Things as Equal." *History of Religions* 9 (October 1969–February 1970): 137–59.

————. *Chuang Tzu: The Seven Inner Chapters and Other Writings from the Chuang Tzu*. London: George Allen and Unwin, 1981.

————. *Disputers of the Tao*. LaSalle, IL: Open Court Press, 1989.

————. *Studies in Chinese Philosophy and Philosophical Literature*. Albany: State University of New York Press, 1990.

————. "The Date and Composition of *Lieh Tzu*." In Graham, ed., *Studies in Chinese Philosophy and Philosophical Literature*, pp. 216–82. First published in *Asia Major* (new series) 8.2 (1961).

————. "How Much of *Chuang Tzu* Did Chuang Tzu Write?" In Graham, ed., *Studies in Chinese Philosophy and Philosophical Literature*, pp. 283–321.

————. "The Origins of the Legend of Lao Tan." In Graham, ed., *Studies in Chinese Philosophy and Philosophical Literature*, pp. 111–24.

————. *The Book of Lieh-tzu: A Classic of the Way*. Translations from the Oriental Classics. 1st ed., London: John Murray, 1960. 2d ed., with a new preface by the author, New York: Columbia University Press, 1990.

Gregory, Peter, ed. *Sudden and Gradual: Approaches to Enlightenment in Chinese Thought*. Honolulu: University of Hawaii Press, Studies in East Asian Buddhism no. 5, 1987.

Haloun, Gustav. "Legalist Fragments: Part I: *Kuan-tsï* 55 and Related Texts." *Asia Major* (new series) 2.1 (April 1951): 85–120.

Hansen, Chad. "Linguistic Skepticism in the Lao Tzu." *Philosophy East and West* 31.3 (July 1981): 231–46.

Han-shu i-wen chih [漢書藝文志]. Taipei: Hua-lien, 1973.

Harper, Donald. "The Sexual Arts of Ancient China as Described in a Manuscript of the Second Century B.C." *Harvard Journal of Asiatic Studies* 47.2 (1987): 539–93.

———. "Tekhnê in Han Natural Philosophy: Evidence from Ma-wang-tui Medical Manuscripts." In Kidder J. Smith, ed., *Sagehood and Systematizing Thought in Warring States and Han China*, pp. 33–45.

———. "The Bellows Analogy in *Laozi* V and Warring States Macrobiotic Hygiene." *Early China* 20 (1995): 381–92.

———. *Early Chinese Medical Literature: The Mawangdui Medical Manuscripts*. London: Kegan Paul International, Sir Henry Wellcome Asian Series, 1998.

Henricks, Robert. *Lao Tzu Te Tao Ching*. New York: Ballantine Books, 1989.

Ho-pei-sheng wen-wu yen-chiu-so Ting-chou Han-chien cheng-li hsiao-tsu [河北省文物研究所定洲漢簡整理小組]. "Ting-chou Hsi-Han Chung-shan Huai-Wang-mu chu-chien wen Tzu chiao-kan chi" [定洲西中山漢懷王墓竹簡文子校勘記]. *Wen-wu* [文物] 12 (1995): 35–38.

Hsün Tzu yin te [荀子引得]. Peking: Harvard-Yenching Institute, Harvard-Yenching Institute Sinological Index Series no. 22, 1949.

Hu, Chia-ts'ung [胡家聰]. *Kuan Tzu hsin-t'an* [管子新探]. Peking: Chinese Academy of Social Sciences, 1995.

Hu-pei sheng Ching-men shih po-wu kuan [湖北省荆門市博物館]. "Ching-men Kuo-tien i-hao Ch'u-mu" [荆門郭店一號楚墓]. *Wen-wu* 7 (1997): 35–48.

Ivanhoe, P. J. "Zhuangzi on Skepticism, Skill, and the Ineffable Dao." *Journal of the American Academy of Religion* 64.4 (1993): 639–54.

James, William. *The Varieties of Religious Experience*. 1st ed., 1902; repr. New York: Penguin Books, 1982.

Kanaya, Osamu [金谷治]. *Kanshi no kenkyū* [管子の研究]. Tokyo: Iwanami Shoten, 1987.

———. "Taoist Thought in the *Kuan Tzu*." In Koichi Shinohara and Gregory Schopen, eds., *From Benares to Beijing*, pp. 35–40.

Karlgren, Bernhard. *The Authenticity and Nature of the Tso Chuan*. Goteborg: Elanders Boktryckeri Aktiebolag, 1926.

———. *The Poetical Parts in Lao-Tsï*. Goteborg: Elanders Boktryckeri Aktiebolag, 1932.

Katz, Steven, ed. *Mysticism and Philosophical Analysis*. Oxford and New York: Oxford University Press, 1978.

———. "Language, Epistemology, and Mysticism." In Katz, ed., *Mysticism and Philosophical Analysis*, pp. 22–74.

Keegan, David. "The *Huang-ti nei-ching*: The Structure of the Compilation and the Significance of the Structure." Ph.D. diss., University of California, Berkeley, 1988.

Kjellberg, Paul, and Phillip J. Ivanhoe. *Essays on Skepticism, Relativism, and Ethics in the Zhuangzi*. Albany: State University of New York Press, 1996.

Knoblock, John. *Xunzi: A Translation and Study of the Complete Works*. 3 vols. Stanford: Stanford University Press, 1988, 1990, 1994.

Knoblock, John, and Jeffrey Riegel. *The Almanac of Lü Buwei*. Stanford: Stanford University Press (in press).

Kohn, Livia, ed. *Taoist Meditation and Longevity Techniques*. Ann Arbor: University of Michigan Center for Chinese Studies, Michigan Monographs in Chinese Studies, no. 61, 1989.

————. "Guarding the One: Concentrative Meditation in Taoism." In Kohn, ed., *Taoist Meditation and Longevity Techniques*, pp. 125–58.

————. *Early Chinese Mysticism: Philosophy and Soteriology in the Taoist Tradition*. Princeton: Princeton University Press, 1992.

Kroll, Paul. "On 'Far Roaming.'" *Journal of the American Oriental Society* 116.4 (1996): 653–69.

Kuan, Feng. "*Chuang Tzu* wai tsa-p'ien ch'u-t'an" [莊子外雜篇初談]. In staff of *Che-hsüeh yen-chiu* (哲學研究), ed., *Chuang Tzu che-hsüeh t'ao-lun chi*. Peking: Chung-hua, 1962, pp. 61–98.

Kuan Tzu, Ssu-pu pei-yao [四部備要] edition. Shanghai: Chung-hua, 1936.

Kuan Tzu, Ssu-pu ts'ung k'an [四部叢刊] edition. Shanghai: Commercial Press, 1919.

Kuo, Ch'ing-fan [郭慶藩]. *Chuang Tzu chi-shih* [莊子集釋]. 1st ed., 1894. Revised ed. published as *Chiao-cheng* [校正] *Chuang Tzu chi-shih*. Taipei: World Publishing Company, 1974.

Kuo, Mo-jo [郭沫若]. *Ch'ing-t'ung shih-dai* [青銅時代]. Shanghai: Hsin-wen, 1951.

————. "Sung Hsing Yin Wen i-chu k'ao" [宋鈃尹文遺著考]. In Kuo, *Ch'ing-t'ung shih-dai*, pp. 245–71.

————. "Ku-tai wen-tzu chih pien-cheng de fa-chan" [古代文字之辨證的發展]. *K'ao-ku* [考古] 5 (1972): 2–13.

Kuo, Mo-jo, Hsü Wei-yü [許維遹], and Wen I-to [聞一多]. *Kuan Tzu chi-chiao* [官子集校]. Peking: Chung-hua shu chü, 1955.

LaFargue, Michael. *The Tao of the Tao Te Ching*. Albany: State University of New York Press, 1992.

————. *Tao and Method: A Reasoned Approach to the Tao Te Ching*. Albany: State University of New York Press, 1994.

LaFargue, Michael, and Livia Kohn, eds. *Lao-Tzu and the Tao-Te-Ching*. Albany: State University of New York Press, 1998.

Lau, D. C. "On the Expression Zai You 在宥." In Henry Rosemont, Jr., ed. *Chinese Texts and Philosophical Contexts,* pp. 5–20.

Lau, D. C., trans. *Chinese Classics: Tao Te Ching.* Hong Kong: Chinese University Press, 1982.

Lau, D. C., and Chen Fong Ching, eds. *A Concordance to the Huainanzi.* Hong Kong: Commercial Press, Institute of Chinese Studies Ancient Chinese Texts Concordance Series. 1992.

———. *A Concordance to the Wenzi.* Hong Kong: Commercial Press, Institute of Chinese Studies Ancient Chinese Texts Concordance Series, 1992.

———. *A Concordance to the Lüshi chunqiu.* Hong Kong: Commercial Press, Institute of Chinese Studies Ancient Chinese Texts Concordance Series, Philosophical Works no. 12, 1994.

———. *A Concordance to the Zhouyi.* Hong Kong: Commercial Press, Institute of Chinese Studies Ancient Chinese Texts Concordance Series, Classical Works no. 8, 1995.

Li, Hsüeh-ch'in [李學勤]. "*Kuan Tzu Hsin-shu* teng p'ien te tsai k'ao-ch'a" [管子心術等篇的再考察]. *Kuan Tzu hsüeh-k'an* [管子學刊] 1 (1991): 12–16.

Li, Ling [李零]. *Chung-kuo fang-shu k'ao* [中國方術考]. Peking: People's China Press, 1993.

Li, Tsun-shan [李存山]. "*Nei-yeh* teng ssu-p'ien de hsieh-tso shih-chien ho tso-che" [內業等四篇的寫作時間和作者]. *Kuan Tzu hsüeh-k'an* 1 (1987): 31–37.

Liao, W. K., trans. *The Complete Works of Han Fei Tzu.* 2 vols. London: Probsthain, 1939 and 1959.

Liu, Hsiao-kan. *Chuang Tzu che-hsüeh chi ch'i yen-pien* [莊子哲學及其演變]. Peking: Chinese Social Sciences Press, 1987.

——— [Liu Xiaogan]. *Classifying the Zhuangzi Chapters.* Trans. William Savage. Ann Arbor: Center for Chinese Studies, University of Michigan, 1994.

Loewe, Michael, ed. *Early Chinese Texts: A Bibliographical Guide.* Berkeley: Institute for East Asian Studies and the Society for the Study of Early China, Early China Special Monograph Series no. 2, 1993.

van der Loon, Piet. "On the Transmission of the *Kuan-Tzu.*" *T'oung Pao* 41.1–3 (1952): 357–91.

Lopez, Donald S., Jr., ed. *Religions of China in Practice.* Princeton: Princeton University Press, 1996.

Lung, Hui [龍晦]. "Ma-wang-tui ch'u-tu *Lao Tzu* i-pen-ch'ien ku i-shu t'an-yüan" [馬王堆出土老子乙本前古佚書探原]. *K'ao-ku hsüeh pao* [考古學報] 2 (1975): 23–32.

Ma, Fei-pai [馬非白] (also known as Ma Yüan-tsai [馬元材]). "*Kuan Tzu* Nei-yeh p'ien chi-chu" [管子內業篇集注]. *Kuan Tzu hsüeh-k'an* [管子學刊] 1 (1990): 6–13; 2 (1990): 14–21; 3 (1990): 12–21.

Machida, Saburo [町田三郎]. *Kin Kan shisho shi no kenkyū* [秦漢思想史の研究]. Tokyo: Sōbunsha, 1985.

Mair, Victor, ed. *Experimental Essays on Chuang-tzu*. Honolulu: University of Hawaii Press, Asian Studies at Hawaii no. 29, 1983.

————. *Tao Te Ching: The Classic Book of Integrity and the Way*. New York: Bantam, 1990.

––. *Wandering on the Way: Early Taoist Tales and Parables from Chuang Tzu*. New York: Bantam Books, 1994.

––. "Introduction and Notes for a Complete Translation of the *Chuang Tzu*." *Sino-Platonic Papers* 48 (September 1994).

Major, John S. *Heaven and Earth in Early Han Thought: Chapters Three, Four, and Five of the Huainanzi*. Albany: State University of New York Press, 1993.

Maspero, Henri. *Taoism and Chinese Religion*. Translated by Frank Kierman. Amherst: University of Massachusetts Press, 1981.

Mattos, Gilbert L. "Notes on a Warring States Period Jade Inscription: The Xing Qi Yu Inscription." Author's notes for a talk delivered at a meeting of the Warring States Working Group, University of Massachusetts, Amherst, April 25, 1998.

Ma-wang-tui Han-mu po-shu [馬王堆漢墓帛書]. 5 vols. Peking: Wen-wu Press, 1980.

McKnight, Edgar V. *What Is Form Criticism?* Philadelphia: Fortress Press, 1969.

McRae, John R. *The Northern School and the Formation of Early Ch'an Ideology*. Honolulu: University of Hawaii Press, Kuroda Institute Studies in East Asian Buddhism no. 3, 1986.

Meyer, Andrew S. "Late Warring States Daoism and the Origins of Huang-Lao: Evidence from the *Lüshi chunqiu*." Unpublished manuscript. 1996.

Moore, Peter. "Mystical Experience, Mystical Doctrine, Mystical Technique." In Katz, ed., *Mysticism and Philosophical Analysis*, pp. 19–31.

Moore, Stephen D. *Literary Criticism and the Gospels: The Theoretical Challenge*. New Haven: Yale University Press, 1989.

Needham, Joseph. *Science and Civilization in China*. Vol. 2. Cambridge: Cambridge University Press, 1956.

Otto, Rudolph. *The Idea of the Holy*. Translated by John W. Harvey. Oxford: Oxford University Press, 1925.

P'ang, P'u [龐樸]. *Po-shu wu-hsing p'ien yen-chiu* [帛書五行篇研究]. N.p.: Ch'i-Lu shu-she, 1980.

Paper, Jordan. *The Spirits Are Drunk: Comparative Approaches to Chinese Religion*. Albany: State University of New York Press, 1995.

Peerenboom, R. P. *Law and Morality in Ancient China: The Silk Manuscripts of Huang-Lao*. Albany: State University of New York Press, 1992.

P'eng, Hao [彭 浩]. "Lun Kuo-tien Ch'u chien chung te Lao-hsüeh chu-tso" [論 郭店楚簡中的老學著作]. Manuscript of an article submitted to *Wen-wu*, 1996.

Perrin, Norman. *What Is Redaction Criticism?* Philadelphia: Fortress Press, 1969.

Peterson, Willard. "Making Connections: 'Commentary on the Attached Verbalizations' of the *Book of Change*." *Harvard Journal of Asiatic Studies* 42.1 (1982): 67–122.

Porkert, Manfred. *The Theoretical Foundations of Chinese Medicine*. Cambridge, MA, and London, UK: MIT Press, 1974.

Proudfoot, Wayne. *Religious Experience*. Berkeley: University of California Press, 1985.

Pulleyblank, Edwin G. *Outline of Classical Chinese Grammar*. Vancouver: University of British Columbia Press, 1995.

Queen, Sarah A. "A Translation of the Jingmen Guodian Five Conducts Manuscript." Paper presented at the International Conference on the Guodian *Laozi*, Dartmouth College, May 1998.

Radhakrishnan, Sarvepalli, and Charles A. Moore. *A Sourcebook in Indian Philosophy*. Princeton: Princeton University Press, 1957.

Rickett, W. Allyn. *Kuan Tzu: A Repository of Early Chinese Thought*. Hong Kong: Hong Kong University Press, 1965.

————. *Guanzi: Political, Economic, and Philosophical Essays from Early China*. 2 vols. Princeton: Princeton University Press, 1985 and 1998.

————. "*Kuan Tzu*." In Loewe, ed., *Early Chinese Texts*, pp. 244–51.

Riegel, Jeffrey. "The Four 'Tzu Ssu' Chapters of the *Li Chi*." Ph.D. diss., Stanford University, 1978.

Robinet, Isabelle. *Taoism, Growth of a Religion*. Translated by Phyllis Brooks. Stanford: Stanford University Press, 1997.

Rosemont, Henry, Jr., ed. *Chinese Texts and Philosophical Contexts: Essays Dedicated to Angus C. Graham*. LaSalle, IL: Open Court, 1991.

Roth, Harold D. "Filiation Analysis and the Textual History of the *Huai-nan Tzu*." *Transactions of the International Conference of Orientalists in Japan* 28 (1982): 60–81.

————. "The Concept of Human Nature in the *Huai-nan Tzu*." *Journal of Chinese Philosophy* 12 (1985): 1–22.

————. "Psychology and Self-Cultivation in Early Taoistic Thought." *Harvard*

Journal of Asiatic Studies 51.2 (1991): 599–650.

————. "Who Compiled the *Chuang Tzu?*" In Rosemont, ed., *Chinese Texts and Philosophical Contexts*, pp. 79–128.

————. "The Strange Case of the Overdue Book: A Study in the Fortuity of Textual Transmission." In Shinohara and Schopen, eds., *From Benares to Beijing*, pp. 161–86.

————. *The Textual History of the Huai-nan Tzu*. Ann Arbor: Association for Asian Studies, Monograph no. 46, 1992.

————. "Text and Edition in Early Chinese Philosophical Literature." *Journal of the American Oriental Society* 113:2 (1993): 214–27.

————. "Chuang Tzu." In Loewe, ed., *Early Chinese Texts*, pp. 56–66.

————. "Redaction Criticism and the Early History of Taoism." *Early China* 19 (1994): 1–46.

————. "Some Issues in the Study of Chinese Mysticism: A Review Essay." *China Review International* 2.1 (spring 1995): 154–73.

————. "The Inner Cultivation Tradition of Early Taoism." In Lopez, ed., *Religions of China in Practice*, pp. 123–48.

————. "The Yellow Emperor's Guru: A Narrative Analysis from *Chuang Tzu* 11." *Taoist Resources* 7.1 (April 1997): 43–60.

————. "Evidence for Stages of Meditation in Early Taoism." *Bulletin of the School of Oriental and African Studies* 60:2 (June 1997): 295–314.

————. "*Laozi* in the Context of Early Daoist Mystical Praxis." In Csikszentmihalyi and Ivanhoe, eds., *Essays on the Religious and Philosophical Aspects of the Laozi*, pp. 59–96.

————. "Bimodal Mystical Experience in the 'Qiwulun' Chapter of the *Zhuangzi*." Paper presented at the annual meeting of the Association for Asian Studies, Chicago, March 1997.

————. "Early Taoist Wisdom Poetry: The Evidence from Kuo-tien." Paper presented at the International Convention of Asia Scholars, Leiden, June 1998.

————. "Some Methodological Issues in the Study of the Kuo-tien *Lao Tzu* Parallels." In Sarah Allan and Robert Henricks, ed., *Proceedings of the International Conference on the Kuo-tien Lao Tzu* (forthcoming).

Roth, Harold D., and Sarah A. Queen, "On the Six Lineages of Thought by Sima Tan." In Wm. Theodore deBary and Irene Bloom, ed., *Sources of Chinese Tradition*. Rev. ed., New York: Columbia University Press, 1999, pp. 278–82.

Rothberg, Donald. "Contemporary Epistemology and the Study of Mysticism." In Forman, ed., *The Problem of Pure Consciousness*, pp. 163–210.

Ryden, Edmund. "Was Confucius a Confucian? Confusion over the Use of the Term 'School' in Chinese Philosophy." *Early China News* 9 (1996): 5–9, 28–29.

————. *The Yellow Emperor's Four Canons.* Taipei: Ricci Institute, 1997.

Schuessler, Axel. *A Dictionary of Early Zhou Chinese.* Honolulu: University of Hawaii Press, 1987.

Schipper, Kristofer. *The Taoist Body.* Translated by Karen C. Duval. Berkeley: University of California Press, 1993.

Schwartz, Benjamin. *The World of Thought in Ancient China.* Cambridge: Belknap Press of Harvard University Press, 1985.

Sekida, Katsuki. *Zen Training: Methods and Philosophy.* New York: Weatherhill, 1975.

Shih chi [史 記]. Peking: Chung-hua, 1959.

Shinohara, Koichi, and Gregory Schopen, eds. *From Benares to Beijing: Essays on Buddhism and Chinese Religion in Honor of Professor Jan Yün-hua.* Oakville, ON: Mosaic Press, 1991.

Sivin, Nathan. "On the Word 'Taoist' as a Source of Perplexity." *History of Religions* 17.3,4 (1978): 303–30.

Smith, Kidder, Jr., ed. *Sagehood and Systematizing Thought in Warring States and Han China.* Brunswick, ME: Bowdoin College Asian Studies Program, 1990.

————. "Sima Tan's Creation of Daoism *et cetera.*" Paper presented at the workshop on Intellectual Lineages in Ancient China, University of Pennsylvania, September 1997.

Stace, Walter. *Mysticism and Philosophy.* 1st ed., 1960; repr. Los Angeles: Jeremy P. Tarcher, Inc., n.d.

Tart, Charles, ed. *Altered States of Consciousness.* New York: John Wiley, 1972.

Thompson, Paul Mulligan. *The Shen Tzu Fragments.* Oxford: Oxford University Press, 1979.

T'ien, Feng-t'ai [田 鳳 台]. *Lü-shih ch'un-ch'iu t'an-wei* [呂 氏 春 秋 探 微]. Taipei: Student Book Company, 1986.

Ts'ui Jen-i [崔 仁 義]. "Ching-men Ch'u-mu ch'u-t'u te chu-chien *Lao Tzu* ch'u-t'an" [荆 門 楚 墓 出 土 的 竹 簡 老 子 初 探]. *Ching-men she-hui k'o-hsüeh* [荆 門 社 會 科 學] 5 (1997): 31–35.

Underhill, Evelyn. *Mysticism.* 1st ed., 1911. 12th ed., New York: E.P. Dutton, 1961.

Unschuld, Paul U. *Medicine in China: A History of Ideas.* Berkeley: University of California Press, 1985.

Vervoorn, Aat. *Men of the Cliffs and Caves.* Hong Kong: Chinese University Press, 1990.

Wallacker, Benjamin. *The Huai-nan Tzu, Book Eleven: Behavior, Culture, and Cosmos.* New Haven: American Oriental Society, 1962.

———. "Liu An, Second King of Huai-nan (180?–122 B.C.)." *Journal of the American Oriental Society* 92 (1972): 36–49.

Wang, Hsien-ch'ien [王先謙]. *Hsün Tzu chi-chieh* [荀子集解]. 2 vols. 1st ed., 1891. Repr. in *Hsin-pien Chu-tzu chi-ch'eng* [新編諸子集成]. Peking: Chung-hua, 1988.

Wang, Nien-sun [王念孫], and Wang Yin-chih [王引之]. *Tu-shu tsa-chih* [讀書雜志]. 1st ed., 1832. 2d ed., 1870. Repr., Taipei: Shih-chieh, 1963.

Watson, Burton. *Chuang Tzu.* New York: Columbia University Press, 1968.

Wilber, Ken, Jack Engler, and Daniel Brown, ed. *Transformations of Consciousness and Contemplative Perspectives on Development.* Boston: Shambala, 1986.

Woods, Richard, ed. *Understanding Mysticism.* Garden City, NY: Doubleday, 1980.

Wu, Kuang [吳光]. *Huang-Lao che-hsüeh t'ung-lun* [黃老哲學通論]. Hangchow: Chekiang People's Press, 1985.

Yates, Robin D. S. "The Yin-yang Texts from Yinqueshan." *Early China* 19 (1994): 74–144.

———. *Five Lost Classics: Tao, Huang-Lao, and Yin-yang in Han China.* New York: Ballantine Books, 1997.

Yearley, Lee H. *Mencius and Aquinas: Theories of Virtue and Conceptions of Courage.* Albany: State University of New York Press, 1990.

Yen, Kuo-ts'ai [燕國材]. *Hsien-Ch'in hsin-li hsüeh ssu-hsiang yen-chiu* [先秦心理學思想研究]. Ch'ang-sha: Hunan People's Press, 1980.

Yü, Ming-kuang [余明光]. *Huang-ti ssu-ching yü Huang-Lao ssu-hsiang* [黃帝四經與黃老思想]. Harbin: Heilungchiang People's Press, 1989.

Yü, Ying-shih. "Life and Immortality in the Mind of Han China." *Harvard Journal of Asiatic Studies* 25 (1965): 80–122.

———. "'O Soul, Come Back!' A Study of the Changing Conceptions of the Soul and Afterlife in Pre-Buddhist China." *Harvard Journal of Asiatic Studies* 47.2 (December 1987): 363–95.

INDEX

Page numbers in **bold** type refer to the complete translation in chapter 2.

an (calmness): of body, 92, 110; of mind, 50, 72, 117, 118, 139; and vital essence, 74, 105, 106

Analects.(Confucius), 16, 176, 178, 194, 207n14, 213n47

An-cheng T'ang edition (*Kuan Tzu*), 37

Baxter, William: on *Lao Tzu*, 15–16, 17, 144, 173, 186, 192; on literary genres, 27, 40, 130, 157, 168, 185

Bhagavad-gita, 137

breathing, 41, 100, 101, 103; alignment of, 110–11, 134, 165, 167, 171; as apophatic practice, 155, 161, 163, 173; in *Chuang Tzu*, 160, 170, 172; and Confucianism, 33; "Duodecagonal Jade Tablet Inscription" on, 161–63;

in early Taoism, 126–27; and inner cultivation, 126, 142, 172; and inner power, 101, 104, 145, 219n28; in *Lao Tzu*, 137, 150; and meditation, 4, 136, 166, 224n80; in mystical practice, 2, 131, 148; and physical hygiene, 5, 21, 127, 168, 197; and yoga, 137. *See also ch'i* (vital energy/breath)

Brown, Daniel, 131–32, 135–36, 137, 151

Buddhism: meditation in, 118, 135, 136, 227n109; mirror metaphor in, 151; mysticism in, 128, 129, 130; Tibetan, 136, 137; Zen, 141, 151

calmness. *See an* (calmness)

Celestial Masters rebellion, 5

Chang Nieh, 36
Chang P'ei-lun, 40
Chang Ping-lin, 40
Chang Shou-cheng, 42
Chang Ying, 36, 37
Chang-chia shan texts, 1, 4, 221n53;
    physical hygiene in, 110, 168,
    169, 170
Chao, state of, 21
chao chih (illumined knowing),
    68, 108
chao (illumination, intuition),
    222n61
Chao Shou-cheng, 12, 40, 209n5,
    220n34
Chao Yung-hsien edition (Kuan Tzu),
    36, 37–38, 39
Ch'en Huan, 40
cheng (to square up, alignment), 95,
    100; benefits of, 60, 76, 86, 88,
    120, 121, 122; of body, 56, 66,
    82, 104, 221n48; in Chuang Tzu,
    156, 158, 171, 172; and Confu-
    cianism, 30; fourfold, 134, 136;
    of heavens, 58; in Lü-shih ch'un-
    ch'iu, 164–65; of mind, 4, 70,
    106, 109, 110, 112, 113, 134,
    135; in stages of meditation, 166,
    167; and techniques of the Way,
    184; in "Ten Questions," 170;
    and tranquility, 109–12, 134,
    135; and vital energy, 4, 109,
    110, 221n48
Ch'i, state of, 162; and Kuan Tzu,
    18, 19, 201; and Lao Tzu, 187;
    in Lü-shih ch'un-ch'iu, 28–29,
    182; scholars at, 20–22, 27, 168;
    Taoism in, 197, 201. See also
    Chi-hsia Academy

ch'i (equanimity), 28, 50, 113, 135,
    154
ch'i (vital energy/breath), 41–42,
    43; and alignment, 4, 109, 110,
    221n48; and breathing medita-
    tion, 110–11, 150, 162; in
    Chuang Tzu, 155; and Confu-
    cianism, 33; and divination, 107;
    and eating, 90; Five Phases of,
    22; fount of, 74, 227n108; and
    inner cultivation, 12, 62, 74, 80,
    100, 126, 142, 196; and inner
    power, 13, 48, 144, 145; in Lao
    Tzu, 148; and mystical experi-
    ence, 140; and mystical practice,
    148, 184; and the numinous,
    107, 108; and physical hygiene,
    144, 168; and political power,
    152; and Tao, 92, 115–16, 118,
    143–44, 147; and tao-yin exer-
    cises, 221n53; in "Ten Questions,"
    169; and tranquility, 54, 82, 96,
    103; and vital essence, 60, 74,
    82, 101, 102, 105, 106, 114,
    118, 119, 150, 167, 219n27;
    and vitality, 120–21, 122
chia (home, lineage, school), 175,
    176, 236n7
Chia I, 22
Chieh Tzu, 21
Ch'ien Mu, 20, 186, 187, 201
chih-i (holding fast to the One): and
    inner cultivation, 62, 99, 116,
    117, 140, 148, 167; in Lao Tzu,
    149, 150, 221n54; in Lü-shih
    ch'un-ch'iu, 164, 166; and po-
    litical power, 191
Chi-hsia Academy, 21–25, 168,
    201, 212n39; and date of Inward

Chuang Tzu (cont.)

"Keng-sang Ch'u" chapter of, 158–59, 164, 165, 191, 225n87, 236n98; "Knowledge Wanders North" chapter of, 158; and *Lao Tzu*, 16, 159, 195, 198; lore of the Way in, 192, 202; and *Lü-shih ch'un-ch'iu*, 164; "Mastery of Nourishing Life" chapter in, 157; mirror metaphor in, 151; mysticism in, 2, 8, 127, 130, 132, 167; on physical hygiene, 4, 160, 170–71, 172; political thought in, 200; Primitivism in, 7, 153, 155–56, 216n69, 239n48; rhymes in, 24, 157, 158, 186; Syncretic Taoism in, 8, 153, 160, 170, 234n70; and Taoism, 5, 19, 193, 195, 209n17; on techniques of the Way, 182, 183, 184; on tranquility, 156, 157, 160, 166; transmission of, 192–93; on vital essence, 155, 156, 160–61, 171, 239n39; "Way of Heaven" chapter of, 180

Chuang Tzu (Chuang Chou), 5, 6, 7, 153, 160, 175; and authorship of *Inward Training*, 25, 28; at Chi-hsia, 21, 201, 212n39; on "sitting and forgetting," 110, 133, 157

Chung-li ssu tzu chi edition (*Kuan Tzu*), 37, 38, 39

Chung-yung (Doctrine of the Mean), 32, 33

Confucianism: at Chi-hsia Academy, 20, 21; in *Inward Training*, 30–33, 100, 216n68, 222n59, 225n92, 226n98; *Lao Tzu* on, 188, 238n33;

and political thought, 196; practice of, 32, 237n14; as school, 175–81, 194–95; in Syncretist texts, 8, 164; and Taoism, 5, 31, 151, 198, 199–200; on techniques of the Way, 182, 184. *See also Analects*

Confucius, 32, 154, 155, 182, 198

cosmic consciousness, 128, 229n8

cosmology: of *Inward Training*, 5, 12, 25, 101–3; *kai-t'ien* (Canopy Heaven), 224n77; in *Kuan Tzu*, 19; Taoist, 7, 8, 174, 177, 195–97; yin-yang, 21–22

dialects, 27, 32, 40

divination, 21, 82, 107, 158

"Duodecagonal Jade Tablet Inscription on Breath Circulation," 161–63

eating, 84, 90, 100, 101, 122, 226n99; and macrobiotic hygiene, 2, 21

Eckhart, Meister, 128, 131

emotions, 224n81, 233n56; in *Chuang Tzu*, 160; and inner cultivation, 32, 126, 171, 196; in *Inward Training*, 31, 50, 58, 86, 88, 94, 113, 114, 116, 121, 135, 167, 220n35; in *Lao Tzu*, 147–48; in *Lü-shih ch'un-ch'iu*, 164; and techniques of the Way, 183. *See also particular emotions*

emptiness (*hsü*), 152, 189, 196

Endō Tetsuō, 40

Eno, Robert, 178, 210n25

extrovertive mystical experience. *See* mystical experience: types of

Fa-chia. See Legalism
Fang Hsüan-ling, 38
fang shih (formula-scholars), 22,
240n54
filiation analysis, 18–19, 35–36,
217n6
Five Phases cosmology, 21, 22, 25,
162
Forman, Robert, 127–29, 131, 132,
135, 139, 140
Four Classics. See Huang-ti ssu-ching
(Four Classics of the Yellow
Emperor)
Fung Yu-lan, 189

Gimello, Robert, 127
Graham, A. C.: on Chuang Tzu, 28,
153, 195; on "disputers of the
Tao," 20; on Inward Training, 2, 31;
on Lao Tan, 198, 199; on Lieh
Tzu, 207n14; on the numinous,
43, 107, 134; on philosophical
schools, 177; on political thought,
196; on shamanism, 189, 201;
on Taoism, 5, 7, 186

Haloun, Gustav, 14, 35, 39, 209n4,
219n26
Han, state of, 162
Han dynasty, 5, 23, 198–99, 200;
Wu, emperor of, 183, 184
Han Fei, 236n9
Han-fei Tzu, 43, 205n1, 212n37
Han shu (History of the Former Han
Dynasty), 30, 33, 176, 206n2,
212n37, 240n54
happiness. See hsi (joy, pleasure); le
(happiness)
harmony. See ho (harmony)

Harper, Donald, 2, 4, 168, 179,
227n115
the heavens. See t'ien (the heavens)
hermeneutics: historical, 207n10;
mystical, 3–4
Hinduism: meditation in, 118, 135,
136, 137; mysticism in, 128,
129, 130
ho (harmony): in Chuang Tzu, 158;
in eating, 90, 100; of the mind,
50, 113; and Tao, 54, 103, 143;
and vital essence, 74, 106; and
vitality, 86, 121
Ho Ju-chang, 40
Ho-kuan Tzu, 2
hsi (joy, pleasure): in Chuang Tzu, 160;
and sages, 58; and vital essence,
50, 113; and vitality, 31, 86,
88, 94, 121
Hsiang, king of Ch'i, 21
hsin (heart, mind), 42–43; alignment
of, 4, 70, 106, 109, 110, 112,
113, 134, 135; and breathing
meditation, 110–11; in Chuang
Tzu, 154–55; in Confucianism,
33; cultivated, 56, 103, 112–15;
forms of, 50, 60, 72, 80, 114,
219n34; and inner cultivation,
12, 82, 86, 92, 100, 109, 112–
15, 118–19, 126, 172; in Lao
Tzu, 147, 152; within the mind,
72, 107–8, 109, 117, 118, 134,
167, 191, 221n55; and mysticism, 139, 142; numinous, 68,
70, 106–8, 112, 113, 115, 116,
118, 134, 152, 154, 166; and
Profound Mirror, 151; and Tao,
52, 54, 102–3, 115–16, 117; in
"Ten Questions," 170; tranquility

hsin (cont.)
of, 54, 66, 96, 103, 104, 105, 113–14; and vital energy, 80, 96, 105; and vital essence, 50, 74, 99, 112, 113, 143; well-ordered, 64, 66

Hsin shu (New Writings; Chia I), 22

hsing (body, form): alignment of, 4, 56, 66, 100, 104, 109, 110–11, 134, 135, 221n48; in *Chuang Tzu*, 158, 160, 171; and eating, 90; and inner cultivation, 100, 172; of mind, 50, 60, 72, 80, 114, 219n34; and Tao, 52, 102; in Taoist cosmology, 196; and vital essence, 74, 143; and vitality, 86, 121

hsing (innate nature), 31, 32, 88, 216n69; development model of, 151; discovery model of, 151

hsü (emptiness), 152, 189, 196

Hsü Wei-yü, 35, 36, 38, 39

Hsüan, king of Ch'i, 20–21, 22

Hsün Tzu, 21, 180, 186, 198

Hsün Tzu, 33, 175, 184, 194, 205n1, 212n37

Hu Chia-ts'ung, 19

Huai-nan, court of, 23, 25, 168, 214n52

Huai-nan Tzu: astronomy in, 44; authorship of, 205n1; "Ching-shen" essay in, 165, 166; and *Chuang Tzu*, 234n70; and *Inward Training*, 198, 223n71; and *Kuan Tzu*, 22, 36, 37; language of, 157, 165; and mysticism, 2, 140; on the numinous, 43, 108, 228n5; on physical hygiene, 4, 170; on political power, 180, 191; on

sages, 224n78; stages of meditation in, 166; Syncretic Taoism in, 8, 32, 200; and Taoism, 177, 202, 209n17; on *tao-yin* exercises, 221n53; on techniques of the Way, 183, 184; "T'ien-wen" essay in, 44; translations of, 218n24; transmission of, 15; on vital energy, 41

Huan duke, of T'ien family (r. 375–58 B.C.), 20

Huan, duke (7th c. B.C.), Ruler of Ch'i, 19

Huan Yüan, 21

"Huang-Lao" Taoism, 173, 197, 212n37, 236n9; and Chi-hsia Academy, 21, 24; and early Taoism, 181, 193; and *Four Classics*, 6, 19; as Han term, 212n39; and Mohism, 215n55; and Ssu-ma T'an, 184; as Syncretic Taoism, 32, 177; texts of, 8, 19, 189, 200

Huang-ti ssu-ching (Four Classics of the Yellow Emperor), 1, 2, 206n2; classification of, 8, 193–94, 209n17; essays in, 157, 165, 166, 191, 223n71, 225n87; and "Huang-Lao" Taoism, 6, 19; and *Inward Training*, 223n71, 224n87; language of, 24, 157, 165; on political power, 191

Hui Shih, 175

I ching (Book of Change), 43, 108

Igai Hikohiro, 40

immortality, 2, 5, 22, 202, 240n54

India, 110, 137, 138

Individualist Taoism, 6, 7, 18, 195, 196, 197

inner cultivation, 7–9, 99, 101, 109–23; benefits of, 118–23, 140–42, 164, 166, 169; and breathing, 126, 142, 165, 172; *Chuang Tzu* on, 29, 153–61, 170, 171, 172, 234n70; and Confucianism, 30, 32–33; dating of, 190; and inner power, 104, 109, 120, 126; *Lao Tzu* on, 147, 148, 149–50, 152–53, 187; in *Lü-shih ch'un-ch'iu*, 29, 216n63; metaphors of, 151, 168; and mind, 12, 82, 86, 92, 100, 109, 112–15, 118–19, 126, 172; and mysticism, 135, 140; and the numinous, 109, 172, 196; and physical hygiene, 138, 142, 168–72; and political power, 26, 29–30, 181, 186, 187–88, 191, 211n35; and stages of meditation, 161–68; in Syncretist texts, 8, 19; and Tao, 11, 12, 33, 62, 99, 116, 117, 126, 140, 143, 148, 167, 196, 239n39; and Taoism, 7, 18, 125–27, 138, 173–74, 195, 201; technical terms for, 196–97; in *Techniques of the Mind* texts, 24; and techniques of the Way, 181–85; and tranquility, 11, 104, 109, 120, 134, 167, 196; transmission of, 191–93, 202; and vital energy, 12, 62, 74, 80, 100, 126, 142, 196; and vital essence, 12, 106, 109, 126; and vitality, 11, 126, 142; writing on, 130

inner power. *See te* (inner power)

introvertive mystical experience. *See* mystical experience: types of

Inward Training (*Nei-yeh*): authorship of, 23, 27–30; commentaries on, 39–40; date of, 8–9, 17, 23–27, 185–87, 213n45; divisions of, 14–15, 41, 209n4; as earlier than *Lao Tzu*, 187–90; editions of, 35–41; emendations to translation of, 39; linguistic features of, 213n45; literary genre of, 12–17; locations for, 187; rhetoric of, 16–17, 167–68, 187; significance of, 4–5, 198; structure of, 99–101; terms in, 41–44, 213n45; textual variations in, 38; title of, 11–12; verse I, 12–13, **46–47**, 99, 101, 105, 107, 219n27; verse II, 13–14, 17, **48–49**, 99, 102, 103, 135, 143–44, 145, 169; verse III, 28, **50–51**, 99, 113, 135, 220n35; verse IV, **52–53**, 99, 102, 135, 140, 142–46; verse V, 17, 38, **54–55**, 99, 102–3, 111, 112, 135, 140, 142–44, 146; verse VI, 17, 38, **56–57**, 99, 140, 142, 143, 145, 146; verse VII, 17, 38, **58–59**, 99, 113, 114, 135; verse VIII, 17, **60–61**, 99, 101, 105, 106, 109–10, 112, 126, 133, 135, 211n36, 219n27, 220n34; verse IX, **62–63**, 99, 116, 118, 140, 148, 149, 150, 152, 189; verse X, **64–65**, 100, 112; verse XI, 38, **66–67**, 100, 104, 110, 112, 134–35, 135, 216n68, 221n48; verse XII, 38, **68–69**, 100, 108; verse XIII, **70–71**, 100, 106, 108, 112, 115, 118, 135, 150, 219n32;

Training, 2, 28, 134–44; language
of, 109, 132–33, 134, 151;
writings on, 129–30, 134, 138,
139

Nan-jung Chu, 193
Nan-kuo Tzu-ch'i, 193
Naturalists (yin-yang), 175, 179,
180, 181
Needham, Joseph, 162
negative particles, 213n45
Nei-yeh. See Inward Training
non-action. *See wu-wei* (non-action)
nu (anger): in *Chuang Tzu*, 160; and
Confucianism, 31, 88; and mind,
50, 58, 113; and vitality, 86, 94,
121
numen/numinous. *See shen* (numen/
numinous)

the One. *See chih-i; shou-i;* Tao (the
Way/the One)
oral transmission, 213n47, 224n80;
and divisions of texts, 15, 41;
of *Inward Training*, 186–87, 188,
190; of *Lao Tzu*, 16, 26, 186–87,
188, 190; and rhymes, 14, 25,
168, 192, 202
Otto, Rudolph, 133–34

Pan Ku, 176, 212n37, 240n54
pao i (embracing the One), 148,
149–50
Paper, Jordan, 189
P'eng Meng, 21, 175, 240n52
P'eng Tzu (P'eng-tsu; Ancestor
P'eng), 4, 29, 160, 182
Peterson, Willard, 43
philosophical schools, 175–81,

194–95, 197; and Taoism, 176–
77, 193, 200, 201; and techniques, 178–81, 184; Western
definitions of, 177–78
physical hygiene, 2, 202; and breathing, 5, 21, 127, 168, 197; in
Chang-chia shan texts, 110,
168, 169, 170; *Chuang Tzu* on,
4, 160, 170–71, 172; and inner
cultivation, 168–72; and vital
energy, 144, 168
pleasure. *See hsi* (joy, pleasure)
p'o and *hun* souls, 231n47
poetry, 31, 32, 130, 192. *See also*
rhymes
political power: *Chuang Tzu* on, 160;
Huai-nan Tzu on, 180, 191; and
inner cultivation, 26, 29–30,
181, 186, 187–88, 191, 211n35;
Inward Training on, 27, 152, 181,
200; *Kuan Tzu* on, 19; *Lao Tzu*
on, 26, 152, 181, 185, 186, 200;
Lü-shih ch'un-ch'iu on, 29; and
mystical practice, 125, 164, 182,
191–92, 193; "Purified Mind"
on, 211n35; and shamanism,
189; Shen Tao on, 215n58; and
Syncretic Taoism, 181, 192, 195,
196, 202; and Taoism, 7, 174,
180, 195–96, 202; *Techniques of
the Mind* texts on, 24, 26
Primitivist Taoism, 7, 195, 196, 197,
202; in *Chuang Tzu*, 7, 153, 155–
56, 216n69
psychic energy (*ching-shen*), 43
psychology, 42, 104–9
Pulleyblank, Edwin, 213n45
Pure Consciousness Event (PCE),
131, 132, 139–40, 141

Shih chi (Records of the Grand Historian), 21, 22, 175, 240n54; on "Huang-Lao" Taoism, 177, 212n37

Shih ching (Book of Poetry), 15, 186, 209n17, 214n53, 233n60

shih ku (therefore), 13, 14, 31

"Shih-wen" (Ten Questions), 169–70

shou-i (maintaining the One): in *Four Classics*, 191; and inner cultivation, 92, 100, 111, 115–17, 148, 196; in *Lao Tzu*, 149, 192; and meditation, 126, 136, 227n109

shu (techniques), 20, 131, 178–81, 210n25. *See also* techniques of the Way

Sivin, Nathan, 174

Sixteen Canons (*Shih-liu ching; Four Classics*), 157, 191, 225n87

"skin's webbed pattern" (*tso li*), 96, 105, 169, 227n115

sorites chain arguments, 17, 31, 162–66

Ssu-ma Ch'ien, 175, 187, 237n10

Ssu-ma T'an, 182, 185, 197, 200, 208n21, 234n70; on philosophical schools, 8, 175–81, 184

Ssu-pu pei-yao, 37–38

Ssu-pu ts'ung-k'an, 36, 37, 39, 40

ssu-t'i (four limbs), 74, 106, 232n56; alignment of, 4, 60, 82, 109, 110, 111, 134

Stace, Walter, 128, 129, 131, 132, 138, 139, 141, 142

statecraft. *See* political power

Sung, state of, 21

Sung Hsiang-feng, 40

Sung Hsing, 21, 24, 28, 175, 211n37, 215n55

Syncretic (Syncretist) Taoism, 7–8, 27, 177; in *Chuang Tzu*, 8, 153, 160, 170, 234n70; in *Huai-nan Tzu*, 32; in *Lü-shih ch'un-ch'iu*, 29, 164, 198, 199; and political power, 181, 192, 195, 196, 202; and "Purified Mind," 211n35; technical terms in, 196, 197, 215n63; and techniques of the Way, 182, 183; texts of, 8, 18

Tai Wang, 40

"T'ai-i sheng shui" (Grand Unity Generates Water), 26

T'ao Hung-ch'ing, 40

Tao Te ching. See Lao Tzu

Tao (the Way / the One): and alignment, 111, 112; and breathing, 101, 164, 165; *Chuang Tzu* on, 28, 154, 155, 158, 161, 172; of eating, 90, 122; and inner cultivation, 11, 12, 33, 62, 72, 99, 100, 116, 117, 121, 122, 126, 140, 143, 148, 167, 196, 239n39; *Inward Training* on, 56, 78, 86, 90, 94, 96, 115–18, 144–50, 189; *Lao Tzu* on, 102, 115, 144–50, 152, 188, 189, 192, 221n54; lore of, 190–93, 202; and meditation, 137, 167; and mind, 52, 54, 102–3, 104, 107–8, 115–16, 117; and mysticism, 131, 135, 138–42, 170; and the numinous, 108–9, 116, 117, 133–34; and political power, 149, 180; and Taoism, 44, 173, 174, 177, 195, 196; unity with, 44, 132, 166; and vital energy, 92, 115–16, 118, 143–44, 147;

Tao (cont.)

    and vital essence, 42, 52, 101–5, 106, 143–44, 146, 147, 169, 239n39. *See also chih-i; shou-i;* techniques of the Way

"Tao-chia" (Taoists), 181, 185, 208n21

Taoism, 173–203; and *Chuang Tzu,* 5, 19, 193, 195, 209n17; and Confucianism, 5, 31, 151, 198, 199–200; definition of early, 174–97; eremiticism in, 172; evolution of, 193–97; and inner cultivation, 7, 18, 125–27, 138, 173–74, 195, 201; inner power in, 177, 195, 196; labels for, 181–82; and *Lao Tzu,* 7, 19, 193, 194, 198–203; and Legalism, 6, 8, 24, 212n41; literary genres in, 157, 202; and meditation, 116, 161, 227n109; metaphors of, 41, 151; and mystical practice, 8, 122–23, 194, 201, 202; mysticism in, 127, 129, 132; and physical hygiene, 42, 170; and political power, 7, 174, 180, 181, 192, 195, 196, 202; as a "school," 174, 175, 176–77, 193, 200, 201; and shamanism, 189–90; and Tao, 44, 173, 174, 177, 195, 196; technical terms in, 195–97; three aspects of early, 6–9, 195–97; vitality in, 122–23; wisdom poetry of, 192; and yoga, 137–38. *See also* "Huang-Lao" Taoism; Individualist Taoism; "Lao-Chuang" Taoism; Primitivist Taoism; Syncretic Taoism; techniques of the Way

Taoist religion, 5–6, 8, 174, 200, 202–3

Tao-shu. See techniques of the Way

tao-yin (guiding and pulling) exercises, 170, 221n53

te (inner power): and alignment, 66, 110, 112, 135; and breathing, 101, 104, 145, 219n28; *Chuang Tzu* on, 160, 164; and inner cultivation, 14, 48, 104, 109, 120, 126; *Lao Tzu* on, 145, 152, 188; and mysticism, 135, 138, 169; and Tao, 52, 76, 78, 99, 143, 146; in Taoism, 177, 195, 196; and vital energy, 13, 48, 103, 144, 145; and vital essence, 52, 102, 104, 106, 145, 219n28

Techniques of the Mind I (*Hsin-shu, shang; Kuan Tzu*), 15, 18, 151; authorship of, 27, 30; and *Chuang Tzu,* 28, 234n70; on cleaning out lodging place of the numinous, 151, 190, 211n36, 222n64; date of, 25, 27, 214n52; and *Inward Training,* 23, 24, 25–26, 191, 213n43; and *Lü-shih ch'un-ch'iu,* 30; and *Purified Mind,* 211n35; rhetoric of, 16, 165, 166; stages of meditation in, 166

Techniques of the Mind II (*Hsin-shu, hsia; Kuan Tzu*), 18; authorship of, 27, 30; and *Chuang Tzu,* 234n70; date of, 25, 27, 214n52; and editions of *Kuan Tzu,* 37; and *Inward Training,* 23, 24, 25–26, 191, 212n43, 222nn57, 59, 62, 223n71, 224n87; and *Purified Mind,* 211n35

Yellow Turbans rebellion, 5
Yen, state of, 22
Yen Hui, 154, 155
Yin Chih-chang, 38
Yin Wen, 21, 24, 28, 175, 212n37, 215n55
Yin-ch'üeh shan (Shantung), 1
yin-yang thought, 21–22, 25, 108; and Naturalists, 175, 179, 180, 181

yoga, 137–38
yü (desire), 50, 94, 113, 121
yu (sorrow, worry), 31, 50, 84, 88, 113; in *Chuang Tzu*, 160; and vitality, 94, 121
Yü Ying-shih, 231n47
Yü Yüeh, 40, 233n57

Zen Buddhism, 141, 151

OTHER WORKS

IN THE COLUMBIA ASIAN STUDIES SERIES

TRANSLATIONS FROM THE ASIAN CLASSICS

Major Plays of Chikamatsu, tr. Donald Keene 1961

Four Major Plays of Chikamatsu, tr. Donald Keene. Paperback ed. only. 1961; rev. ed. 1997

Records of the Grand Historian of China, translated from the Shih chi of Ssu-ma Ch'ien, tr. Burton Watson, 2 vols. 1961

Instructions for Practical Living and Other Neo-Confucian Writings by Wang Yang-ming, tr. Wing-tsit Chan 1963

Hsün Tzu: Basic Writings, tr. Burton Watson, paperback ed. only. 1963; rev. ed. 1996

Chuang Tzu: Basic Writings, tr. Burton Watson, paperback ed. only. 1964; rev. ed. 1996

The Mahābhārata, tr. Chakravarthi V. Narasimhan. Also in paperback ed. 1965; rev. ed. 1997

The Manyōshū, Nippon Gakujutsu Shinkōkai edition 1965

Su Tung-p'o: Selections from a Sung Dynasty Poet, tr. Burton Watson. Also in paperback ed. 1965

Bhartrihari: Poems, tr. Barbara Stoler Miller. Also in paperback ed. 1967

Basic Writings of Mo Tzu, Hsün Tzu, and Han Fei Tzu, tr. Burton Watson. Also in separate paperback eds. 1967

The Awakening of Faith, Attributed to Aśvaghosha, tr. Yoshito S. Hakeda. Also in paperback ed. 1967

Reflections on Things at Hand: The Neo-Confucian Anthology, comp. Chu Hsi and Lü Tsu-ch'ien, tr. Wing-tsit Chan 1967

The Platform Sutra of the Sixth Patriarch, tr. Philip B. Yampolsky. Also in paperback ed. 1967

Essays in Idleness: The Tsurezuregusa of Kenkō, tr. Donald Keene. Also in paperback ed. 1967

The Pillow Book of Sei Shōnagon, tr. Ivan Morris, 2 vols. 1967

Two Plays of Ancient India: The Little Clay Cart and the Minister's Seal, tr. J. A. B. van Buitenen 1968

The Complete Works of Chuang Tzu, tr. Burton Watson 1968

The Romance of the Western Chamber (Hsi Hsiang chi), tr. S. I. Hsiung. Also in paperback ed. 1968

The Manyōshū, Nippon Gakujutsu Shinkōkai edition. Paperback ed. only. 1969

Records of the Historian: Chapters from the Shih chi of Ssu-ma Ch'ien, tr. Burton Watson. Paperback ed. only. 1969

Cold Mountain: 100 Poems by the T'ang Poet Han-shan, tr. Burton Watson. Also in paperback ed. 1970

Twenty Plays of the Nō Theatre, ed. Donald Keene. Also in paperback ed. 1970

Chūshingura: The Treasury of Loyal Retainers, tr. Donald Keene. Also in paperback ed. 1971; rev. ed. 1997

The Zen Master Hakuin: Selected Writings, tr. Philip B. Yampolsky 1971

Chinese Rhyme-Prose: Poems in the Fu Form from the Han and Six Dynasties Periods, tr. Burton Watson. Also in paperback ed. 1971

Kūkai: Major Works, tr. Yoshito S. Hakeda. Also in paperback ed. 1972

The Old Man Who Does as He Pleases: Selections from the Poetry and Prose of Lu Yu, tr. Burton Watson 1973

The Lion's Roar of Queen Śrīmālā, tr. Alex and Hideko Wayman 1974

Courtier and Commoner in Ancient China: Selections from the History of the Former Han by Pan Ku, tr. Burton Watson. Also in paperback ed. 1974

Japanese Literature in Chinese, vol. 1: *Poetry and Prose in Chinese by Japanese Writers of the Early Period*, tr. Burton Watson 1975

Japanese Literature in Chinese, vol. 2: *Poetry and Prose in Chinese by Japanese Writers of the Later Period*, tr. Burton Watson 1976

Scripture of the Lotus Blossom of the Fine Dharma, tr. Leon Hurvitz. Also in paperback ed. 1976

Love Song of the Dark Lord: Jayadeva's Gītagovinda, tr. Barbara Stoler Miller. Also in paperback ed. Cloth ed. includes critical text of the Sanskrit. 1977; rev. ed. 1997

Ryōkan: Zen Monk-Poet of Japan, tr. Burton Watson 1977

Calming the Mind and Discerning the Real: From the Lam rim chen mo of Tsoṇ-kha-pa, tr. Alex Wayman 1978

The Hermit and the Love-Thief: Sanskrit Poems of Bhartrihari and Bilhaṇa, tr. Barbara Stoler Miller 1978

The Lute: Kao Ming's P'i-p'a chi, tr. Jean Mulligan. Also in paperback ed. 1980

A Chronicle of Gods and Sovereigns: Jinnō Shōtōki of Kitabatake Chikafusa, tr. H. Paul Varley 1980

Among the Flowers: The Hua-chien chi, tr. Lois Fusek 1982

Grass Hill: Poems and Prose by the Japanese Monk Gensei, tr. Burton Watson 1983

Doctors, Diviners, and Magicians of Ancient China: Biographies of Fang-shih, tr. Kenneth J. DeWoskin. Also in paperback ed. 1983

Theater of Memory: The Plays of Kālidāsa, ed. Barbara Stoler Miller. Also in paperback ed. 1984

The Columbia Book of Chinese Poetry: From Early Times to the Thirteenth Century, ed. and tr. Burton Watson. Also in paperback ed. 1984

Poems of Love and War: From the Eight Anthologies and the Ten Long Poems of Classical Tamil, tr. A. K. Ramanujan. Also in paperback ed. 1985

The Bhagavad Gita: Krishna's Counsel in Time of War, tr. Barbara Stoler Miller 1986

The Columbia Book of Later Chinese Poetry, ed. and tr. Jonathan Chaves. Also in paperback ed. 1986

The Tso Chuan: Selections from China's Oldest Narrative History, tr. Burton Watson 1989

Waiting for the Wind: Thirty-six Poets of Japan's Late Medieval Age, tr. Steven Carter 1989

Selected Writings of Nichiren, ed. Philip B. Yampolsky 1990

Saigyō, Poems of a Mountain Home, tr. Burton Watson 1990

The Book of Lieh Tzu: A Classic of the Tao, tr. A. C. Graham. Morningside ed. 1990

The Tale of an Anklet: An Epic of South India—The Cilappatikāram of Iḷaṇkō Aṭikaḷ, tr. R. Parthasarathy 1993

Waiting for the Dawn: A Plan for the Prince, tr. and introduction by Wm. Theodore de Bary 1993

Yoshitsune and the Thousand Cherry Trees: A Masterpiece of the Eighteenth-Century Japanese Puppet Theater, tr., annotated, and with introduction by Stanleigh H. Jones, Jr. 1993

The Lotus Sutra, tr. Burton Watson. Also in paperback ed. 1993

The Classic of Changes: A New Translation of the I Ching as Interpreted by Wang Bi, tr. Richard John Lynn 1994

Beyond Spring: Tz'u Poems of the Sung Dynasty, tr. Julie Landau 1994

Modern Japanese Drama: An Anthology, ed. and tr. Ted. Takaya. Also in paperback ed. 1979

Mask and Sword: Two Plays for the Contemporary Japanese Theater, by Yamazaki Masakazu, tr. J. Thomas Rimer 1980

Yokomitsu Riichi, Modernist, Dennis Keene 1980

Nepali Visions, Nepali Dreams: The Poetry of Laxmiprasad Devkota, tr. David Rubin 1980

Literature of the Hundred Flowers, vol. 1: Criticism and Polemics, ed. Hualing Nieh 1981

Literature of the Hundred Flowers, vol. 2: Poetry and Fiction, ed. Hualing Nieh 1981

Modern Chinese Stories and Novellas, 1919–1949, ed. Joseph S. M. Lau, C. T. Hsia, and Leo Ou-fan Lee. Also in paperback ed. 1984

A View by the Sea, by Yasuoka Shōtarō, tr. K„ren Wigen Lewis 1984

Other Worlds: Arishima Takeo and the Bounds of Modern Japanese Fiction, by Paul Anderer 1984

Selected Poems of Sŏ Chŏngju, tr. with introduction by David R. McCann 1989

The Sting of Life: Four Contemporary Japanese Novelists, by Van C. Gessel 1989

Stories of Osaka Life, by Oda Sakunosuke, tr. Burton Watson 1990

The Bodhisattva, or Samantabhadra, by Ishikawa Jun, tr. with introduction by William Jefferson Tyler 1990

The Travels of Lao Ts'an, by Liu T'ieh-yün, tr. Harold Shadick. Morningside ed. 1990

Three Plays by Kōbō Abe, tr. with introduction by Donald Keene 1993

The Columbia Anthology of Modern Chinese Literature, ed. Joseph S. M. Lau and Howard Goldblatt 1995

Modern Japanese Tanka, ed. and tr. Makoto Ueda 1996

Masaoka Shiki: Selected Poems, ed. and tr. Burton Watson 1997

Writing Women in Modern China: An Anthology of Women's Literature from the Early Twentieth Century, ed. and tr. Amy D. Dooling and Kristina M. Torgeson 1998

American Stories, by Nagai Kafū, tr. Mitsuko Iriye 2000

The Paper Door and Other Stories, by Shiga Naoya, tr. Lane Dunlop 2001

Grass for My Pillow, by Saiichi Maruya, tr. Dennis Keene 2002

For All My Walking: Free-Verse Haiku of Taneda Santōka, with Excerpts from His Diaries, tr. Burton Watson 2003

The Columbia Anthology of Modern Japanese Literature, ed. J. Thomas Rimer and Van C. Gessel, vol. 1, 2005

The Ōnin War: History of Its Origins and Background, with a Selective Translation of the Chronicle of Ōnin, by H. Paul Varley 1967

Chinese Government in Ming Times: Seven Studies, ed. Charles O. Hucker 1969

The Actors' Analects (Yakusha Rongo), ed. and tr. Charles J. Dunn and Bungō Torigoe 1969

Self and Society in Ming Thought, by Wm. Theodore de Bary and the Conference on Ming Thought. Also in paperback ed. 1970

A History of Islamic Philosophy, by Majid Fakhry, 2d ed. 1983

Phantasies of a Love Thief: The Caurapañatcāśikā Attributed to Bilhaṇa, by Barbara Stoler Miller 1971

Iqbal: Poet-Philosopher of Pakistan, ed. Hafeez Malik 1971

The Golden Tradition: An Anthology of Urdu Poetry, ed. and tr. Ahmed Ali. Also in paperback ed. 1973

Conquerors and Confucians: Aspects of Political Change in Late Yüan China, by John W. Dardess 1973

The Unfolding of Neo-Confucianism, by Wm. Theodore de Bary and the Conference on Seventeenth-Century Chinese Thought. Also in paperback ed. 1975

To Acquire Wisdom: The Way of Wang Yang-ming, by Julia Ching 1976

Gods, Priests, and Warriors: The Bhṛgus of the Mahābhārata, by Robert P. Goldman 1977

Mei Yao-ch'en and the Development of Early Sung Poetry, by Jonathan Chaves 1976

The Legend of Semimaru, Blind Musician of Japan, by Susan Matisoff 1977

Sir Sayyid Ahmad Khan and Muslim Modernization in India and Pakistan, by Hafeez Malik 1980

The Khilafat Movement: Religious Symbolism and Political Mobilization in India, by Gail Minault 1982

The World of K'ung Shang-jen: A Man of Letters in Early Ch'ing China, by Richard Strassberg 1983

The Lotus Boat: The Origins of Chinese Tz'u Poetry in T'ang Popular Culture, by Marsha L. Wagner 1984

Expressions of Self in Chinese Literature, ed. Robert E. Hegel and Richard C. Hessney 1985

Songs for the Bride: Women's Voices and Wedding Rites of Rural India, by W. G. Archer; ed. Barbara Stoler Miller and Mildred Archer 1986

The Confucian Kingship in Korea: Yŏngjo and the Politics of Sagacity, by JaHyun Kim Haboush 1988

Approaches to the Oriental Classics, ed. Wm. Theodore de Bary 1959

Early Chinese Literature, by Burton Watson. Also in paperback ed. 1962

Approaches to Asian Civilizations, ed. Wm. Theodore de Bary and Ainslie T. Embree 1964

The Classic Chinese Novel: A Critical Introduction, by C. T. Hsia. Also in paperback ed. 1968

Chinese Lyricism: Shih Poetry from the Second to the Twelfth Century, tr. Burton Watson. Also in paperback ed. 1971

A Syllabus of Indian Civilization, by Leonard A. Gordon and Barbara Stoler Miller 1971

Twentieth-Century Chinese Stories, ed. C. T. Hsia and Joseph S. M. Lau. Also in paperback ed. 1971

A Syllabus of Chinese Civilization, by J. Mason Gentzler, 2d ed. 1972

A Syllabus of Japanese Civilization, by H. Paul Varley, 2d ed. 1972

An Introduction to Chinese Civilization, ed. John Meskill, with the assistance of J. Mason Gentzler 1973

An Introduction to Japanese Civilization, ed. Arthur E. Tiedemann 1974

Ukifune: Love in the Tale of Genji, ed. Andrew Pekarik 1982

The Pleasures of Japanese Literature, by Donald Keene 1988

A Guide to Oriental Classics, ed. Wm. Theodore de Bary and Ainslie T. Embree; 3d edition ed. Amy Vladeck Heinrich, 2 vols. 1989

Introduction to Asian Civilizations

Wm. Theodore de Bary, General Editor

Sources of Japanese Tradition, 1958; paperback ed., 2 vols., 1964. 2d ed., vol. 1, 2001, compiled by Wm. Theodore de Bary, Donald Keene, George Tanabe, and Paul Varley; vol. 2, 2005, compiled by Wm. Theodore de Bary, Carol Gluck, and Arthur E. Tiedemann

Sources of Indian Tradition, 1958; paperback ed., 2 vols., 1964. 2d ed., 2 vols., 1988

Sources of Chinese Tradition, 1960, paperback ed., 2 vols., 1964. 2d ed., vol. 1, 1999, compiled by Wm. Theodore de Bary and Irene Bloom; vol. 2, 2000, compiled by Wm. Theodore de Bary and Richard Lufrano

Sources of Korean Tradition, 1997; 2 vols., vol. 1, 1997, compiled by Peter H. Lee and Wm. Theodore de Bary; vol. 2, 2001, compiled by Yŏngho Ch'oe, Peter H. Lee, and Wm. Theodore de Bary

Instructions for Practical Living and Other Neo-Confucian Writings by Wang Yang-ming, tr. Wing-tsit Chan 1963

Reflections on Things at Hand: The Neo-Confucian Anthology, comp. Chu Hsi and Lü Tsu-ch'ien, tr. Wing-tsit Chan 1967

Self and Society in Ming Thought, by Wm. Theodore de Bary and the Conference on Ming Thought. Also in paperback ed. 1970

The Unfolding of Neo-Confucianism, by Wm. Theodore de Bary and the Conference on Seventeenth-Century Chinese Thought. Also in paperback ed. 1975

Principle and Practicality: Essays in Neo-Confucianism and Practical Learning, ed. Wm. Theodore de Bary and Irene Bloom. Also in paperback ed. 1979

The Syncretic Religion of Lin Chao-en, by Judith A. Berling 1980

The Renewal of Buddhism in China: Chu-hung and the Late Ming Synthesis, by Chün-fang Yü 1981

Neo-Confucian Orthodoxy and the Learning of the Mind-and-Heart, by Wm. Theodore de Bary 1981

Yüan Thought: Chinese Thought and Religion Under the Mongols, ed. Hok-lam Chan and Wm. Theodore de Bary 1982

The Liberal Tradition in China, by Wm. Theodore de Bary 1983

The Development and Decline of Chinese Cosmology, by John B. Henderson 1984

The Rise of Neo-Confucianism in Korea, by Wm. Theodore de Bary and JaHyun Kim Haboush 1985

Chiao Hung and the Restructuring of Neo-Confucianism in Late Ming, by Edward T. Ch'ien 1985

Neo-Confucian Terms Explained: Pei-hsi tzu-i, by Ch'en Ch'un, ed. and tr. Wing-tsit Chan 1986

Knowledge Painfully Acquired: K'un-chih chi, by Lo Ch'in-shun, ed. and tr. Irene Bloom 1987

To Become a Sage: The Ten Diagrams on Sage Learning, by Yi T'oegye, ed. and tr. Michael C. Kalton 1988

The Message of the Mind in Neo-Confucian Thought, by Wm. Theodore de Bary 1989